The Telegraph and

The Atlantic Cable

Beginning of the Modern World

Chronology

1684	Hooke suggests use of the telescope to build an optical telegraph.
1745	Leyden jar, for storing electrical charge, invented by Pieter van Musschenbock.
1763	Optical telegraph built in Liverpool, England, to signal return of ships.
1791	Chappe demonstrates optical telegraph in France.
1794-1844	Hundreds of optical telegraph lines built in France, Russia and other countries.
1816	Francis Ronalds demonstrates a dial telegraph, over 8 miles of wire, in England, using Leyden jar.
1823-25	Schilling develops, demonstrates a working telegraph in Russia.
1828	Chemical telegraph demonstrated by Harrison Gray Dyar in Long Island, NY, US.
1831	Joseph Henry publishes paper on increasing power of a magnet.
1832	Return voyage of the *Sully*; Morse conceives electrical telegraph.
1833	Gauss, Weber, Steinheil develop a galvanometer telegraph in Germany.
1835-7	Cooke, Wheatstone develop electrical telegraphs in England.

1837	Morse develops first simple telegraph.
1843	US Congress funds Morse $30,000 for initial telegraph line.
1844	Baltimore-Washington telegraph line completed, first major line in U.S.
1846	Royal House, in Vermont, US, develops a needle telegraph.
1846	Alexander Bain, in Edinburgh, Scotland, develops a chemical telegraph.
1851	Hiram Sibley, others form a company to consolidate industry.
1851	John and Jacob Brett lay submarine cable across the English Channel, connecting England with Europe for the first time.
1853	USS *Dolphin* carries out survey of North Atlantic sea bottom from Ireland to North America.
1855	Cooper, Field and others form American Telegraph Company to cover New England, NE Canada, Atlantic Cable terminal.
1857	First attempt to lay trans-Atlantic cable.
1858	The *Great Eastern*, largest ship yet built, launched in London.
1858	Second, third trans-Atlantic cable attempts.
1864	The Inquest, investigation of the causes of the cable failures.
1865	Fourth Atlantic cable attempt.

1866	Trans-Atlantic Cable successfully laid, 1865 cable recovered and completed.
1866	Telegraph consolidation completed, creating Western Union telecom monopoly in US.
1870	Telegraph nationalized in Britain.
1876-77	First two telephone patents by Bell in US.
1881	Jay Gould's American Union merges with Western Union, reconsolidating the telegraph industry.
1896	Marconi demonstrates wireless telegraph in Britain.
1915	First coast to coast long distance telephone line in US.
1954	First trans-Atlantic Telephone Cable.

Also by Bert Lundy

Telegraph, Telephone and Wireless: How Telecom Changed the World,
2008

Learn for Excellence: How to Prepare Your Children for College and
Life, 2021

Telegraph & The Atlantic Cable: Beginning of the Modern World
Copyright © 2021 by Bert Lundy

Published in the United States of America
ISBN Paperback: 978-1-956780-14-7
ISBN Hardback: 978-1-956780-15-4
ISBN eBook: 978-1-956780-13-0

ReadersMagnet, LLC
10620 Treena Street, Suite 230 | San Diego, California, 92131 USA
1.619. 354. 2643 | www.readersmagnet.com

Book design copyright © 2021 by ReadersMagnet, LLC. All rights reserved.
Cover design by Ericka Obando
Interior design by Mary Mae Romero

The Telegraph and

The Atlantic Cable

Beginning of the Modern World

B e r t   L u n d y

ReadersMagnet, LLC

Acknowledgments

First, I wish to acknowledge all of the heroes of this book, for their contributions to human progress, especially telecommunications.

Secondly, I wish to acknowledge those authors and others who wrote down this history for their contemporaries and those us who came later. Without these accounts, it would have been impossible for me to write this story.

I also wish to thank the many students at the Naval Postgraduate School who sat through my classes on telecommunications, including the business and history. Their comments and the interest shown was helpful and at times inspiring. To this there were also several faculty who showed interest.

A special thanks goes to Bill Burns, who maintains the cable site on the Atlantic Cable, Atlantic-Cable.com, for giving permission to use many photos and maps from this web site. These complement the story in Part 2 wonderfully.

Another special thanks goes to Bernard Finn, longtime curator of the Smithsonian Institute, who read the manuscript and made several helpful comments and corrections. These included details on the mirror galvanometer, Morse's battery, and several others.

Most importantly of all, my wife, Minerva Lundy, encouraged me enthusiastically throughout the entire project, and was very patient with the many hours I spent on it. The enthusiasm she showed was very encouraging.

Table of Contents

Part 1:   The Telegraph

Part 2: The Atlantic Telegraph Cable

Tables Figures Photos

Introduction

Those who don't know history are destined to repeat it.
−Edmund Burke (1729-97), British Statesman and Philosopher

It is difficult for us living in the twenty-first century to imagine life without modern telecommunications. No one alive today in America or most of the rest of the world has ever lived in a world without modern communications. Together with the advances in transportation and agriculture which have been made in the last century, life on this planet has been made infinitely easier for most of today's human population.

Most recently, since the 1990's, we have seen to proliferation of the cell phones and their latest networks, along with the smart phone and the Internet. These alone have made a huge change in life just since 1990.

Earlier, in the 1980's, we had the explosion of the use of personal computers, with two newly founded companies − Apple and Microsoft − making their founders and many employees and investors rich. And of course, about the same time came the birth and early growth of the Internet.

The year 1984 was an important one, which marked the breakup of the AT&T system, leading to an explosion of competition in the telephone and telecom business. AT&T had held a monopoly or near monopoly in the telephone business for nearly a century; this undoubtedly slowed technological progress, because AT&T had been protected from competition.

Prior to the 1970's, few people possessed calculators, which greatly eased mathematical calculations. It was in the late 1960's that calculators, developed by companies like Texas Instruments began to be used. Prior to this, the slide rule was a method of calculation which was still taught in high schools.

In the 1940's, computers were under development, and were used by the allies to break the German encryption system known as the **Enigma**, as

1

well as the Japanese encryption methods. The first great US computer company, IBM, dominated commercial computing for several decades, and some talked of breaking it up as was done with AT&T. In the 1970's, IBM was THE computer in use for businesses, and Apple and Microsoft did not yet exist.

Also by the 1940's, the wired telephone had been in use for decades, and was widely used in both American and Europe, but long distance was still quite expensive, and it is worth remembering that telephone conversations across the Atlantic Ocean were still unknown; the first trans-Atlantic telephone cable was not laid until 1954. Trans-Atlantic communication was by telegraph messages. Even so, there were still areas of the U.S. – mostly rural or remote – which still did not have telephone service

One hundred years ago, as this is being written – 1920 – telephone was widely used, but quite primitive compared to today. It was possible to speak by long distance from coast to coast (as of 1915) but also quite expensive, so most people didn't do it. Even as late as the 1970's, long distance telephone was still quite expensive, so that most people were careful about the number and length of long distance calls.

In the 1920's, radio was just beginning to be developed as a broadcast communication, and revolutionized communications during the 1920's and after. Telegraph was still quite important for long distance and especially intercontinental communication.

In the early 1900's and late 1800's, telephones were just beginning to be used in major cities. Most homes were still without telephones, in fact most people had never seen one. Radio was just beginning to be developed.

Throughout the last three decades of the 19th century – from about 1870-1900 – the way for most people to communicate personally with someone was by writing a letter and sending it by mail. The telegraph was in wide use, but mostly used by newspapers and other commercial and government. Communication between the US and Europe was possible, due to the existence of trans-Atlantic telegraph cables (since 1866).

The American Civil War, 1861-65, was the first major war in which the telegraph communications played a major role. It is well known that President Lincoln spent much, if not most of his time at the telegraph office in Washington, D.C., in constant communication with his generals.

Before 1850, the only way for communication from the US to Europe was by sending written letters or other documents on ships. At the time of the American Revolution (1775-83), a voyage across the Atlantic took from 6 weeks to 3 months, each way, depending on weather and route. By about 1850, the development of fast steamships had cut this to about 10 days to 2 weeks – in each direction.

One hundred eighty years ago – about two to three human lifetimes – 1840 – there were no telephones, no computers, and for most practical purposes, no way of speaking with anyone out of hearing distance, except by writing a note or letter, and sending it physically, by post or other type of messenger.

Each of the major advances I've mentioned in this very short review of telecom history has made a huge impact. The cell phone, the Inter- net, wireless communications, the computer, the telephone, the Telegraph – all made a big difference in the way life was lived – in short, they "changed the world." To those living before and after one of these changes came along, it is tempting to say "Ah, this is the biggest change, the world will never be the same!"

But of all of these advances, which was the **most important**? Which made the **biggest impact**?

I suggest that, out of all of these advances, the answer to both these questions – though both questions don't necessarily have the same an- swer – is the subject of this book, *The Telegraph* and the *Atlantic Cable*. If we take these together – the Atlantic Cable was an extension of the telegraph overseas, but as shown in this history, it took a huge effort and advances to do so – it is easy to imagine the impact.

Simply to be able to send a note or letter across hundreds or thousands of miles; to be able to learn of the important news in other cities or continent within a day of it's occurrence, rather than waiting weeks or months, long after the event was a huge improvement. Though each certainly had a tremendous impact on many people, I argue than **none** of the others made such a tremendous difference. So I claim that out of all the technology advances in telecommunications over the last 2 centuries, the telegraph, including the Atlantic cable, had the biggest impact of all.

Was the telegraph and cable the *most important* of these advances? Here one can make an argument for the technical advances of the computer, of wireless, and of just about every advance mentioned. Certainly the technical advances made by some, or even all of the others were more complex and scientifically advanced than the telegraph itself (though the Atlantic Cable required some major improvements).

Yet I would still argue, not only that the telegraph and cable made the *biggest impact* on the world, but that it was also the *most important* of all of these – because without it, none of the others would have been possible.

It took *thousands of years* since the development of language and writing systems to get the telegraph. But from the telegraph to the telephone was matter of about three decades, to wireless a couple more, and computers a few more after that. Each of these earlier advances made others possible. But the telegraph was the first. So I argue that of all of these, it was the most important, because it made all of them possible.

The telegraph proved that long distance – across a city, a continent, and oceans – was possible, and its success inspired thousands of others to improve on it, eventually leading to the telephone, wireless and the rest.

Of course these are subjective arguments, and someone else not agree. Even so, I think you have to admit there is a good case for this – certainly enough of a case to read my book, and see what you think then.

In Part 1 I cover the invention and early development of the telegraph, both in America and in England. Looking back almost two hundred years, I find it a bit overwhelming to just imagine the difficulties of life in those days, and in the obstacles that Morse and others had to overcome. Part 2 discusses the conception and ultimate realization of the dream to connect Europe and American by telegraph. The overwhelming difficulties, disappointments which had to be overcome, were heartbreaking, but the ultimate success was inspiring. I trust that you, the reader, find it as inspiring as I did.

In the rest of this introduction I will review a bit of basic telecom terminology. This may be helpful to less technically trained readers.

Basic Telecom Terminology

Telecommunications is the moving of information through a distance. Specifically, telecommunications is the movement of symbols such as letters of the alphabet, numeric characters such as 0 or 1, punctuation, or other symbols.

The distance which the symbols are transported can be millions of miles, as in deep space communications, or just across the room, as in sending a document to be printed.

In this book about the telegraph we are mainly interested in moving the letters of the alphabet and punctuation from one telegraph station to another, usually in a distance city. But telecommunications could also be a telephone call, email, or wireless radio.

A *signal* is a physical mechanism or quantity which is used to convey some type of information between two different physical locations.

Countless examples of signals abound from the history of communications. "One if by land, two if by sea," recalls the famous signal used by Paul Revere and his colleagues at the start of the American Revolution in 1775. One lantern, two or none would be hung in a church tower.

Smoke and fire have been used for thousands of years as signals. Flashes of light using Morse or other code has been used by ships.

A telegraph signal takes the form of electrical current flowing through a wire, which in the early days was often iron. A short burst of current (dot) or a longer burst (dash), with carefully specified time intervals between bursts.

There are two major types of signals. First, a *digital signal* is assumed to have only a finite, relatively small number of possible values. Light on or light off, in the simplest case. Paul Revere's signal was digital: one lantern, two, or none.

Telegraph signals are also digital. In the case of the Morse telegraph, the signal was a longer burst of electricity, or dash, a shorter one, a dot, or no current, such as the time between letters and words.

The second signal type, an *analog signal* has a range of possible values which is continuous and has an infinite number of possible values. This type of signal was used in the telephone network for many years.

In order to move from one point to another, both digital and analog signals must be *transmitted*, or generated and sent through the wire or wireless medium. At the receiving point, the signal must be received, or detected.

A *detector* is an instrument which senses or detects the signal and recovers the information which the signal carries. An incoming electromagnetic wave causes a current in a wire or other conductor to be generated, which has the same frequency as the incoming wave and which

can be amplified. The galvanometer developed by Clerk Maxwell for the Atlantic Cable, described in Part 2, is an example in this book.

Attenuation is the weakening of the signal as it passes through the medium, and *noise* refers to other unwanted signals or physical quantities which can *interfere* with the signal. It is harder to hear the professor on the back row of the classroom (unless an *amplifier* is used to strengthen the signal) than on the front, because the sound waves *attenuate* with the distance they travel. If other students are talking during the lecture, they make noise which also interferes with the professors' voice.

Attenuation was a **major** issue – perhaps *the* major issue, in the Atlantic Telegraph Cable, Part 2 of this book. A cable stretching some 2000 miles on the bottom of the Atlantic was a long way to carry a cur- rent without its becoming so attenuated as to be undetectable.

An *amplifier* strengthens an analog signal, so that the signal can be detected at greater distances. A *repeater* detects, interprets and regenerates a digital signal, for the same reason. Amplifiers and repeaters had to be invented for long distance communications to be possible.

Repeaters were critical in the use of the telegraph, and still are in other telecommunications also.

The *transmission medium* is the physical wire, cable, material or space through which a signal must pass. In the telegraph, the major medium was the wire carrying the signal. Later, when wireless signals were used such as on ships, the medium was air or space.

There are two major categories of media: *guided* or *unguided*. These are also called *wired* and *wireless*.

The telegraph, at least in the beginning, used guided media – the wire. Later, when radio became somewhat developed, telegraph codes were also used in wireless communications, especially on ships. The *Titanic* sent out distress wireless telegraph signals as it was sinking, and a ship arrived from 58 miles away to pick up the survivors.

In order to communicate, in addition to the physical signals, there must be a *communication protocol*. The protocol defines how the signals are transmitted, received, and interpreted.

Paul Revere's protocol was: "When the British troops start on their way, hang one or two lanterns in the church tower; one if by land, two if by sea." The British troops could see the lanterns; but since they were unaware that they were being used as signals with a protocol for communication with the rebels, the lights meant nothing to them. (To avoid provoking suspicions, the lanterns were only left hanging for a short time).

The *protocol* described what is to be done, when, and how; the *signal* was the actual mechanism used to pass information.

Most signals today make use of light and/or electricity, including electromagnetic waves. One very important characteristic of all signals is the speed at which they can travel, or *propagate*. The speed of light in a vacuum or in space, generally denoted in physics by the letter c, is very close to 3×10^8 meters/second; that is, 300 million meters/second. ($10^8 =$ $100, 000, 000$). The speed of signals in wires, including the telegraph, is a bit less. A good rule of thumb for the speed in a wire is 2/3 the speed of light – which is still very fast. So the comparisons of the telegraph speed to lightning in its early days were actually quite reasonable.

Part 1: The Telegraph

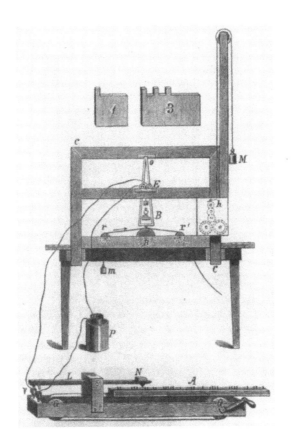

Early Morse Telegraph Instruments

Chapter 1
Primitive Communications

Canst Thou send lightnings, that they may go, and say unto thee, here we are?
– Job 38:35

No one alive today, early in the 21st century, can remember a time when long distance electronic communications were *not* available. In fact, very few alive can remember when it was not possible to speak to one's family members, friends or colleagues by voice, over local or long distance wired telephone, by cell/mobile phone, or by radio.

None of us can even remember when news of important events, even events overseas, was not almost instantly available. In this first chapter, I invite you, the reader, to pause for a few moments, and to try to imagine what life was like just 200 years ago – before the existence of modern communications.

This chapter is a brief review of early communications – before the telegraph. It also serves as an introduction to the history of the Telegraph.

Thousands or perhaps millions of years ago, early humans learned to communicate through spoken language. More recently – perhaps five thousand years ago – people learned to communicate through written language. This made it possible to communicate through longer distances, by writing letters, though the speed was still limited by that of a horse, boat or man on foot.

Transportation was also very slow until the arrival of the railroad and the steam engine in the middle of the nineteenth century. It is interesting to note that the use of horses for transportation was at one time, a few centuries ago, a great advance. When Europeans brought horses to America, life was revolutionized for many of the indigenous people. Similarly, advances in water transportation greatly improved life over thousands of years.

Early methods of communications included drums, smoke, horn blasts, carrier pigeons, mirrors reflecting sunlight, and various types of signal fires. Ancient Greeks and Persians used signal fires. Ancient historian Thucydides described various signal fires used during the Peloponnesian War. In about 429 BC, for example, a Spartan fleet of fifty-three ships was lying off Sybota on the western shore of Greece. It was warned by beacons from the island of Leucas that an Athenian fleet was stealing up the coast.

Fires were used for signaling for 2,000 years, probably more. The Romans also used fire and smoke. Many references to beacon fires are found in the writings of ancient poets and dramatists.

The Talmud, a collection of ancient writings on Jewish law, tells of a systems of signal fires used by the Jews between Jerusalem and Babylonia: "One went to the top of the mountain and lighted them, and waved the flame to and fro, up and down, until he could perceive his companion doing so at the second mountain, and so on to the third mountain . . . "

Some early telegraph-like systems used the human voice, shouted from point to point by men with "leathern lungs." Diodorus Siculus wrote that the Persian King Cyrus established lines of signal towers extending in several directions from his capital, manned by men with leathern lungs who shouted sentences to one another. Voice telegraphs were used by the Gauls during and following the time of Julius Caeser. When Gallic tribes massacred a group of Romans near Orleans, the news is said to have traveled one hundred sixty miles between sunrise and nine A.M. Similar voice systems were used Albania, Montenegro, South Africa, Switzerland and elsewhere.

The reflection of sunlight by mirror or polished surface was also used by the ancient Greeks. Herodotus tells of a signal flashed from Athens to Marathon – a distance of twenty five miles – by means of a burnished shield in 480 B.C., when the Greeks were about to meet the army of Darius. King Dimetrius of Macedonia is said to have given the signal for battle at Salimis in Cyprus by displaying a gilded shield.

The Roman emperor Tiberius used the heliograph – which uses a movable mirror to reflect the sun's rays – for sending signals from the island of Capri, from which he ruled Rome. The Moors in Algeria were using the heliograph in the eleventh century.

In 1455, the Scottish parliament passed an act fixing the "signal code." One bale (bonfire) burned at a station signaled that the English were coming; two bales, that they had arrived; and four bales, side by side, that they were in great force. In the time of Queen Elizabeth (1533-1603), a system of watchmen was set up around the English coast, to warn with signal fires of the arrival of invaders.

The heliostat, a device by which a flash may be sent (reflected by mirror) in any desired direction, regardless of the sun's motion, was in- vented by Willen Jakob van's Gravesande (1688-1742), a Dutch physicist. In the early nineteenth century, Johann Gauss, the German mathematician, discovered by experimentation that a one-inch square mirror could reflect sunlight a distance detectable for seven miles.

The British used the heliograph in the Afghan and Boer Wars, as well as in World War I. The British Navy used flags for signaling, as early as the seventeenth century. The invention of the rocket in that century provided another possible means of signaling for the armies and navies of the world.

In the next chapter, the development of the optical telegraph, also called semaphore, is described. These optical telegraph networks were well developed in several countries, particularly in France, long before the electrical telegraph was invented.

In Chapter 3, advances in electricity which made electronic communication possible are reviewed, including some early electrical telegraph systems. In Chapter 4, the invention and early development of the electrical telegraph of Cooke and Wheatstone in England is described. The telegraph was invented and developed in England independently from that of Morse in the US. There are some interesting differences between the two telegraph systems, each with advantages and disadvantages.

Chapter 5 describes the invention and early years of Morse's telegraph in the U.S. This led to the development of electrical telegraph networks in the U.S, Europe, and much of the world, which are discussed in the following chapters. In the U.S., this led to the establishment of the first great industrial monopoly in the U.S., Western Union.

The electrical telegraph had a major impact on the world in the nineteenth and early twentieth centuries. Practically every important aspect of life was affected. Transportation systems, such as railroads and shipping, for example, were made much more safe and efficient due to telegraph communications. News was much more up to date, and news of international events in foreign lands, such as wars, was now possible within days or even hours of the event. International finance was also greatly improved. It was a major advance towards the modern communications we have today, including the telephone, wireless, and the Internet.

Chapter 2
Optical Telegraphs

He said to his friend, "If the British march
By land or sea from the town tonight,
Hang a lantern aloft in the belfry arch
Of the North Church Tower as a signal light, --
One, if by land, and two, if by sea;
And I on the opposite shore will be,
Ready to ride and spread the alarm
Through every Middlesex village and farm,
For the country-folk to be up and to arm."

From The Midnight Ride of Paul Revere,
--by Henry Wadsworth Longfellow (1807-82

The first true telegraphs did not use fire, voices, or electrical signals, but optical ones. Communication was achieved by building a series of towers, each a short distance from the next – at most a few miles, but always with a direct line of sight. Messages were sent from one tower to the next, then relayed to the following tower. One of the earliest known optical telegraphs was in Greece, about 200-125 B.C. The letters of the alphabet were divided into five groups, with each letter in each group numbered (up to five letters in each group). At each tower a wooden frame was built, several meters long, the height of a man. The beginning of a message was announced by raising two torches. Next, a letter was indicated by raising up to five torches first, to indicate the group, and again, to indicate the letter within the group. Between each letter, the torches were lowered behind the frame.

This procedure for using the Greek telegraph is an early example of a *communication protocol*, the algorithm or set of rules which must be understood by all in order to exchange information. All communications systems must have protocols. The raising of the two torches to announce the beginning of the message is an early example of *synchronization*, another process inherent in communication. The representation of the letters was an example of *coding*, another important component of most communications and information systems.

A major improvement in optical telegraphs was made possible by the invention of the telescope. In England, Dr. Robert Hooke (1635-1703) suggested the use of the telescope in telegraphing symbols. The symbols could be placed in a visible area, such as a tower, and read from a distance through a telescope. He wrote a report describing his idea and presented it to the Royal Society in 1684. Hooke suggested reducing the alphabet to a few letters, and having special symbols for often used words and phrases, such as "ready to communicate," "go slower," and so on. A single right angled symbol, showed in eight different positions, could represent eight different letters of the alphabet. He wrote "I do not in the least doubt but that with a little Practice thereof, all Things may be made so convenient that the same Character may be seen at Paris, within a Minute after it hath been exposed in London, and the like in Proportion, for greater Distances." As we know now, Hooke had a good idea, but another century passed before the idea was implemented.

In 1763, another type of optical telegraph was constructed in the port city of Liverpool, England – intended to operate only within the city. A series of about seventy-five tall masts were constructed. A signal station was placed at Bidon, where there was a clear view to sea. From here it was possible to see a ship some hours before it reached port. Each of the masts represented a Liverpool ship owner, and when his vessel approached, his flag would be raised. The signal could be seen at several vantage points throughout the city, so preparations could be made to receive the incoming cargo. In those days, the homecoming of a ship from foreign ports was one of the most important events to the city and to the nation. The masts were later replaced with a semaphore, and in 1827 these were connected by a series of optical telegraph stations to Holyhead, some seventy miles away, where the incoming vessels could be sighted sooner.

The first extensive networks of optical telegraphs appear to have been built in France, after being invented by the Chappe brothers. Claude Chappe (1763-1805) was born into a well-to-do French family. Like a number of others, he tried unsuccessfully to use electricity to send messages. He also tried a system of sound signals, devising a method using the clanging of pots synchronized with clocks to send messages.

With the help of his brother Rene, standing a few hundred meters away, he was able to send simple messages. He devised a simple code using a dictionary. However, this system was limited by the distance at which sound could be detected, and also was very difficult and noisy to use. This led him to experiment with the use of sight, or optical signals. He used a wooden panel, about five feet tall, painted black on one side and white on the other. With the help of telescopes and clocks, which he used to synchronize the signals, he devised a code for sending the letters from one telegraph tower to the next.

In 1791, Chappe and his brothers used the panels, clocks and telescopes to send a message from a castle in Brulon to a house in Barcé a distance of about ten miles. Witnessed by local officials, they sent a message of about ten words in about four minutes. Following this demonstration Chappe tried to get support for his invention from the government; another brother, Ignace, was a member of the legislature. In 1792, the brothers staged another test in Belleville, near Paris, but a mob destroyed the equipment, suspecting that the Chappes were trying to communicate with Royalist prisoners in a nearby jail.

Chappe soon developed a new, better design, eliminating the synchronized clocks. He used a bar which rotated, on the end of which were two rotating arms, which could be aligned in several different positions. Together, bar and arms could be aligned to form ninety-eight different positions. A code was designed which, with the use of a codebook, could represent more than eight thousand different words and phrases.

Abraham-Louis Bréguet (1747-1823), perhaps the best clock maker of his time, helped Chappe design a system of pulleys to facilitate control of the arms by the operator. With the pulleys, a larger bar and arms could be constructed and controlled by the operator inside the tower below. Chappe expected it would be possible to send messages great distances rapidly by constructing a series of such towers.

In early 1793, Chappe sent his plan to the National Convention. A committee of this body agreed to allocate money for the construction of three stations in Belleville, Ecouen and Saint-Martin-de-Tertre, span- ning a distance of about twenty miles. By July the towers were ready, and on July

12, 1793 a message of about twenty-seven words (Translated "Daunou has
arrived here. He announced that the national convention has just authorized
his committee of general security to put seals on the papers of the deputies.")
was sent in eleven minutes. The reply came back in nine minutes.

Joseph Lakanal (1762-1845), one of the committee members who had
authorized the money and witnessed the demonstration was very favorably impressed and addressed the convention two weeks later, praising
the invention. Following his speech, the construction of a fifteen station line from Paris to Lille, 130 miles to the north, was proposed. The
Paris-Lille line, the first branch of what was to become the French State
Telegraph, began operation in May, 1794, and on August 15 was used to
report the recapture of a town, only an hour after the end of the battle.
By 1798, another line was built to the east as far as Strasborg, and the
Lille line had been extended to Dunkirk.

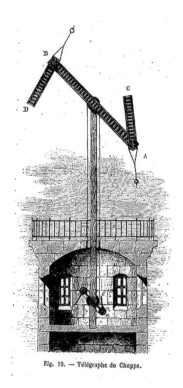

Fig. 19. — Télégraphe de Chappe.

Chappe Telegraph

In 1799, Napoleon Bonaparte seized power in France. He understood well the value of the telegraph. He ordered further extensions of the telegraph network, including a line to Boulogne in preparation for an invasion of England. He asked Abraham Chappe, younger brother of Claude, to design a telegraph capable of signaling across the English Channel. A prototype was built, and a station on the French side of the channel was also built, though the invasion never took place.

Other European nations recognized the value of the (optical) telegraph and soon began constructing their own. In Britain, in 1795, a line of telegraphs from London to the coast was ordered constructed, to help communication in case of war. The British telegraph was designed by George Murray, consisting of six wooden shutters; each shutter had two positions, for a total of sixty-four possible combinations.

Claude Chappe was disappointed in the use of his invention by Napoleon for military purposes. He wanted it to be used for peaceful purposes, such as business and commerce. He also was criticized by rivals, who claimed to have invented it before, or to having a better design. In 1805, he committed suicide by jumping into a well outside the Telegraph Administration building in Paris. His tombstone was decorated with a telegraph tower showing the sign for "at rest."

By the mid 1830s, optical telegraph networks covered much of western Europe, with additional networks in Britain, Sweden, Denmark, Germany, and Russia. By the end of Napoleon's era France had more than a thousand miles of telegraph lines with 224 stations. By 1844, this had grown to 533 telegraph stations and more than 3,000 miles of telegraph lines. In Russia, Czar Nicholas I had a network built connecting St. Petersburg with Warsaw, Moscow and other key cities. In Russia the towers were built of stone, tall enough to see over the tall pines of the forest, five to six miles apart. The line from St. Petersburg to Warsaw required 220 stations, each manned by six men, or 1,320 operators. Supervisors and administrative support also were needed.

Optical telegraphs also were used to a limited degree in the United States, such as to signal the appearance of incoming vessels in ports such as Boston, New Orleans and San Francisco. But optical telegraph networks were never as extensively developed in the U.S. Optical Telegraph systems continued to operate in Algeria until 1860, and in a few isolated areas until the early twentieth century.

The optical telegraph designed by Claude Chappe and other similar ones made major advances in communications. They made it possible to send messages hundreds of miles in a matter of hours. However, they suffered from a number of serious limitations, which meant that their use would be limited to government officials or to the rich.

First, they were expensive. Only governments could afford to construct the series of towers necessary, the equipment, and to train and pay the skilled operators necessary.

Second, they were also severely limited by the properties of light: they could not be used at night or when foggy or rainy weather prevented the towers from seeing each other. The users of today's optical and microwave systems are quite familiar with these limitations.

Third, the amount of information which could be sent was severely limited; as we would say today, they had "very low bandwidth." Any messages had to be brief. Anyone wanting to send a book was better off using a horse. Thus, it never became a medium for the masses.

Despite their handicaps, optical telegraph networks proved that timely communication was possible over long distances, through a network of stations linked together. If a better method of communications be- tween stations could be found, communications could be improved, and indeed a better method was already on the horizon. For more than one hundred years, a number of scientists and thinkers had known of the existence of electricity, and many had suspected that it would be possible to use it as a means of rapid communications.

Chapter 3
Progress in Electricity and Early Systems

Chagrined a Little that we have hitherto been able to produce nothing in this way of use to mankind, and the hot weather coming on, when electrical experiments are not so agreeable, 'tis proposed to put an end to them for the season, somewhat humorously, in a party of pleasure on the banks of theSkuylkill. Spirits at the same time are to be fired by a sparksent from side to side through the river ... a turkey is to be killed for our dinner by the electrical shock, and roasted bythe electrical jack, before a fire kindled by the electrified bottle, when the health of all the famous electricians in England Holland, France and Germany are to be drank in electrifiedbumpers, under the discharge of guns from an electrical battery.
–Benjamin Franklin (1706-90)

By the eighteenth century, awareness and knowledge of electricity was growing. Many throughout Europe and elsewhere attempted to use electricity for communications.

Lodestone, or magnetic iron ore, was discovered several centuries ago, and the possibility of using it for communications was mentioned as early as 1569 in a book Magis Naturalis by Italian natural philosopher Giambattista della Porta (1535?-1615). He wrote, "I do not fear that with a long absent friend, even though he is confined by prison walls, we can communicate what we wish by means of two compass needles circumscribed with an alphabet."

In *Prolusiones Academica*, published in 1617, Faminianus Strada of Rome wrote that a certain lodestone had the property that if it touched two needles, when one of the needles began to move the other, though separated by a distance, moved at the same time and manner. Strada and a friend Addison each had a needle set on a pivot in the middle of a dial plate having the letters of the alphabet around its circumfer- ence. When one friend turned his needle so that it pointed at a letter, the other needle did the same. This was an early indication of the possibility of wireless communications.

By the middle of the 18th century, a number of people had thought seriously about the possibility of using electricity and/or magnetism for long distance communication. In 1729 Stephen Gray, an Englishman, excited an electroscope through 293 feet of wire. In 1730 he increased the distance to 886 feet. He described these experiments in a letter to the Royal Society of London in 1731.

Around 1745, the Leyden jar, which can store an electrical charge, was invented by Pieter van Musschenboek. The Leyden jar is a device for storing electric charge, and is considered to be the first capacitor. This provided for the first time a method of storing electrical charge; it was a precursor to the battery. Its discovery spurred a number of experiments throughout Europe. In 1746, Daniel Gralath discharged a shock of three leyden jars through a circle of twenty people holding hands. Later that year Joseph Franz, in Vienna, discharged a shock through 1500 feet of iron. Many other similar experiments were conducted as more was learned about the properties of electricity. Abbe Nollet and Lemonnier of Paris extended the length to over 12,000 feet. In April, 1746, a French scientist, Jean-Antione Nollet, conducted an experiment with about 200 monks, showing that electricity could travel a great distance, apparently instantaneously. He had them line up in a long file, each monk holding a wire in each hand. Nollet connected a primitive electrical battery to the wire, giving them all a shock.

In 1748 Benjamin Franklin (1706-90), the famous American statesman, sent electrical impulses across the Schuylkill River. In a letter to his friend Peter Collinson of London that summer he showed a considerable amount of imagination and vision as to what electricity would someday bring in the quotation at the beginning of this chapter.

One of the first documented uses of electricity came in 1753, in a letter written at Renfrew, Scotland, published in the Scots Magazine of Edinburgh, entitled "An Expeditious Method of Conveying Intelligence." The letter suggested that insulated wires be strung between distant points, one wire for each letter of the alphabet, through which "electrical discharges should separately exhibit themselves by the diverging balls of an electroscope, or the striking of a bell by the attraction of a charged ball." The letter was signed only with the initials "C.M." and the actual author is unknown.

Joseph Bozolus, a Jesuit and lecturer in Rome, suggested an electric telegraph shortly afterward. His idea is described in a Latin poem published in 1767. He suggested that two wires be strung between two stations, with a Leyden jar at one of them. The discharge through the wires could produce a spark; he suggested that an alphabet of such sparks could be devised. However, he apparently never implemented his idea.

Perhaps the first known telegraph instruments were in Geneva, in 1774. Georges Louis Le Sage set up a line consisting of twenty-four insulated wires, representing letters of the alphabet. Each wire terminated with an electroscope, where a ball of pith became excited when the key at the other end of the wire was depressed. The receiving operator, watching the balls, spelled out the words. In a letter written in 1782, he said that he had been contemplating the idea for thirty or thirty-five years. In 1787, a pith ball telegraph was operated in Paris by Lomond. Its operation was witnessed by an English visitor, Arthur Young.

In 1794, a telegraph device with thirty-six wires was built in Geneva by Reizen. The wires were connected to thin strips of tin foil pasted on glass, each representing a letter of the alphabet or a digit. The flash of sparks at breaks in these strips spelled the message. But it quickly became evident that such devices, requiring a wire for each letter of the alphabet, were not feasible. Tiberius Cavallo in England and D. F. Salva in Spain also experimented with electrical communications, around 1795-96.

Around 1800 Gian Somenico Romagnosi of Trent discovered that a galvanic-charged wire held near a compass needle deflects the needle. He was one of several who discovered that there is a relationship between electricity and magnetism.

The discovery of galvanism – the ability to produce an electrical current by a chemical reaction – by Luigi Galvani (1737-98) around 1770 led to the invention of the voltaic battery by Alessandro Volta (1745-1827), his colleague, which made possible a sustained electrical current. This led to the development of several other kinds of telegraphs. Von Soemmering of Munich was among the first to use Volta's battery for telegraph communications. He used the current to cause water to decompose into its base elements, hydrogen and oxygen. Thirty-five wires were strung, connected at one end to a voltaic pile, and at the other to a test tube of water. Flowing current caused bubbles to appear in the test tube, thus signaling the letter or digit. He eventually demonstrated his device through 10,000 feet of wire. His device was bulky and inconvenient, however, and never was widely used.

A few years later, in 1816, John Redman Coxe, professor of chemistry at the University of Pennsylvania in Philadelphia, suggested telegraphy by either water decomposition or metallic salts. He had evidently not heard of Von Soemmering's apparatus. Years later, in about 1843, a Scotsman named Robert Smith used the idea to build a telegraph. At first he used individual wires for the letters and digits; later he reduced the number of wires to just two, by having lines of varying lengths drawn by the receivers' instruments.

Also in 1816, Francis Ronalds demonstrated a telegraph at his home in Hammersmith, England. He strung eight miles of wire, suspended by silk strands, on his lawn. Electric charge, or power, was provided by a Leyden jar. Two synchronized clocks with dials were used. This was the first known dial telegraph, which made it possible to send letters with only a single wire.

In 1819, Hand Oersted of Copenhagen and J. S. C. Schweigger of Halle developed the galvanometer, an instrument for measuring electrical current. This important advance made several others possible in the next several years.

In 1820, Andre Mari Ampere (1775-1836) in France affirmed the possibility of deflecting a magnetic needle through a wire at a great distance from the pile or battery and proposed a telegraph using this idea. He said that Laplace suggested the idea to him.

Pavel Ludovitch Schilling, a Russian baron, made use of the idea of electricity to develop an electro-magnetic telegraph. Schilling was in Munich when Von Soemmering's telegraph was shown at the Academy of Sciences there, and was greatly interested in it. In 1812 he attempted to insulate a cord so that galvanic current could be carried through water or earth. He was hoping to perfect a telegraph for the use of the Russian Army. It took him until 1823 to make his instrument into a working telegraph. He demonstrated this model to Czar Alexander I in 1824 or 1825. This model of Schilling might well be considered the first electro-magnetic telegraph.

Schilling's telegraph consisted of five needles, each connected to its own circuit, and each able to move in two directions. He contrived a code enabling him to send the letters and digits. Later he improved his Telegraph so that only a single wire was needed, with a more complex code. The Czar Alexander I showed interest in Schilling's telegraph, visiting Schilling's home in 1830 to see it. In 1835 Schilling demonstrated his device to a group of German physicists in Bonn, and later, with their assistance, operated it in Vienna. However, he died in 1837, and there was no one to continue his work.

In 1820, Dominique Arago of Paris discovered that with the galvanic instruments of Oersted and Schweigger he could develop magnetic power in bars of iron, and give them permanent magnetism. In 1824, William Sturgeon, in England, carried this idea further, and invented the electromagnet. It was of soft iron, in the now typical horseshoe shape. A wire of copper was wound around its limbs loosely. By connecting the ends of wire to a galvanic pair, causing an electric current to flow, he created a temporary magnet powerful enough to sustain several pounds of weight. On breaking the circuit, the magnet lost its power immedi- ately.

In the United States, a chemical telegraph was devised by Harrison Gray Dyar in 1828. Electric current caused a chemical reaction to make red marks on a roll of blue litmus paper. Dyar wound his single wire around a race track on Long Island several times, a distance of several miles. He supported it with glass insulators strung from tress and poles. Witnesses of his demonstration testified that the marks made on the paper were satisfactory.

Joseph Henry (1797-1878) was born in Albany, New York, of Scotch descent, and was to play an important part in the story of the telegraph. He would also become the leading American physicist of the nineteenth century. According to one source, as a young teenager he once chased a rabbit which led him to the foundation of a small church. There was a small hole in the foundation. Curious, he crawled through it and discovered a small library.

The books fascinated him, especially those on science, and the course of his life had been found. He knew that he was interested in science, but exactly what branch of science changed as he grew. At first he was interested in medicine, later in engineering, and, by his late twenties, became interested in electricity. In 1826, he accepted a position as professor of mathematics at the Albany Academy, and in this position he found time for considerable experimentation.

Henry was especially interested in electrically induced magnets. In 1828, he exhibited an electromagnet wound with insulated copper wire. In 1831, he suspended a mile of copper wire around the walls of a large classroom, creating a circuit between a battery and an intensity magnet. A rod was placed in contact with one of the limbs of the soft iron core. When the magnet was excited the rod was repelled from it, causing it to strike a bell. Henry explained to his class that such a device could be used for signaling; but he made no attempt to patent it or make any commercial profit from it. In 1831 he published a paper explaining how to increase the power of an electromagnetic magnet. A few years later, this work helped S. F. B. Morse and others improve the distance through which their telegraphs could communicate.

Joseph Henry

It has been claimed by followers of Henry that this experiment and others he conducted entitled him to be considered the inventor of the electric telegraph. The work he did certainly had many of the key elements of an electric telegraph. Years later, in a letter to a friend, Professor Samuel Dod, Henry wrote:

> I think that the first actual line of telegraph using the earth as a conductor was made in the beginning of 1836. A wire was extended across the front campus of the college grounds, from the upper story of the Library Building to Philosophical Hall on the opposite side, the ends terminating in two wells. Through this wire signals were sent from time to time from my house to my laboratory. The electro-magnetic telegraph was first invented by me in Albany in 1830. . . At the time of making my original experiments on electro-magnetism in Albany, I was urged by a friend to take out a patent, both for its application to machinery and to the telegraph, but this I declined, on the ground that I considered it incompatible with the dignity of science to confine the benefits which might be derived from it to the exclusive use of any individual. In this, perhaps, I was too fastidious.

> In briefly stating my claims to the invention of the electro- magnetic
> telegraph, I may say that I was the first to bring the electro-magnetic
> into the condition necessary to its use in telegraphy, and also to point
> out its application to the telegraph and to illustrate this by constructing
> a working telegraph . . .

In 1833, Charles Friedrich Gauss and William Edward Weber constructed a galvanometer telegraph in Gottingen, Germany. It was about
1.5 miles long. Two wires making up a single circuit were strung over
the city's housetops by insulators. A needle in the receiving station,
alternately attracted and repelled, caused a small mirror suspended by
a silk thread to move slightly to the right or left. The small movements
of the mirror were observed through a telescope about ten to twelve
feet away.

At Gauss's request, Karl August Steinheil, professor of mathematics
and physics in Munich took up the telegraph project, in order to further
develop it. Steinheil added new features such as two bells which rang
when magnetic bars were attracted or repelled. He also added fountain
pens to the two bars, capable of writing on a roll of paper moved by
clockwork. He also discovered that the earth could be used as half of
the circuit, and thus reduced the two wire circuit to one.

Steinheil generously gave credit for the telegraph to his predecessors:
"To Gauss and Weber is due the merit of having, in 1833, actually
constructed the first simplified, galvano-magnetic telegraph." Of his own
work he said, "I by no means look on the arrangement I have selected as
complete; but as it answers the purpose I had in view, it may be well to
abide by it until some simpler arrangement is contrived." The Bavarian
Government built many miles of telegraph under Steinheil's system for its
own use over part of its railway system. This was the first government
to give its support to electrical telegraphs.

Chapter 4
Cooke and Wheatstone's
Telegraph System
In Britain

One day, to the surprise of the bookseller, he coveted a volume on the discoveries of Volta in electricity, but not having the price, he saved his pennies and secured the volume. It was written in French, and so he was obliged to save again, till he could buy a dictionary. Then he began to read the volume, and, with the help of his elder brother, William, to repeat the experiments described in it, with a home-made battery, in the scullery behind his father's house. In constructing the battery the boy philosophers ran short of money to procure the requisite copper plates. They had only a few copper coins left. A happy thought occurred to Charles, who was the leading spirit in these researches, 'We must use the pennies themselves,' said he, and the battery was soon complete.
–John Munro, *Heroes of the Telegraph*

William Fothergill Cooke was born in Middlesex, England in 1806. His father, William Cooke, was a medical doctor. Cooke was educated at Durham and the University of Edinburgh. From 1826 to 1831 he served in the East Indian Army. In 1836, Cooke was a medical student in Paris and Heidelberg, Germany, where he attended a lecture about electricity. A demonstration of a telegraph was given. It was the telegraph invented by the Russian baron Pavel Lvovitch Schilling, mentioned above, in the mid-1820s. Based on a galvanometer, it used left and right swings of the needle of a galvanometer to indicate letters and numbers. Professor Muncke of Heidelberg University had a copy of Schilling's apparatus, which he demonstrated at the lecture.

Cooke was eager to make himself a fortune, and recognized the potential of the apparatus at the lecture. He dropped his medical studies and dedicated himself to building an electric telegraph based on improvements in it. Within a few weeks he had built a prototype of an electric telegraph. It used a set of three needles controlled by three circuits of two wires each, for a total of six wires. Depending on the current in the wires, the needles were made to point to the right, the left, or straight up. The combination of pointing needles indicated letters or numbers. Cooke was able to make his telegraph operate through thirty or forty feet of wire, but when he attempted to make it work over longer distances, found that the current became too weak to turn to needles.

Searching for help, Cooke visited Michael Faraday (1791-1867), the eminent British scientist, who was investigating the relationship between electricity and magnetism. Faraday confirmed that the telegraph was technically Cooke also turned to a friend, Peter Roget, compiler of the first thes Roget was also a scientist, and had published a treatise on electricity 1832. Roget introduced Cooke to Professor Charles Wheatstone.

	Five-needle	Two-needle	One-needle
A	/|||	\\\ |	\\\ (7)
B	/|||	\\\ |	\\\ (8)
C		\/ | (1)	\\\
D	|/||	√ | (2)	\/ (9)
E	/|\\|	/ | (3)	\/ (0)
F	|/||	// |	\\\
G	||/|	/// |	\/ (+)
H	/|||	| \ (4)	\\
I	|/||	| \\	\
J		(subst. G)	
K	||/|	| \\\	\\ (Wait)
L	|||/	| \/ (5)	\\\ (Express)
M	\/|||	| √/ (6)	/ (1)
N	|\/||	| / (7)	// (2)
O	||\/|	| //	/// (3)
P	|||\/	| ///	//// (4)
Q		(subst. K)	
R	\\|/||	\ \ (8)	√ (5)
S	|\\|/|	\\ \\	√/ (6)
T	||\\|/	\\\ \\\	√//
U	\\||/|	\/ \/ (9)	√/
V		√/ √/ (0)	√//
W	|\\||/	/ /	√/
X		// //	/√ (Substitute)
Y	\\|||/	/// ///	√√ (Repeat)
Z		(subst. S)	
+ (stop)		\ |	\
Number shift		Ŧ÷	
Letter shift		Ħ÷	

Cooke & Wheatstone Codes

Wheatstone was born in 1802 in Gloucester, England. As a youth he built musical instruments, became interested in the laws of sound, and by the 1830's became interested in electricity. In 1834, he devised an ingenious method for measuring the speed of electricity in a wire. Though the speed he measured turned out to be inaccurate, it did show the speed to be finite, which was a major contribution to physics; up to that time, many still believed that speed to be instantaneous. Also in 1834, Wheatstone was appointed Chair of Experimental Physics at King's College, in London. In 1835, Wheatstone discussed Shilling's telegraph in a lecture, and began experimenting with the idea of an electrical telegraph. By 1836, he had devised one similar to that of Shilling, using five needles and five wire circuits.

Meeting with Wheatstone, Cooke learned that he had already been experimenting with a telegraph. But Wheatstone, as a professional scientist, and not shown any interest in developing a commercial system.

Cooke asked Wheatstone to help him, and the two formed a partnership. Working together, they soon devised an improved telegraph device, using five needles. They strung an experimental line about two kilometers long in early 1837, which was somewhat successful.

In April, 1837, Joseph Henry visited Wheatstone, and most likely discussed their telegraphs. As Henry had knowledge of how to get better distance out of the signals, he seems to have helped Wheatstone solve this problem.

Cooke and Wheatstone obtained a British patent for it in July, 1837. The device required a separate wire for each of the five needles. An alphabet of twenty letters was used, as the pointing of the needles only allowed this many. Though the design required five wires, it could transmit messages easily without the need for a codebook.

To demonstrate the usefulness of their invention, Cooke sought out the railroads. After receiving some rejections, the Great Western Railway agreed to a 13-mile telegraph line between Paddington and West Drayton. Another was also installed in the Blackwall Railway, a small line in London.

It took some time before the usefulness of the lines became clear to the public. But on August 6, 1844, the birth of the second son of Queen Victoria was announced, and the news traveled quickly along the telegraph lines. Suddenly, many realized its power to provide urgent news rapidly.

Another milestone came when it was used to apprehend a famous criminal gang known as Fiddler Dick. He and his gang would rob persons at railway stations, then stage their getaway by jumping quickly on a leaving train. When this occurred on one occasion at a station with a telegraph, the news was sent to the next station, where the authorities were waiting to arrest them.

A still more famous incident occurred when a murderer who had escaped was apprehended due to a telegraph lines on the railroad. This was John Tawell, who on January ———, murdered his mistress. He escaped on a railway headed for London, but telegraph messages alerted the authorities there who arrested him on his arrival. He was tried, convicted and hanged. The telegraph wires in England soon gained fame as the "wires that hung John Tawell."

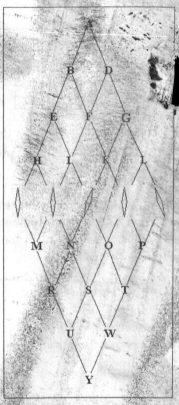

These and other similar incidents served to excite the public, and also authorities and investors with the means to help. The admiralty soon needed a contract to build an 80-mile link from London to Portsmouth. The success of this line brought more business, and soon plans to build telegraph lines all over England were being made. In September, 1845 Cooke and John Lewis Ricardo, a member of Parliament and a prominent financier, bought the patents of Cooke and Wheatstone and formed the Electric Telegraph Company. The electrical telegraph revolution was now well underway in England.

In later years, disputes arose as to which of the two had been the real "inventor" of the telegraph. As seems to have been the case in America with Henry and Morse, the dispute may have pushed by the partisans of each. In 1841, Isambard Brunel – perhaps the greatest English engineer of the

Cooke & Wheatstone 5 Needle Telegraph Receiving the Letter G

century, who is discussed later – and Professor Daniell – who invented a type of battery named after him, which was widely used – were called upon to adjudicate the question. After considerable investigation, they drew up the following statement:

Whilst Mr. Cooke is entitled to stand alone, as the gentleman to whom this country is indebted for having practically introduced and carried out the electric telegraph as a useful undertaking, promising to be of national importance, Professor Wheatstone is acknowledged as the scientific man, whose profound and successful researches had already prepared the public to receive it as a project capable of practical application. It is to the united labors of two gentleman so well qualified for mutual assistance that we must attribute the rapid progress which this important invention has made during the five years since they have been associated.

In other words, the panel gave a more or less equal measure of credit to both inventors. And it seems a fair assessment. Wheatstone was clearly the more competent from a technical and scientific viewpoint; but it is doubtful he would have ever made an attempt to commercialize the telegraph. He simply had little interest in business. Without Cooke's initiative, it might have been years before a working telegraph was brought to the public in Britain.

The telegraph soon became a big success in Britain, and a very prosperous one for the owners of the telegraph lines. Later, in the 1860's, there were many complaints about the high prices charged by the companies for the sending of telegraph messages. There were also complaints that the service was not brought into small towns and villages, where there was not enough business to make it profitable. The service was cheaper in nearby European countries, where it was established as a government monopoly. As a result, in 1870 the English government bought out the telegraph companies and made it into a government monopoly. It was operated as a branch of the postal service. Afterwards, services were extended into small towns and villages, and prices were standardized at considerably lower rates.

Chapter 5
Morse: The First
U.S. Line 1832-44

His vast conception of enlisting electricity in the work of civilization
was the grandest thought of time.
–San Francisco city resolution, 1872

Samuel Finley Breese Morse was born in the parsonage in Charlestown, Massachusetts on April 27, 1791. His father was Jedediah Morse (1761-1826), a minister and well-known geographer. Both of Morse's parents were fundamental protestants and this made a strong impression on him. Morse's father, Jedediah, also published a number of books on geography, and through these books became known throughout the U.S. and Europe. On numerous occasions as a young man, Samuel Morse received a warm welcome because of his father's reputation.

Morse studied at Yale College in 1807-10. Letters sent home commented on Dr. Benjamin Silliman's lectures on chemistry and galvanic electricity and on the experiments in electricity of Dr. Jeremiah Day. He studied liberal arts in the college, and wanted to become an artist, but it seems clear that he had some early exposure to the existence, at least, of electricity.

After attending college, Morse went to Europe for about four years to study art with Washington Allston and Benjamin West, two major American artists. He developed a close, long lasting friendship with Allston. After returning from this first trip to Europe, Morse attempted to make a living as an artist. His goal was to become a historical painter, painting works describing important historical events.

In August, 1816, while seeking work doing portraits in Concord, New Hampshire, he met Lucretia Pickering Walker, the daughter of a lawyer. The two soon fell in love, and in the fall of 1818 were married. The next several years, however, were quite difficult financially. Morse did not do well financially in art. He produced a number of impressive portraits, but there was not enough demand for art in early America for him to make a decent living at it.

Not having much financial success in the north, he went to Charleston, South Carolina, where he expected to find more demand for his painting. For a while he did better, painting portraits of well-to-do citizens of that state. His paintings were quite good, accurate likenesses of the subjects, and many of them still exist. Such paintings were not the type of artwork he had hoped to build his reputation with, but he did get some income from them.

In 1821, Morse made a portrait of the interior of the new House of Representatives, which had been recently rebuilt; the British had burned the capital in 1814. The work was eleven feet wide and over seven feet high, and also included portraits of all the House members. It was the largest and most complex work he had yet attempted. Allston, one of the leading artists of the day, admired the portrait: "really a beautiful thing . . . he has brought out more in this picture than I ever anticipated." Allston also said that, if the canvas were shown in London, that Morse would be made an associate at the Royal Academy. The canvas weighed 640 pounds.

Unfortunately for Morse, though the portrait was beautifully done and was admired by art lovers, it brought him little money. It was displayed in Boston, New York and other cities, but brought in barely enough money to pay expenses.

In 1825, the Marquis de Lafayette arrived in New York to begin a one-year farewell tour of the United States. Lafayette was the French officer who had befriended George Washington during the American Revolution, and had helped him defeat the British. He was the last living general from the Revolutionary War, and was a national hero in America. The city of New York desired a portrait of him, and Morse was chosen to do it. Both Morse and his father Jedediah, as well as many Americans of that day, considered Lafayette a hero, of a status near to that of Washington. The painting also would bring a commission of about $1,000 – a nifty sum in 1825, the equivalent of about $18,000 in 2007.

Excited at the prospect, Morse wrote a detailed letter to his wife Lucrece. But he got no reply. Instead, he got a letter from his father Jedediah. "My Affectionately-Beloved Son, My heart is in pain and deeply sorrowful, while I announce to you the sudden and unexpected death of your dear and deservedly-loved wife."

Lucrece died at her parents home in New Hampshire, just three weeks after having given birth to a son. Morse's last visit to her had been a few days earlier. Due to the slow communications of that day, Morse did not receive word of her death until days later, and so was not able to attend her funeral. Ironically, had his own invention been in existence, he might have gotten the word in time to be able to attend his wife's funeral. The death of his wife was a serious blow to him, and he experienced a deep depression at times during the next few years.

Morse's painting of Lafayette brought him more attention, and a few more commissions. The painting was done on a five by eight foot canvas, and depicts the general standing at the top of a flight of stairs, dressed in a black coat and yellow pantaloons. Several newspapers praised it for its accurate likeness, but the portrait also had many symbolic touches. There were busts of Washington and Franklin, and a glowing sunset sky, marking the glorious evening of the life of the Marquis.

In the winter of 1827, Morse attended a series of lectures on electricity by Professor James Freeman Dana at the New York Athenaeum. Years later, Morse remembered the magnet which was used by Dana and was able to draw a diagram of it. It was also reported that he had several evening discussions with Dana during this time. These lectures and discussions provided him with some exposure to the principles of electricity and magnetism.

Several years later, when a detractor claimed that Morse had no knowledge of electricity prior to the storied voyage of 1832 (described below), he pointed out that he had attended the lectures of Dana and had discussions with him.

In 1829, Morse returned to Europe again to study art, and this time stayed for about three years. The famous return voyage was in October of 1832, aboard the packet ship Sully. One of his fellow passengers on that voyage was Dr. Charles T. Jackson (1805-1880), a physician and geologist. During the voyage home, which took about a month, there were some discussions of electricity. According to most accounts, Dr. Charles T. Jackson, aware of recent advances in Europe, discussed some of the properties of electricity, and stated that electricity could pass through a wire instantaneously, through any distance. (Not so, as we now know; however, the actual speed is slightly less than that of light, which in those days was indistinguishable from "instantaneous." Nor for any distance, as Morse later learned).

Through these discussions, Morse conceived of the idea of an electrical telegraph, and after his return to New York, he worked on his ideas. Optical telegraphs were already in use in France and several other European countries, where Morse had spent several years, and it appears certain that he was aware of these. During the voyage he carried a notebook, and in the notebook he made sketches of his ideas of an elec- tric telegraph. The sketches included a magnet which was practically identical to the magnet used in the lectures by Dana he had attended in 1827.

After returning from the voyage to Europe in 1832, Morse spent the next few years working on his telegraph ideas while a professor of art at New York University. He seems to have been in no hurry. By early 1837, he had completed a crude telegraph. He told few people other than his brothers about his work. He apparently believed that he was the only person in the world working on the idea of an electrical telegraph, and kept it to himself.

In 1837, however, some external news speeded up his work. Two Frenchmen traveled to the U.S. and attempted to sell a telegraph system to the U.S. government. The news reached Morse in April, through his brothers, who had seen the news in a newspaper article. The Frenchmen, named Gonon and Servel, claimed that their telegraph would operate as fast as a person could write or talk. Very few Americans knew of the optical telegraph networks in Europe, and had always equated communication time with travel time. The telegraph which the Frenchmen were trying to sell to the U.S. was an optical one, an improved version of that which Chappe had developed and which was in use in France. However, the initial reports which Morse heard did not mention this detail, and he assumed at first that the system was an electrical one.

Also in 1837, news also began arriving from Europe about electric Telegraphs. As discussed above, these had been developed in England and elsewhere in Europe. These developments spurred Morse into action. He now knew that others were also working on electrical telegraph instruments. In October, 1837 he applied for a caveat to the patent office for his telegraph, which he called the "American Electro Magnetic Telegraph." A caveat is a document which is preliminary to a patent; it establishes protection of the inventor's rights, without the details of a patent, but required the filing of a patent within a year.

In an effort to establish himself as the first "inventor" of the electric telegraph, he sent a letter to several of his fellow passengers on the 1832 voyage of the Sully, including the captain. He asked them to verify that he had conceived the idea of the telegraph on that voyage in 1832. Several responded positively, confirming his claims to having conceived of the idea on that voyage. He had also made drawings in his personal log on the voyage, of a possible telegraph apparatus, of which copies still exist.

Morse, Photo by Matthew Brady, 1857

However one passenger, the Dr. Charles T. Jackson, was not so cooperative. Jackson claimed to have been the co-inventor with Morse of the telegraph. Certainly his knowledge of the recent advances in electricity in Europe were shared with Morse, and had some part in inspiring him; but the fact remains that it was Morse who actually built the instruments over the next few years, and later did much more, so Jackson's claims were almost certainly exaggerated or false. Jackson's jealousy would cause more problems for Morse a few years later.

Morse's telegraph of 1837 was still quite crude, but it worked. The basic idea of an electrical telegraph is that an electrical circuit is laid between two points. The "circuit" is simply a wire, or pair of wires, strung between the two points. A battery forms part of the circuit, which provides the power needed to make the electricity flow. A switch can open or close the circuit. When closed, electrons flow; when open, the current ceases. A buzzer or similar device is also attached. When the current flows, the buzzer sounds. A key connected to the switch enables an operator to open or close the circuit at will, causing the buzzer at the other end to sound.   By devising a code, with synchronization   and a protocol, the circuit can be used to send letters, numbers or words.

Seeking to improve his crude instruments, Morse sought help from Professor Leonard D. Gale, a chemistry professor and colleague of Morse at New York University. Gale confirmed that Morse's telegraph worked, but only for short distances – forty feet. Observing that Morse was using a simple 1-cup galvanic battery, Gale replaced it with a more powerful battery of forty cups. Gale also noted that Morse had wound the electromagnet loosely with only a few turns of wire. Gale had read the 1831 scientific paper by Joseph Henry, mentioned earlier, which showed that the power of such a battery could be greatly improved by winding the wire more tightly and for more turns.

Using these ideas from Gale and, through his paper, Henry, Morse improved the distance his telegraph could transmit greatly. On 2 September 1837, he gave the first public demonstration of his telegraph instruments at New York University. At that demonstration, the telegraph successfully transmitted over a wire of 1700 feet. Among the witnesses of that demonstration was Charles Daubeny, a professor of chemistry at Oxford, and a member of the Royal Society.

Another important witness was a young man of about thirty years of age, Alfred Vail (1807-1859). Vail was a recent graduate of New York University, had been a student of Morse, and importantly at this time, was an expert machinist: an expertise Morse lacked but needed. It was also very helpful that Vail's family owned a foundry and machine shop, called the Speedwell Iron Works, in nearby New Jersey.

Vail agreed to work with Morse on improving the telegraph, in exchange for a share of the profits, and soon the two were working together. Vail's family also made the iron works at Speedwell available for their use, and provided financial support to Morse, which was needed desperately.

Following the demonstration of 2 September, Morse wrote a letter to the Secretary of the Treasury, Levi Woodbury. In response to the visits of the Frenchmen, Woodbury had issued a government request for information on the possibility of building an optical telegraph system in the U.S. Morse's response was that his electrical telegraph would be far better, and explained in some detail his experiments and ideas. Morse's response was the only one advocating an electrical telegraph, and impressed Woodbury. As a result, Morse was given the opportunity, early the following year, to demonstrate his telegraph to the Congress in Washington, D.C.

Knowing that a distance of only 1700 feet would not be sufficient for a practical telegraph, Morse worked on improving the distance. (Thus he had already disproved Jackson's claim that electricity would travel through wire "any distance.") Reasoning that the electrical current weakened with distance through the wire, but that at a distance a weak current may still have the strength to open and close another circuit, he developed an instrument which he called a relay. It was a simple instrument that would open and close a new circuit in response to the signals received from the incoming circuit. The new circuit having its own battery, would in effect repeat the same signal, this time with renewed strength, on a new circuit. Today, devices using the same principle are widely used in digital signaling, and are called repeaters. Morse's repeater, or relay as he called it, was perhaps the first, and a significant contribution to the telegraph and to telecommunications.

Morse and Vail worked at improving the telegraph throughout the rest of 1837. By early 1838 they were ready to take their instruments to Washington. Before doing so, on January 6, a private trial was conducted at Speedwell. The message suggested by Judge Stephen Vail, Alfred's father, "A patient waiter is no loser," was sent through two miles of wire wound around a room in the foundry. Four days later the demonstration was repeated, this time for several hundred people.

Morse also worked at developing a dictionary, or code, for sending the signals. His initial idea was to send numbers, making a dictionary with a number for each word. He hoped to make a dictionary/code book of 30,000 words, but it seems he never completed this, as a new and better idea came to him. The better idea, of course, was to make a code for the letters of the alphabet and numerical characters – Morse code. This code, or the earliest versions of it, seem to have been developed by Morse in late 1837 or early 1838. Some have claimed that Vail should be credited with this (his widow claimed this years later), but a letter from Vail himself to his father, written at the time, stated that Morse had developed a new code for letters. This appears a solid indication that it was indeed Morse who developed the famous Morse Code, which still has some applications today in communications.

Alfred Vail

The code which Morse developed was built on the primitive physical states of "current flowing" and "no current flowing." An operator at one end could only detect whether or not a current was flowing in the wire. One method was to have a buzzer connected to the circuit, which would sound when current was present, and be silent otherwise. The code consisted of three primitives, which were called dots, dashes, and spaces. A dot was a short burst of current, while a dash was a longer burst. A space was a break, when no current was flowing. Typically, a space would be a short break between letters of the alphabet.

For example, the code for the letter "S" was three short bursts of electrical flow, represented by three dots, and often written "· · ·." The letter "O" is three longer bursts, represented by three dashes, usually written "− − −". Hence the Morse code for the letters "SOS," which was used as a distress signal for ships, was "· · · − − − · · ·." Dots were also sometimes called *dits* and dashes *dahs*. In this case, the SOS signal would be expressed as "di-di-dit dah-dah-dah di-di-dit".

With the help of Vail, Morse demonstrated his telegraph to Congress in February, 1838. The demonstrations took place over several days, and were quite successful. President Van Buren sent a message coded personally by Morse, and demonstrations were also witnessed by several members of his cabinet. The demonstrations were made over ten miles of wire. Many of the members of Congress were clearly very impressed, even amazed at the invention. Henry Ellsworth, the patent commis- sioner, said the "nothing has ever been in Washington that produced such a noise."

A	· −	K	− · −	U	· · −	1	· − − − −
B	− · · ·	L	· − · ·	V	· · · −	2	· · − − −
C	− · − ·	M	− −	W	· − −	3	· · · − −
D	− · ·	N	− ·	X	− · · −	4	· · · · −
E	·	O	− − −	Y	− · − −	5	· · · · ·
F	· · − ·	P	· − − ·	Z	− − · ·	6	− · · · ·
G	− − ·	Q	− − · −			7	− − · · ·
H	· · · ·	R	· − ·			8	− − − · ·
I	· ·	S	· · ·			9	− − − − ·
J	· − − −	T	−			0	− − − − −

International Morse Code

1. 1 dash = 3 dots.
2. Space between parts of same letter = 1 dot.
3. Space between 2 letters = 3 dots.
4. Space between 2 words = 5 dots.

Morse requested money to fund a fifty mile demonstration of his Telegraph, saying he needed $26,000 to build the line. The committee on commerce recommended that $30,000 be provided for the project. The chairman of the commerce committee was Francis O. J. Smith (1806- 1876), a third term congressman from Maine. Smith was very impressed with Morse's telegraph, and asked Morse to take him in as a partner. Smith could provide business and legal expertise, which Morse lacked and needed.

Morse hesitated, stating ethical concerns, as Smith was a public official. To alleviate this concern, Smith offered to write a letter to his constituents, saying that he would not run again for Congress, and on this condition Morse agreed to take him in as a partner. This decision to take on Smith as a partner was one which Morse would later regret, many times over.

In March, 1838 Morse drew up an agreement with Vail, Gale and Smith. Each of the three was given a fraction of the rights, with Morse retaining 9/16 of the rights in the U.S. and half for any European patents which they might obtain. Paper work was drawn up to apply for a U.S. patent – Morse still had only a caveat – and Morse and Smith left for Europe in May to demonstrate the telegraph there and apply for patents in England, France and other European countries while waiting for Congress to approve the money.

The trip to Europe, which had been planned for three months, extended into eleven. In England first, Morse met one of his competitors, Charles Wheatstone, face to face. He visited Wheatstone and learned of the needle telegraph of Wheatstone and Cooke. Morse paid the required patent fees (with financial support from Smith, part of their agreement) and obtained a hearing with the British attorney general for a patent. However, his patent application was rejected outright, on the claim that it had already been published. Despite efforts to refute the claim, Morse was ultimately unable to get a patent. It is highly likely that his being an American, and that the telegraph of Wheatstone and Cooke (British citizens) was a competitor had some bearing on the rejection.

Morse made demonstrations of his telegraph in France also, where he received a warmer welcome. But he encountered much bureaucratic resistance there as well, failing to obtain the desired patents. Return- ing to the U.S. in March, 1839, he received more discouraging news: Congress still had not approved the $30,000 appropriation for his Telegraph line.

The next few years were discouraging. Morse struggled financially. His partners seemed to lose interest and gave little support. However, Morse persisted in his efforts to obtain funding. Between 1839 and 1842 he corresponded with and visited Joseph Henry, who had visited Europe and was familiar with the needle telegraphs of Wheatstone and Cooke. Henry also was familiar with the needle telegraph of Karl Steinheil in Germany. Henry gave Morse scientific advice and moral support, stating publicly that he preferred the telegraph of Morse to the others.

In December, 1842, Morse traveled to Washington again, and once again demonstrated his telegraph to Congress. The commerce committee again reported on his telegraph favorably, and again recommended that $30,000 be funded for the construction of an experimental telegraph line. This time Morse took no trip to Europe, but instead stayed in Washington, attending the sessions of Congress in which the critical votes were taken.

The Journal of the Senate shows that on the morning of March 3, 1843 – the final day of the session – the bill providing the money was approved, and was signed by President John Tyler a few hours before the session ended. In letters to Smith and Vail dated 3 March 1843, Morse wrote "The Senate have just passed my bill without division and without opposition, and it will probably be signed by the President in a few hours." Morse finally had the capital he needed to build the first telegraph line.

Morse immediately began making plans to build the experimental Telegraph line, the first major electrical engineering project in the United States. He decided to put the line between Baltimore and Washington, a distance of about forty-four miles. The wires would be laid along the route of the Baltimore and Ohio Railroad. The railroad agreed to allow Morse the use of its right-of-way on the conditions that the railroad could use his telegraph for free and that, should any harm be done by the telegraph, the railroad would have the right to stop it. Neither Morse nor the railroad yet had any idea of how helpful the telegraph would become for the railroad.

Once Morse had the money, his partners – Vail, Gale and Smith – returned eagerly to help. Vail was given the job of building the telegraph instruments, for a salary of $1,000. Gale was to inspect the pipe and the line, testing it, for a salary of $1,500. Smith was to handle the legal work and would not receive a salary but would profit by contracting out the construction work and from his 1/4 share in the patent. Morse himself would receive $2,000, the most money he had seen in several years.

One of the first decisions Morse had to make was whether to bury the cable under ground or to place it above ground on poles. Fearing vandalism, he decided to bury it under ground. The plan was to place the wire in lead pipes, 2 1/2 feet deep. (Later experience showed his fear of vandalism well-placed).

Morse hoped to have his line working by December, when Congress returned to Washington. His plans called for 160 miles of wire, insulated by cotton thread and two coats of varnish, and lead pipes for the 44-mile line. He was able to get the wire by July, but getting the lead pipes proved a problem. The first contractor proved unable to complete the tubes on time, only able to manufacture about ten miles of pipes. Thus a second contractor was obtained to begin manufacturing the remaining thirty or so miles.

Another problem was how to efficiently dig a trench, bury the cable, and then close it. Smith obtained Ezra Cornell (1807-1874) for this job. Cornell designed a machine which was a combination plow and cart, pulled by a team of eight mules. A single blade cut a deep slit in the earth. Atop the cart was a large drum wound with the lead pipe and wire, which was laid in the slit as it was cut. The narrow slit or furrow in the earth would then collapse on itself, covering up the pipe as it was laid.

Work was begun on the line on October 21, 1843, beginning in Baltimore. The first two thousand feet of the line, inside the city, had to be laid by hand. Once outside, Cornell went to work with his machine and mules. He found that he could lay from one-half to one mile of cable a day; however, the team following him, responsible for soldering the pipes together, could not keep up, going only about half as fast.

In December, due to several serious problems, Morse ordered construction to be halted. Approximately eight to nine miles of cable had been laid. The company responsible for delivering the lead pipes had been late, and once delivered, many of the pipes were found to be defective: the insulated circuits inside the pipes had been damaged, rendering them useless. Further, a section of the already entrenched pipe was found to contain water.

Morse also experienced problems with some of his partners. Gale, suffering from illness and cold, resigned. Smith was proving to be more a nuisance than help. He was clearly interested in getting the maximum profit from the government, regardless of the ultimate success of the project. Winter was coming on soon, and the money was already more than half spent. Construction was be halted for the winter, to be resumed in the spring.

During the winter months, Morse reviewed the progress, or lack of it, and decided to begin again in the spring, but this time putting the wire on poles above ground, which would be easier and cheaper. Leonard Gale and Joseph Henry had both advised Morse against continuing underground, due to the numerous problems which could cause failure. Ezra Cornell spent much of the time in the winter removing the wires from the tubes.

In March, 1844, work began again, this time beginning from Washington and working towards Baltimore. Cornell headed a work gang of more than twenty-five men. As poles, chestnut trees were used, branches cut off, bark left on, cut to a height of 30 feet. Holes were bored in the ground to a depth of about four feet, and about two hundred feet apart. Two wires ran from post to post, hung on cross arms. Insulation of the wires at the attachment points was a critical problem. Morse used a method suggested by Cornell of wrapping them in shellac-saturated cloth, sandwiched between two glass plates, and held in place with a wooden cover nailed to the cross arm.

By the end of March about seven miles of the poles had been completed, wire put on the poles, and tested. Tests indicated that the circuit functioned as expected, and work continued throughout April. Construction went briskly, adding a mile or more a day. The crew of men under the direction of Cornell worked twelve hours per day, shuttling back and forth on the train between Baltimore and Washington. Some of the men also ate and slept in railroad cars.

Morse stayed in Washington, in one of two rooms which had been given him in the Capitol building. Each day he tested the ever lengthening circuit, telegraphing messages back and forth with Vail or Cornell. As the line was built he and they became more and more adept at tapping out messages in Morse's code, and thus they also tested each new piece of the line immediately after it was added – good engineering practice. Building the line in this manner, by the time it was completed in late May, Morse, Vail and Cornell all had confidence in its capabilities and knew how to use it.

On 1 May, Morse gave the public a glimpse of what was soon to come. The Whig political party was having its convention in Baltimore to choose its candidates for president and vice-president. By then, about 22 miles of line had been laid, as far as the train stop at Annapolis Junction. Morse had Vail stationed there, and he would get the results of the voting from the train en route to Washington. He would then telegraph the results to Morse, so that the news would arrive more than an hour ahead of the train. Vail telegraphed Morse with the news that Henry Clay had been nominated for President. As the news spread, many visitors came to see Morse and his telegraph.

As the line neared completion, public curiosity and excitement grew. Morse and Vail continued sending short messages of news or messages for the passengers on the trains en route.

The Washington-Baltimore Telegraph line officially opened on May 24, 1844. Morse invited a "dear young friend," Annie Ellsworth, to compose the first official message. Although there were some rumors of romantic involvement, Morse explained that his choice was in gratitude to her for having brought him the news when Congress passed the appropriations bill. After consulting with her mother, she suggested the words "What hath God wrought!" taken from Numbers 23:23 in the Bible. On the official day, Morse tapped out the message to Vail at the other end, who telegraphed it back to him as acknowledgment.

That now famous transmission did not attract much attention in the press immediately. However, three days later the Democratic National Convention began in Baltimore, and there was intense interest throughout the country in the result. With Vail at the convention in Baltimore, and Morse in Washington, up-to-the-minute results were passed back and forth between the two cities.

Morse's telegraph station in Washington became the center of attention, as politicians and news correspondents hovered around to get   the latest news. A Washington correspondent of the New York Herald reported that "Little else is done here but watch Professor Morse's Bulletin from Baltimore, to learn the progress of the doings at Convention." When James K. Polk was chosen as the candidate, the news reached Washington within minutes.

The next day brought more telegraph excitement, when the convention nominated Senator Silas Wright, who was then in Washington, as candidate for vice-president. Learning of the news of the nomination within minutes, Morse informed Wright. Wright respectfully declined the nomination, and Morse wired this news back to Baltimore. Another message shortly came back from the convention asking him to reconsider. Wright wired back that his mind was made up. This "long-distance" political negotiating was reported to have taken place "with lightning speed."

These and numerous other similar uses of the telegraph throughout 1844, particularly during the election of 1844, served as proof of the usefulness and possibilities of the telegraph to change the economical, political and social life of the country.

Another interesting application of the telegraph, other than for communications, was in the measurement of time and longitudes. Morse himself had suggested this as a possible use some years earlier. Establishing longitude is the same as knowing the time difference in two distant locations; the east-west difference of one hour is equal to 15 degrees longitude.

Explorer Charles Wilkes conducted experiments between Baltimore and Washington, improving the longitude accuracy of some locations. He wrote that the telegraph provided the means of measuring meridian distances more accurately than ever before.

Morse had considerable help and inspiration from others such as Jackson, Vail, Gale, Cornell, and Smith but often failed or refused to recognize others who helped him. He often attempted to claim all the credit for the invention of the telegraph, not recognizing the many improvements and achievements made by others. This often resulted in resentment, and Morse was the target of numerous lawsuits throughout the rest of his life.

It is worthy of remark, that more business was done by merchants after the tariff was laid than when the service was gratuitus.
–Alfred Vail

Chapter 6
Beginnings of an
Empire 1844-46

On June 3, 1844, Morse officially informed the Secretary of the Treasury that the experimental telegraph line was completed. He pointed out the political, economical and social uses which had already been made of it, citing several examples. He also wrote a report to Congress, asking that Congress take control of the telegraph, for the good of the country. He offered to sell the rights to it for a fair price and supervise its development for the government.

With the help of Vail, Morse demonstrated his telegraph to Congress in February, 1838. The demonstrations took place over several days, and were quite successful. President Van Buren sent a message coded personally by Morse, and demonstrations were also witnessed by several members of his cabinet. The demonstrations were made over ten miles of wire. Many of the members of Congress were clearly very impressed, even amazed at the invention. Henry Ellsworth, the patent commissioner, said the "nothing has ever been in Washington that produced such a noise."

Morse believed that the telegraph was a very powerful new tool with potential to be used for ill as well as for good. He argued that the interest of the country would be better served if the government were to take control of the telegraph and supervise its development.

Another advantage of this, of course, was that it would be easier for Morse himself: by selling out to the government, he could realize an immediate profit, and by supervising the development of the line assure himself of a steady income for many years to come. It would eliminate the need to organize a private company, raise capital, and almost all of the accompanying risks. The job of raising capital to build the telegraph lines would then fall to the government, and thus taxpayers.

Considering his admitted lack of acumen in financial affairs, it is unlikely that Morse gave much thought to the cost this would place on taxpayers. All indications are that Morse sincerely believed that government control would be better for the telegraph development and for the country than private control and competition. That said, experience has shown that, human nature being what it is, it is easy to convince oneself that what is best for one personally is also best for all.

For the next several months, throughout the rest of 1844 and well into 1845, Morse attempted to convince the government to take over the telegraph. He proudly pointed out many examples of its use.

The proceedings of the Democratic National Convention in Baltimore had been reported. A family in Washington had entreated Morse to check on the rumored death of a family member; in minutes he was able to reply that the rumor was false. A Baltimore merchant had telegraphed the Bank of Washington to ascertain whether a check drawn on it was good, and had received the answer in a few minutes. A bill was introduced into Congress to extend the Baltimore-Washington line to New York, but Congress ended its session without taking any action on it.

F. O. J. Smith began attempting to raise capital in 1844. Morse agreed to this with great reluctance; he still had hopes that the government would participate. He also insisted that any agreement with private investors have a clause permitting the government to buy them out, within a specified time, at cost plus 20%. Vail also believed that the government should take over. Smith visited both Boston and New York in an attempt to raise capital to construct a line between those cities, but was unable to generate much interest.

In December, 1844, Morse appealed again to Congress for support for the telegraph. He again pointed out the many advantages which a national communications system would bring. It would aid in national defense, in law enforcement, and in financial business. He declared that the proprietors of the telegraph would be pleased to sell out their interests to the government for a fair price.

He also hinted at what might happen, should Congress fail to act, writing, "For myself, I would prefer that the government should possess the invention, although the pecuniary interests of the proprietors induce them to lean towards arrangements with private companies."

The press also supported government control, as a whole. William Swain of the Philadelphia *Public Ledger* wrote that "the Government . . . possess itself at once with this triumph of American genius, and give to every city throughout the Union the advantages which may be derived from it." James Gordon Bennett wrote in the New York *Herald* that "Government must be impelled to take hold of it" and develop it as a part of the postal service. But as of late 1844, Congress had taken no action to nationalize the telegraph system. The Baltimore-Washington line was placed under the Treasury Department, under the direction and control of the Postmaster General.

On 1 April 1845, the Postmaster General of the U.S. put into place a tariff of one penny per four letters or characters for transmission on the Baltimore-Washington line; up until that time, there had been no charge for its use. Within a few weeks the line was drawing more business than when its use had been free. "It is worthy of remark," wrote Vail, "that more business was done by merchants after the tariff was laid than when the service was gratuitus."

In the first four days of operation, total revenue came to one cent. Dur- ing this time, an office seeker dropped in and asked for a free demon- stration, which Vail refused. When the visitor explained that he had only a penny and a twenty-dollar bill, Vail offered to give him a penny's worth of telegraphy. Vail transmitted a single character to Baltimore, and received a single character in reply. The tariff for this was half a penny; but the visitor, not having the correct change, generously donated half a penny.

The visitor must have passed the word, however, because the next day 12 1/2 cents were taken in; two days later, $0.60; and on April 9, $1.04.

In the first three months of operations with a tariff, receipts totaled $193.56. This was not enough, however, to cover expenses. In the second quarter, income went up slightly, to $219.88. Expenses in the second quarter were $1,425.12; so the line, while bringing in a small income, was still losing money.

On 1 December 1845, Postmaster General Cave Johnson discussed the question of government investment and control of the telegraph in his annual report to the Congress. He pointed out that the Morse patent group had already negotiated agreements with private interests for the construction of telegraph lines between the major cities of the U.S., and that their success would diminish the revenues of the Postal Department.

In his report, he wrote that "It becomes then a question of great importance, how far the government will allow individuals to divide with it the business of transmitting intelligence – an important duty confided to it by the Constitution, necessarily and properly exclusive? Or will it purchase the telegraph, and conduct its operations for the benefit of the public?"

Although the Postmaster General did not believe that the revenue of the telegraph would be sufficient to pay its expenses under any feasible rate of tariffs, he firmly believed that the government should control it. Its importance was not based on its potential revenue, but "as an agent vastly superior to any other ever devised by the genius of man for the diffusion of intelligence . . . The use of an instrument so powerful for good or evil cannot with safety to the people be left in the hands of private individuals uncontrolled by law."

Still, no action was taken by the Congress during the following year, and the Postmaster General addressed the issue once more in his report for 1846. "It is the settled conviction of the undersigned that the public interest, as well as the safety of the citizen, requires that the government should get control of it [the telegraph], by purchase, or that its use should be subjected to the restraint of law."

His report pointed out that privately owned telegraph lines were already in operation between New York and Boston, Buffalo, Philadelphia, and

Washington, and that others were being planned; that in a few years, telegraph lines would undoubtedly extend to all the cities of the Union. He warned of the irreparable damage that might be done if this private enterprise were allowed to proceed unchecked.

The comments of the Postmaster General of the United States in his official reports to the Congress brought up other questions in addition to that of government control of the new telegraph.

First, he seems to have feared that the new invention would take away revenue from the postal service. One of his concerns was protection of the postal monopoly. Protection of an existing service or business is often given as an argument for impeding the establishment of a new one, despite the potential of the new one to greatly improve the quality of life of many.

A second issue the comments brought up was whether the new line and the new telegraph network would make money. The postmaster said that the government should take control, despite the fact that it would not make money. As would be proven a few years later, the new service would make a tremendous amount of money.

A third issue was government control of the transmission of intelligence, the Postmaster General's primary objection to private control. He claimed that the constitution limited the powers of transmitting intelligence to the government. This claim was debatable, and the remarks imply distrust of private enterprise and of individuals. The source of his comment was in the control which the constitution gave to the government of the postal system.

Finally, we come to the issue which was at hand, that of government funding for and control of the telegraph. Samuel Morse, Alfred Vail, Postmaster General Cave Johnson, and a large portion of the press were in favor of a government established monopoly over the telegraph system. If they had had their wish, the history in this chapter and this book would be quite different.

As it turned out, the U.S. Congress rejected their pleas and chose to leave the development of the telegraph system – or lack thereof – up to private individuals and the free market. The United States was at war with Mexico, and it has been suggested that the Congress was simply too busy to concern itself with the telegraph at the time. Whatever the reason, telegraph and telecommunications development was not taken over by the government, but was left up to private enterprise.

There were numerous other countries in which government did take over the telegraph industry and make it into a government monopoly. The issue came up again a quarter century later, amid numerous complaints of the Western Union telegraph monopoly.

In early 1845, Morse and his fellow patentees despaired of getting any more help from Congress, and began looking for private capital in earnest. Realizing his own inadequacies in dealing with matters of business, Morse brought in Amos Kendall (1789-1869) as his representative.

On March 10, 1845 they signed a contract making Kendall the agent for three-fourths of the Morse patent interest in the U.S. Kendall had been trained as a lawyer, had also been a journalist, and had served as Postmaster General under President Andrew Jackson from 1835-40. In that capacity, as a member of Jackson's cabinet, he had done a commendable job in turning that organization around. He also had a reputation for honesty, and he and Morse soon became friends and colleagues.

While Kendall thus became the agent for three-fourths of the Morse patent rights, the remaining one-fourth was held by F. O. J. Smith, and his consent was required for the conveyance of any patent rights. In a letter to Kendall dated March 10, 1845, Smith warned that his cooperation in any plans for the development of the telegraph would not be given unless his claims against his co-patentees were satisfied. For his part, Kendall believed that a satisfactory arrangement could be reached with Smith through compromise and mutual best interest.

Kendall's experience as Postmaster General served him well in this new venture. He laid out a master plan for a national telegraph network, with New York City as the major hub, with trunk telegraph lines planned to be run to Boston, Buffalo, Philadelphia, and Washington. Plans were also made to build a line to the southern cities of Richmond, Charleston, Mobile and New Orleans. Money would be raised from private capital to construct the major trunk lines, after which feeder lines could be added to serve the rest of the country.

Kendall first attempted to find capital to fund the entire network; but when that failed, he set out to capitalize each major trunk line separately. He himself took responsibility for the New York-Washington line; Smith agreed to take the Boston-New York line. John J. Butterfield, the famous stagecoach owner, was found and enlisted to take charge of a line from Buffalo to New York. In the west, Henry O'Rielly, as will be discussed, was granted a contract to extend from the east coast to the Mississippi River and the Great Lakes.

Kendall set out to organize a company to finance the New York – Washington line, but after several weeks of canvassing, had not succeeded in raising the necessary capital. He then decided to build a line from New York to Philadelphia first, which was roughly halfway between New York and Baltimore.

Kendall tried to raise $15,000, the amount needed for the shorter line. He hoped that the success of this line would then help him raise the capital to build the link from Philadelphia to Baltimore. He finally got an opening pledge from William Corcoran, a prominent Washington financier, for $1,000. Kendall himself pledged $500, as did Ezra Cornell, and Kendall finally succeeded in getting pledges for the $15,000 from a total of twenty-five subscribers. The only pledge for more than $1,000 was from F.O.J. Smith, who pledged $2,750.

On 15 May 1845, the "Articles of Association" of the new company were adopted, and the Magnetic Telegraph Company, the first telegraph company in the United States, was established, for the purpose of building a telegraph line from New York to Philadelphia, and eventually to Washington, D.C. For each $50 in capital provided, the subscriber was assigned a $100 share in the company. That is, for the original $15,000 in capital given, the subscribers were given $30,000 in company stock.

The Morse patentees were also assigned $30,000 in stock, in accordance with their agreement. In other words, the original value, or capitalization, of the New York-Philadelphia line was set at $60,000, with half-ownership going to the original subscribers and half to the Morse patentees.

Kendall agreed to take charge of the line's construction. Initially, he and Smith were to be joint contractors, but Smith resigned when the board refused to accept wires and other telegraph equipment which he had on hand as part of his subscription. He also failed to pay his $2,750 at the time it was needed, forcing Kendall to use personal funds for the completion of the line. This was only one of the lesser of many difficulties that Smith would cause for the other Morse patentees.

For the construction, Kendall selected Ezra Cornell and Dr. A. C. Goell as his assistants in the field. Cornell was in charge of construction from Newark, New Jersey (Newark lies across the Hudson River from New York City) towards Philadelphia, while Goell was to supervise construction starting from Philadelphia.

Construction contracts called for the use of unannealed copper wire, poles set two hundred feet apart, and insulators of a "glass bureau knob pattern." Work began in the fall of 1845, and due to vigilant supervision on the part of Kendall, the line was completed on 20 January 1846, from Newark to Philadelphia. The final hop from Newark across the Hudson River to New York City, however, proved to be more of a problem than had been expected.

Early in the construction phase, Cornell attempted to lay a cable under the river from nearby Fort Lee, New Jersey into New York. A copper wire was covered with cotton, soaked with pitch, placed in lead pipes, and laid under the river. Before the line was tested, however, a ship brought it up, together with the ship's anchor, breaking and losing the cable.

Various means were tried with little success, including carrier pigeons, balloons, tall masts, and anchored ships. The problem was not permanently resolved until about a decade later, when cable insulated with gutta-percha (described in Part 2) was found to be suitable. In the meantime, Newark served as the New York terminus of the wire, and messages were sent into New York by ferry or other available means.

Once the line was completed in early 1846, the shareholders met in New York for a final organizing meeting. A board of directors was appointed, and Kendall was made president, with an annual salary of $2,250. A secretary and a treasurer were also chosen with salaries of $350 and $300 per year, respectively. The salaries of chief operators were set at $600; assistant operators and clerks at $500; and assistant clerks at $350.

The shareholders laid out the rules of operation in considerable detail. The telegraph was to "be opened alike to all men . . . and the first to come shall be first served." No one would be allowed to occupy the line for more than fifteen minutes while others were waiting. Exceptions were permitted in the case of public emergencies, or for the prevention of crime, or the hunting or notice of fugitives.

Among some sixty-six detailed provisions, it was provided that "the Telegraph Offices . . . should be open every day from sunup until 10 o'clock P. M. except the ordinary hours for morning and afternoon services on the Sabbath." Operators were to observe the strictest decorum towards customers, and to listen to all complaints, however unreasonable, with good temper. They were also advised that "all angry or impertinent messages sent along the wire from operator to operator . . . were absolutely prohibited, or if sent, must be paid for as other messages not pertaining to the business of the line."

The line was tested to make sure it would work, and Kendall sent out advertisements to the major New York and Philadelphia papers. He also sent out the following circular letter to major prospective customers:

Sir:

The Magnetic Telegraph between New York and Philadelphia via Newark, will be opened to the public on Tuesday, January 27. [1846] Messages will be dispatched from the Telegraph Office, No. 10 Wall Street (basement) New York, at 9, 11 A.M. and 12 o'clock, M. – 3,4 and 7 P.M., and will be received by Philadelphia via Newark, at 8 1/2, 9 1/2, and 11 1/2 A.M., and 2 1/2, 4 1/2 and 10 P.M. Communications which must all be pre-paid, will be sent in the order in which they are received.

The following are the rates established for ten words and under: – For the transmission and writing out of every communication, not exceeding ten words, every figure being counted as a word, exclusive of the signature and address, and the direction of the writer, as to the disposition of the communications, from New York to Philadelphia, Twenty- five Cents. For every addition, not exceeding ten words, the same rate of charge as in the first ten.

Yours truly,
Amos Kendall, President

In the first four days of operation, the new line brought in $100. The company treasurer, Sidney Doane, wrote to Smith: "When you consider that we anticipate the mails by only a few hours, are obliged to send to Newark, can only send a few times daily, that business is extremely dull, that editors do nothing for us, and we have not yet the confidence of the public and that on 2 of the 4 days we have been delayed and lost business in Philadelphia through mismanagement – when you consider all these things you will see that we are all well satisfied with results so far. In one month we shall be doing $50 business a day."

Morse was even more enthusiastic. He wrote, "Telegraph matters are looking very well. We are operating between Newark and Philadelphia and the point is decided that the stock is a dividend paying stock; the stockholders are in good spirits and prepared to push forward. We are troubled with the river and that is the reason we cannot communicate direct to New York, but hope to be able in a few weeks."

However, the line encountered two important problems from its first days of operation. The glass used for insulation glistened in the sunlight, and became targets for the marksmen in the area. These were destroyed by the dozen.

The other unexpected problem was related to the copper wire. In harsh winters the lines often contracted and snapped apart. One solution to this problem was to take care not to string the wires too tightly between the poles. Wires strung too loosely, however, had other problems: they could become caught on branches, blow in the wind and drag on the ground. A better solution was eventually found: use iron wires rather than copper. Though not as good a conductor, these were stronger and less vulnerable to cold and heat, and were found to conduct electricity well enough for the telegraph.

Despite the problems, the line made a small profit in the first six months of operation. In July, 1846, the company treasurer reported profits of $293.17 on the New York office for the preceding five months, and a similar figure in the Philadelphia office; these on a total income of $4,228 in the first six months of operation. Though this was not as much as hoped for, the line had been out of operation due to breaks for almost a quarter of the days in operation. The Postmaster General's remark that the telegraph could not make money was already proving to be mistaken.

Some of the earliest customers for the new telegraph line were stockbrokers. Since the board of brokers met much earlier in Philadelphia than in New York, speculators could telegraph the prices of stocks in Philadelphia to the terminal point in Newark, and then sent across the river by pre-arranged semaphore codes. This enabled speculators to profit from the difference in prices between two markets – an early form of "hedging."

The best customer, however, was the press. Before the line was opened, it was discussed and decided to give rates of one-third the regular price after the first hundred words. A provision giving credit accounts led to problems when some of the papers refused to pay their accounts, because the transmissions had been delayed.

As soon as Kendall had made the arrangements for the construction of the New York-Philadelphia line, he started raising capital for the Philadelphia-Baltimore link. By January of 1846 he was able to obtain pledges of $10,000 from nine subscribers. However, most of the money came from just two sources. Henry O'Rielly of New York pledged $4,000 and William M. Swain pledged $3,500. To O'Rielly, the telegraph became more than just a business; it became a "cause," to which he was to dedicate his life. Swain, of the Philadelphia *Public Ledger*, had understood the potential of the telegraph early on.

Kendall asked for construction bids on the new line, and O'Rielly bid $12,000, which Kendall accepted. This amount was later raised to $14,000. Kendall admitted to doubts that the work could be completed for that amount. O'Rielly began work in late 1845, and despite a number of difficulties, the line was completed by June, 1846.

Once this line was connected to the government line in Baltimore, it became possible to send telegraphs between New York City (actually Newark, until the link across river was completed) and Washington, a distance of 260 miles. The possibilities of the telegraph to improve communications were now becoming clear to a larger number of people. Benjamin French – who had invested $1,000 in the initial line – a politician and speculator, wrote to his brother, "The Telegraph is doing wonders – we are now taking in hundreds of dollars daily and have a great deal more work than we can do on one wire. We can communicate from here [Washington] to Jersey City in a second, and next week we shall probably communicate with Boston! The telegraph stock must be the best stock in the country – our line will pay for itself in one year."

O'Rielly's expenses for the Philadelphia-Baltimore section went well beyond the $14,000 which he had bid, and the board of directors refused to pay him beyond that amount. There was a long and bitter quarrel in which O'Rielly claimed that Kendall had authorized him for additional expenses. The board refused to go along, however, so O'Rielly ended up with little or no profit on the construction of the line.

Line	length	capital	time	who
Baltimore-Wash.,D.C.	44 mi.	30,000; Congress	May, 1844 1844	Morse patentees
New York-Baltimore	260	(divided at Philadelphia)	1845-46	Kendall
New York-Philadelphia	130	15,000	Jan., 1846	Kendall
Philadelphia-Baltimore	130	14,000	Jun., 1846	O'Rielly
New York-Boston	260	40,000 needed 28,000 raised	1846	Smith
New York-Buffalo	500	200,000	1845-46	Faxton, Butterfield

Projected Morse Telegraph Lines

By early 1846, then, construction was underway on routes from New York to Philadelphia, and from Philadelphia to Baltimore. These were both completed that year. Lines northward to Boston and northwestward to Buffalo had also been started, as is described in the next section.

The route to New Orleans from Washington was much longer, and would come later. This required more capital, and took Kendall more time. In November, 1846, a contract for the this route was signed by John J. Haley, a small restaurant owner in New York. This was planned to run from Washington south through Richmond and Petersburg,Virginia; then to Raleigh, North Carolina; Charleston, South Carolina; Savannah, Georgia; Mobile, Alabama; and finally on to New Orleans.

From his experience as Postmaster General, Kendall expected this route to be the most profitable of all the early routes. As Postmaster General, he had established an express route between New Orleans and New York which proved quite profitable. However, despite Kendall's plans, several years would pass before his hopes for the New Orleans line were realized.

insulate *1. to cover with a material that prevents or reduces the passage or transfer of heat, electricity or sound.*
2. to place in an isolated situation.
–Webster's School and Office Dictionary

Chapter 7
The North: New York to Boston, Buffalo and Canada

F. O. J. Smith had agreed to take responsibility for the New York-Boston line. His performance of this task was dismal. The New York-Boston line could have paid major dividends for the Morse patentees, had it been well built; instead, it was a major disappointment.

One of the problems had nothing to do with Smith, however, but with another man who harbored ill feelings toward Morse from years earlier, Dr. Charles T. Jackson. Jackson had been one of the passengers on the voyage of the *Sully* in 1832, and had tried to claim credit for inventing the telegraph. Jackson did his best to discourage the citizens of Boston from having anything to do with the "Morse telegraph."

In addition, Smith himself had a reputation throughout New England as an "unsavory" character. He had served as a New Hampshire Congressman earlier. The result of this and Jackson's campaign was strong negative feeling in Boston towards Morse, and practically zero capital was raised for the line there. Smith then tried to raise the capital in New York.

The construction cost for the line was estimated at $40,000, or $160 per mile. By the end of 1845, only $28,000 of the needed $40,000 had been raised, but Smith was determined to proceed. Thus on 7 January 1846, it was decided to go ahead and begin construction, and to try to raise the remaining capital later in Boston. Once Bostonians saw the benefits of communications with New York, they might be more willing to help finance it.

However, the construction of the line went even worse than had the fundraising. Smith's construction program was careless and workers were poorly supervised, or not at all. A comment written by one of the workers on the line illustrates. W. Y. Deere, member of a construction gang wrote to Smith:

> Arrived in Springfield on the 28th. Reported to Mr. Strong [foreman] that I was ready for work. But neither Mr. Merrill nor Mr. Fairbanks was there and the freight had not arrived and Mr. Strong knew nothing of the tools. The 29th was the same reason for delay. The 30th Mr. Merrill and myself and a man I hired went to work. Took 1/2 day to get glass and staples down to starting point. My man and I had to carry all irons two miles on our backs. Saturday I was out of stock to do with.

Smith's policy of paying labor as cheaply as possible also resulted in problems. Robert Right, a foreman, wrote: "They are first class workmen and I think you would do well to pay them $13 a day and keep them, rather than try to get a new crew out from Boston." Another foreman, J. E. Strong reported that a number of men had left because the pay was not sufficient for the work required.

One of the most serious problems on Smith's line was his lack of understanding of and attention to insulation. He once considered it entirely unnecessary. Later, he modified this attitude, but still stated that too much attention was being given to insulation.

His thinking was the opposite of Kendall's, who had every alternate pole cut down along a section of the Magnetic line to reduce the number of contact points with the ground. In a letter to O'Rielly in December, 1845, Smith described his plan: "I put my wires up in both a more useful and, in milder latitudes, cheaper form. I use no glass cap, nor crossbar, but only blocks saturated thoroughly with tar and resin, also a tin cover and saturated cloth."

As the work on the line progressed, it became obvious that there were serious problems. Other causes such as short circuits and improper connections were blamed at first, but it soon became clear that the major one was faulty insulation. "Yesterday I examined 59 posts and found the wires resting on the screws in 74 instances," wrote a foreman in April. "They had not the appearance of being drawn down by the weight of the wire, but were probably left so at the time they were put up. It there were no further difficulty, what I have found would be sufficient to account for failure to get the circuit through."

Smith was finally forced to admit his mistake, and at the end of April, the wires were coming down, and the wooden blocks were being replaced by glass knob insulators.

Despite the difficulties, progress continued on the line, and by early June, 1846, it reached New York City. In preparation for the grand opening, Smith himself personally connected the instruments in every station along the route. When the line first reached New York, the New York station could not even connect to New Haven, Connecticut, the nearest neighboring station, due to faulty connections. More checking of the connections was needed, and on June 27 the line was finally opened to the public.

The New York-Boston line, once opened for operations, was not what its builders had promised, nor what it should have been. One problem was that the copper wires had been hung slackly from the poles, in order to avoid the breaks such as had occurred on other lines when the they contracted with the cold. As a result the lines often became crossed, interfering with each other.

The line had been cheaply and carelessly built, and this showed in its operation from the start. There were frequent breaks, causing inter-ruptions in service. When the first storm passed through, some 130 breaks were reported in a distance of thirty miles. During the first four months of operation, the line was out of service more than half the time.

Public opinion along the Boston-New York corridor was turning against the Morse telegraph, causing the Morse patentees much concern. In

August, Morse wrote to Vail, "You see how F.O.J. Smith gets on with his Boston line!! A little less boasting, a little less self-confidence, a little more confidence in our experience, would not have been of any harm. Let them work out their trouble since they will have things their own way."

In a letter to Smith dated 1 September 1846, Kendall mentioned the many inquiries he received concerning the Boston line. People wanted to know when the line would be working. There was no question that there would be a tremendous mutual benefit with the other lines, once interconnection became possible. "It would be a great matter for us if your line could be got to work well," Kendall's letter said. "I passed along some 20 miles of it west of New Haven a few days ago and saw the wires in contact with the limbs or leaves of the trees in five or six places."

In the first six months of operation, the New York-Boston line earned no money. Its outside structure already needed extensive repairs. Of the original $40,000 capital needed, only $28,000 had been raised, and considering its poor performance, the raising of more capital from the public seemed still less likely than before. Under the circumstances, Smith had no alternative but to turn to his personal resources for support. With this, he took over complete control of the line. It seemed that, for better or worse, he would dominate its future.

At the same time that Smith was stringing wires between Boston and New York City, another group was working on a much longer link, from New York City to Buffalo, in western New York state, and passing through the cities of Albany, Utica, Syracuse, and Rochester. This was based on an agreement which John Butterfield (1801-69) – still remembered as the father of the Butterfield Overland Mail – signed with Kendall on May 30, 1845.

The Articles of Association for the proposed New York, Albany and Buffalo Company were adapted in Utica in September. They called for a line of two copper wires, insulated by glass knobs, and no less than twenty-five poles per mile. The total length of the line was 500 miles, and the capitalization of the company was set at $200,000, with the Morse patentees having 50% ownership and the rest going to the original subscribers.

The trustees of the new company were Theodore Faxton, John Butterfield, Hiram Greenman, Henry Wells, and Crawford Livingston, and these also became the contractors for the construction of the line. Faxton and Butterfield had both been involved in stagecoach lines, and worked well together as partners on several successful enterprises.

They made frequent business trips to Washington, and in 1844 had observed the progress of the Baltimore-Washington line with interest. When it became clear that the government was not going to take control of development of the telegraph, they were ready to take charge in bringing it to western New York State. This led to Butterfield's agreement with Kendall.

The group led by Faxton were experienced businessmen and took much care in the construction of the line. Due attention was given to insulation, to the trimming of tree branches which might interfere with the wires, to the proper placing of the posts, and other important details in construction.

The people of the state along the route showed much more interest in the line than had the people in New York City or Boston. One can easily surmise that, living hundreds of miles from any major city, they were much more appreciative of the potential of the telegraph.

Construction began in late 1845 and progressed rapidly. Some sections were open in February, 1846, others by May, and the entire 500-mile line was completed in September, 1846. According to Ezra Cornell, who had helped build part of the line, receipts for September 10, the second day of operation, were $125, even though no announcement had yet been made of the opening. "Eighty dollars per day will pay all expenses and 7 percent on all the stock. Receipts will go up to $200 per day. Mark that," he predicted.

Morse was also optimistic. "Our receipts on the Buffalo line for 23 days only (not one month) were 2,960 odd dollars; that is at the rate after expenses are all paid, of 14 percent." At the end of the year, the stock for the line was selling at a twenty percent premium over its par value.

While the New York-Buffalo line was undoubtedly the best constructed so far, like any new business, it also experienced problems and difficulties. The glass insulators, so important to the operation of the line, glistened in the New York state sun just at they had in New Jersey and Pennsylvania, and sharpshooters there were just as happy to use them for target practice in the "Empire State" as they were in the other states. As a result, many breaks occurred.

Faxton had attempted to prevent this problem, by getting the New York legislature to pass a law on May 13, 1845 making the destruction of telegraph property a crime. The problem was so widespread that the company offered a $100 reward for the apprehension of violators.

A second problem which the line experienced was the constant conflict between "way business" and "through business." The line was needed the majority of the time for the transmission of messages between New York and Buffalo. This left insufficient time for the business between the cities along the route, such as Albany, Syracuse, and Rochester. Because of the slowness of the "way service," people along the route became disenchanted with the telegraph and it lost much potential business.

Yet another problem which surfaced very early was a disagreement between Faxton and Kendall, only one of many bitter quarrels which occurred between the Morse patentees and their licensees. The disagreement was over the terms by which feeder lines could connect to the main one.

The contract which Faxton acccepted required him to allow feeder lines (authorized by the patentees) to connect to the main one, and as tariff pay one-half of the total charged by the side line. Faxton did not like this agreement because it gave him less profit that he thought reasonable.

Kendall felt compelled to insist on the original terms, as some feeder lines had already been built with these conditions, and Faxton's terms would leave them with little or no profit. Kendall threatened to build another line for the feeders before an agreement was reached on October 29. Faxton ended up getting most of what he wanted, but the hard bargain caused bitter feelings against him from the Morse patentees, especially Kendall.

In the fall of 1846, the telegraph also took root in Canada. A group of Toronto businessmen, observing the success of the line to Buffalo, financed a telegraph from that city to Niagara so that the news from Europe and New York which now reached Buffalo so quickly could also get to Toronto almost as quickly. That line was opened on 19 December 1846.

Then hurry along the wire, boys, the sooner we get through
To New Orleans, the sooner we will have a chance to blow
For there's no stopping this O'Rielly; it may happen very soon
He'll get the notion in his head to telegraph the moon.
–Line Builders' Song, 1848

Chapter 8
Henry O'Rielly
and the West

As Kendall was pushing the line from New York to Philadelphia and Baltimore, Smith was working on the line from Boston to New York, and Faxton was building out west to Buffalo, an enthusiastic young immigrant was making grand plans for a telegraph network which would stretch from the east coast to the Mississippi River, and from the Great Lakes to the Ohio River valley. He quickly became an enthusiastic advocate of the telegraph, and once involved in its development, he dedicated himself to it with a zeal exceeded by none.

His name was Henry O'Rielly, born in Carrickmacross, County of Ulster, Ireland, in 1806. At the age of ten the boy emigrated from Ireland to New York City with his father, and soon became an enthusiastic new American, identifying himself strongly with the life of the new country and its causes.

As a youth O'Rielly served an apprenticeship with the *Columbian*, and also took another job with the *Patriot*, where his political thinking seems to have matured. At the age of twenty he moved west to Rochester with a friend, Luther Tucker, to organize a newspaper. Rochester was just a village at the time, and the Rochester *Daily Advertiser* was a welcome addition to the community. O'Rielly took up a number of the important issues of the day, supporting the re-election of Andrew Jackson, the improvement of the Erie Canal, Irish independence, and other social issues.

In 1836, he ran for the state legislature, but was defeated. The next year, Postmaster General Amos Kendall appointed him as head of the Rochester post office. This position was too mundane for O'Rielly, however, and in 1842 he left to take an editorial position at the Albany *Atlas*, where he was better positioned to crusade for his causes. There he played a part in advocating state constitutional reform, which eventually led to the drafting of a new state constitution in 1846.

In June, 1845, O'Rielly was returning from New York on the Albany night boat, when he met John Butterfield. Butterfield was returning from the trip to Washington, where he had just made the agreement with Amos Kendall for the New York-Buffalo line. Butterfield discussed his plans for the line with O'Rielly, who quickly became so excited about the issue that within two weeks he made a trip to Washington to see Kendall and had his own agreement with the Morse patentees.

O'Rielly's contract with Kendall was signed on June 13, 1845. The contract had a stipulation that would later become the cause of a serious dispute: that O'Rielly was required to complete the section of the line to Harrisburg, Pennsylvania within six months of the signing date, or the agreement would be nullified.

O'Rielly's Projected Lines	approx. length (miles)
Pittsburgh-Philadelphia, via Harrisburg, Lancaster	260
Pittsburgh-St. Louis	610
St. Louis-Chicago	290
Buffalo-Chicago, via Erie, Cleveland, Detroit	540
Pittsburgh-Cleveland	130

O'Rielly's Major Planned Lines

After signing the contract, O'Rielly returned to Rochester, where he was well known and respected. He sought out Hervey Ely, one of the leading businessman in the area. The Ely family had long been prominent in the economic life of the community. After examining the contract and discussing it with O'Rielly, Ely was favorably impressed with the possibility, and he helped O'Rielly make contact with other investors in the area. The Atlantic Lake and Mississippi Telegraph Company was soon formed.

In addition to O'Rielly, there were six other original signers. These were two nephews of Hervey Ely: Elisha and Heman Ely; two attorneys who were brothers, Samuel Selden and Henry Selden; and George Dawson and Alvah Strong. These last two were editor and proprietor, respectively, of the Rochester *Daily Democrat*. The lawyer brothers were also related to the Ely family through their mother.

The six investors pledged $2,800 to O'Rielly for his immediate use, with more capital promised to follow as needed for the construction of the telegraph lines.

On 14 September 1845 the stockholders met in Rochester to formally organize the company. At this meeting, another $4,200 was pledged for the construction of the Philadelphia-Harrisburg line so that O'Rielly could build the line without delay.

In the meantime, O'Rielly had developed his plans and begun to publicize them in a series of pamphlets which were widely circulated. The plans called for two lines running from the east coast to the Mississippi River. The northern line would run from Buffalo – the terminal of Faxton's line from New York City – to Erie, Pennsylvania and then follow the shores of Lake Erie to Cleveland and Toledo, in Ohio; to Detroit, Michigan; and finally, to Chicago.

Chicago would be connected by a north-south line to St. Louis, Missouri, which was the western terminal of the southern line. The southern line would connect to the Morse line at Philadelphia or thereabouts, and lead to Harrisburg and Pittsburgh, Pennsylvania, and to Wheeless, Virginia. From there it was to continue westward, following generally the course of the Ohio River, to St. Louis.

In addition to the Chicago-St. Louis line, two other north-south links were planned: one from Dayton to Toledo, the other between Pittsburgh and Cleveland. The entire network was divided into six parts, and each part would be subscribed and built as an independent com- pany.

As far possible, the capital for each line should be raised from investors along its route, but when that failed, the members of the parent Atlantic, Lake and Mississippi Telegraph company were committed to raise the capital. Thus, this agreement guaranteed to O'Rielly all the capital necessary for the entire network. It was also understood that the parent company was to have the final voice in shaping the general policy for the entire O'Rielly system.

O'Rielly had thus been far more successful in raising the capital for a much bigger network than had been either Kendall or Smith, and in a shorter time. Faxton had also done well in raising capital for and building his 500-mile line, but O'Rielly's planned network dwarfed even the New York-Buffalo line in size.

The contract which O'Rielly signed on June 13, 1845 with the patentees – Francis O. J. Smith, Samuel F. B. Morse, and L. D. Gale – must have been hastily written, and had a requirement that would cause much grief to both O'Rielly and Kendall.

In his history of telegraphy, *Wiring a Continent*, Luther Thompson describes the contract as "a masterpiece of ambiguity." In O'Rielly's eagerness to get an agreement with the Morse group, he clearly failed to make a careful assessment of it, and also made the mistake assuming that the other signers of the document would be reasonable in their interpretation of it and/or in their dealings with him. The entire contract contained less than a thousand words. The second paragraph follows:

> That the said O'Rielly undertakes on his part, at his own expense, to use his best endeavors to raise capital for the construction of a line of Morse's Electro-Magnetic Telegraph, to connect the great Seaboard Line at Philadelphia, or at other such convenient point on said line as may approach nearer to Harrisburg in Pennsylvania, and from thence through Harrisburg and other intermediate towns to Pittsburgh; and

thence through Wheeling and Cincinnati, and other such towns as the said O'Rielly and his associates may elect, to St. Louis, and also the principal towns on the Lakes.

On the date that the contract was signed, the line which O'Rielly was to connect to had not yet been built, its route had not even been decided yet, and was not decided until late the following fall.

Kendall had experienced considerable difficulty in raising sufficient capital for its construction. The route which Kendall wanted to follow was along the Philadelphia, Wilmington and Baltimore Railroad. In this case, O'Rielly's eastern connection would be Philadelphia.

But Kendall experienced considerable difficulty in getting that right-of-way, and he wrote to O'Rielly on 12 July 1845 that he would probably have to build west to Lancaster, Pennsylvania, which was seventy miles west of Philadelphia, and from there on to Baltimore. In this case, O'Rielly's eastern connection would be Lancaster. Coupled with this uncertainly over the route was the contract's time limit:

> Unless this line, from the point of connection with the seaboard route, shall be constructed within six months from date, to Harrisburg, and capital provided for its extension to Pittsburgh, within said time, then this agreement, and any conveyance in trust that may have been made in pur- suance thereof, shall be null and void thereafter; unless it shall satisfactorily appear that unforeseen difficulties are experienced by said O'Rielly and his associates in obtain- ing from the State Officers of Pennsylvania the right of way along the public works; and in that event, the conditional annulment shall take effect at the end of six months after such permission shall be given or refused.

Thus, having received the letter in July from Kendall, O'Rielly began construction of a line from Lancaster to Harrisburg in September, 1845. He did so without any other explicit authority from Kendall than the letter, and expected this to satisfy the six-month stipulation.

O'Rielly placed his brother, Captain John O'Rielly, and Bernard O'Conner in charge of the construction. Other members of the construction crew were James Reid, Anson Stager, David Brooks, and Henry Hepburn.

Reid and Stager had worked at the Rochester newspaper. All left their jobs to join up with O'Rielly's telegraph company.

O'Rielly and his crew attracted a lot of attention from the farmers in the countryside along the route, not much of it positive. "We were looked upon as the denizens of another world come to break the quiet and honest industry and sobriety of Pennsylvania," Reid wrote in a report to the stockholders.

The crew made up for their lack of experience with an abundance of enthusiasm, and construction of the line proceeded at a rapid pace. Chestnut poles were planted along the tracks of the Harrisburg & Lancaster Railroad at two-hundred foot intervals. A black walnut crossarm was inserted through the top of each pole to support the two wires. Reid wrote, "As to insulation, it was a long word that few of us understood." The crew attempted to follow the instructions in a pamphlet written by Alfred Vail, which suggested the cotton cloth dipped in beeswax be wrapped around the pole.

The wire was of unannealed copper, according to the prevailing scientific opinion of the day. Since it was thought that a curving wire might affect the destination of the messages, the wires were drawn taught.

"The line looked very trim and handsome," Reid wrote, "as in the evening of a fine October day we looked at our first day's work. We noticed that some enterprising bees . . . came to our waxed rags, no doubt to replevin on their lost stores." When fall rains and frost arrived, the beeswax and cotton soon disappeared.

On Thanksgiving Day, 24 November, "four hungry, dirty, unkempt and unshaven men . . . on the verge of the canal near the railroad depot" in Harrisburg, Pennsylvania, connected the last thread of wire to the last post at its destination. The wire and posts were in place, but the telegraph instruments to connect it, which were to be made by Ezra Cornell, had not yet arrived.

The waited-for instruments finally arrived on 10 December, just three days before the six-month deadline. However, they were not Morse instruments. With the instruments was a note from Cornell, explaining that he had designed a new type of instrument, which was an improvement on the Morse type, and that he intended to apply for a patent on them.

He requested that O'Rielly sign and return an enclosed paper which recognized his rights to the new type of instruments. Suspecting something improper, O'Rielly returned Cornell's instruments, denouncing Cornell's claim as unjust to Morse, and thus lost the opportunity to complete the line within the six-month deadline.

The line was opened for business in the second week of January, 1846. At the end of the first week of January, Brooks wrote to O'Rielly, "The thing is accomplished. We have communicated with Reid by telegraph this forenoon." Hepburn commented that "The section of the 'Atlantic, Lake & Mississippi Telegraph' between Lancaster and Harrisburg is in the full tide of successful operation."

The line was slow to bring in business. "The receipts of the week up to last night were $4.50," reported Brooks from the Lancaster office, the first week in February. J. N. Lindsay in Harrisburg reported receipts of $8.50 for the same time period. Unlike the longer lines, the situation did not improve soon. The link was not yet connected to the Washington-New York line, and Harrisburg and Lancaster were smaller cities, so there was less demand, but the line also had many technical difficulties.

Two months after its construction was completed, it was practically worthless as a communication link. The tightly strung wires caused many breaks, and the poor insulation was also a likely cause of the frequent disconnections. It became a daily routine for Brooks to come into the Lancaster office at 4:30 AM, check for current, and on finding none, set out along the route with a bundle of wire to find the problem. The operation of the line as a commercial enterprise soon became impossible, and after three months of futile operation, the service was shut down, and the copper taken down and sold to pay the operators debts.

O'Rielly probably would have quickly made the needed changes to get the Lancaster-Harrisburg line back into service, but he was fully occupied, helping the Morse patentees on another line. In November, 1845, as O'Rielly's line was nearing completion, Kendall asked for bids on the line from Baltimore to Philadelphia, even though he had not yet raised all the capital necessary.

O'Rielly offered the lowest bid of $12,000 (later amended to $14,000). Since his line to Lancaster was nearing completion, he reasoned that he would be able to handle the Baltimore-Philadelphia line. The route which the line was to follow still had not been finalized.

Thus, O'Rielly did Kendall another favor, in negotiating with the Philadelphia, Wilmington and Baltimore Railroad for the right of way along its railroad. O'Rielly thus proved himself more able to negotiate with the railroad companies than Kendall had been. This provided a more direct route, but is also meant that the line would not pass through Lancaster; making it necessary for O'Rielly to extend his Harrisburg-Lancaster line another seventy miles to Philadelphia.

O'Rielly told Kendall that he would be able to work on both lines – the extension of his line from Lancaster to Philadelphia, and the Philadelphia-Baltimore line – at the same time, and would be able complete them by February, 1846.

In this estimate he was overly optimistic, and the Philadelphia-Baltimore line was not completed until June, 1846. Further, his own line from Harrisburg to Philadelphia, which needed to be rebuilt to Lancaster and extended to Philadelphia, was not completed until September, 1846, nine months after the six-month deadline in his original contract. These delays provided the pretext for an unfortunate attack on him.

The reason for the six-month deadline is not spelled out clearly in the contract. One possibility is that it was put in as a method rescinding the contract for the patentees, in the case that the contract was not carried out in good faith. At any rate, the six month time limit seems quite unreasonable; the point at which O'Rielly was to connect was not even determined until near the end of the time limit. Under these circumstances, it is difficult to imagine how he could be faulted.

By the end of 1846 − 2 1/2 years after the completion of the experimental Baltimore-Washington line − the telegraph had become the talk of the nation. It had been sufficiently tested that its worth was now clear. The telegraph had already begun to make a major impact on all aspects of life and on the economic development of the U.S.

F. O. J. Smith now began to look for a way to get a bigger piece of the pie for himself. It was now clear to him that O'Rielly's ambitious plan for the western network had tremendous potential. Smith monitored O'Rielly's progress carefully and found the six-month limit had not been met. This gave him a pretext to try to wrest O'Rielly's network away and keep it for himself.

At first, Smith tried to negotiate with O'Rielly. In July, 1846, Smith sent his brother-in-law, Eliphalet Case, to talk with O'Rielly. Case brought an offer for financing for a line from Cincinnati to Pittsburgh, but under conditions which were not compatible with O'Rielly's plans. When O'Rielly refused his offer, Smith hardened his position.

"On referring to your contract respecting the Telegraph and the West," he wrote to O'Rielly on 2 October 1846, "you will perceive it has long since expired by its limitations. I hope, however, you have the section to Harrisburg so nearly completed, as to have that section disposed of under your contract. Its retardation has greatly delayed the progress farther west." Smith, in other words, was offering to let O'Rielly hold on to the Harrisburg-Philadelphia line, which had just been completed, but the rest of his planned network − the vast majority of it − was to be reapportioned.

O'Rielly was enraged at Smith's blatant attempt to dismiss him and take over his network. For a while, Kendall tried to mediate between them. He urged O'Rielly to accept the Case proposal, and when O'Rielly refused, on 15 October wrote, "Neither you nor I can get along with our enterprise without consulting to some extent the views of Mr. Smith. Never intending to take advantage of a failure to meet the time limited in your contract, I had not examined it minutely; but now I would ask, whether your line was, in fact, constructed from the connecting point to Harrisburg within six months from its date or from the time that point was finally fixed at Philadelphia? I ask the question, not for my own satisfaction, but to fix your attention on that point and to say that if you treat Mr. Smith as not entitled to be consulted by you it is not difficult to see how this matter is to end."

At the same time, Kendall was urging moderation on Smith. He urged Smith to meet him in Philadelphia to work out a solution. In a letter to Smith on 6 October, he wrote, "If we manage with prudence and act in concert, the revenues of a nation are within our reach. If we are divided in counsel or raise the public against us, we jeopardize everything and shall live in constant turmoil."

This was same cooperative business philosophy Kendall had vainly urged on Smith from the beginning of their relationship. But his conciliatory words, as before, had little influence on Smith.

Unfortunately for O'Rielly, some new developments caused Kendall to turn against him. O'Rielly was not one with a great deal of legal expertise or financial acumen. He made the mistake of issuing a few stock certificates on his line without consulting either the patentees or his associates. He explained to Kendall that these were issued to editors who could help the telegraph cause, that no general issue of stock had been made nor would be made until the line was completed. His intentions were positive; his methods were not quite within the letter of the law of his agreement.

Kendall was not a man with a great deal of patience or understanding. He took a hard line against O'Rielly for this seemingly minor infraction. On 15 October, he wrote to Smith, "As you turn over Faxton & Co. to me, I believe I must turn over O'Rielly and Co. to you."

In a joint letter to O'Rielly, dated 4 November 1846, Smith and Kendall wrote that, due to irregularities of organization and failure to meet the time limit set out in the contract, the O'Rielly contract as "absolutely null and void."

But O'Rielly and his associates had no intention of backing down. They held tightly to the validity of their contract, while at the same time offering to negotiate a settlement. Speaking for his associates three days after the notification of nullification, Hervey Ely told Kendall that they considered their rights under the contract unchanged and that he believed that the Morse patentees would be forced to accept this view. In an attempt to avoid a long battle, the O'Rielly associates appointed a committee to negotiate with the Morse patentees. Several proposals were made to reach a compromise agreement.

Unfortunately for any who wished a peaceful settlement, however, Kendall had "referred the matter to Smith," and Smith was not interested in a peaceful settlement: he wanted the whole O'Rielly telegraph pie.

In the meantime, while its diplomats argued fruitlessly with the Morse patentees, O'Rielly's Atlantic, Lake and Mississippi Telegraph Company was building its network. A program to build out the two planned trunk lines – the northern one, along Lake Erie to Chicago, and the southern one, through Pittsburgh, and along the Ohio River to St. Louis – was launched. The company hoped to get its network built and in operation before any opposition could respond.

The company also sought means to free itself from dependency on the Morse telegraph patents, should that prove necessary. Judge Samuel L. Selden, who was the brother of Henry Selden, the company president, took actions in this regard; aid and encouragement were given to inventors who were developing a competing telegraph system.

Ralph E. House in Vermont was working on a telegraph system which would print the message. Charles B. Moss, in Philadelphia, was developing a system which he claimed would be superior to all other telegraph systems in existence. If a reasonable settlement was not possible with the Morse patent group, perhaps other telegraph instruments could be found. It was the building out of the network of wires, after all, which required the bulk of the capital investment and labor.

Smith also had gone to work building lines in the west. Even before he had formally notified O'Rielly of the nullification of his contract, Smith contracted the construction of a line from Buffalo to Milwaukee, Wisconsin. (This violated the agreement which the Morse patentees had made with O'Rielly). This became the Erie and Michigan Telegraph Company, and the subscribers agreed to issue one-half of the total stock to the Morse patentees, for the privilege of using the Morse instruments on the line.

Along the Ohio River valley, Smith issued Morse patent rights to his brother-in-law, Eliphalet Case, and the Western Telegraph Company was formed. These would compete, it was expected, with O'Rielly's northern and southern trunk lines.

Smith also launched a series of bitter attacks in the press against the O'Rielly companies. "The patentees publicly disavow all acts of H. O'Rielly and all other persons, in building or operating telegraph lines under their appointments," stated a notice in the Philadelphia Pennsylvanian on December 12, 1846. Operators of Morse instruments were warned that they could be guilty of lawbreaking through association with O'Rielly. Legitimate telegraph companies were to avoid making connections with the "pirate" telegraph lines of O'Rielly.

The O'Rielly group argued that the real reason for the attempt by the patentees to repudiate their contract was that it only gave them a quarter interest in the company, rather that the half interest of the other contracts. As of the end of 1846, the Smith-Morse patentee group and the O'Rielly group appeared to be preparing for a protracted struggle. These quarrels between and the other Morse patentees, and between the Morse patentees and O'Rielly, would be the cause of much grief, and delay the establishment of a quality telegraph network in the country.

The steed called Lightning (says the Fates)
Is owned in the United States.
'Twas Franklin's hand that caught the horse;
'Twas harnessed by Professor Morse.
By Smith and Kendall injured – vilely,
But driven westward by O'Rielly.
–Popular Doggerel, 1848

Chapter 9
O'Rielly, Smith, Kendall: Fighting and Divorce, 1847

The next few years saw an explosion in the number of telegraph lines in the US. By 1847, the public had learned of the incredible new telegraph, and was eager to be connected to the rest of the world. Many new lines were constructed hastily. Due to poor planning and lack of knowledge, many of these lines were unreliable. Much of the lack of coordination between the developers of the new lines was caused by endless and destructive quarreling between Smith, Kendall, and O'Rielly. Two new telegraph systems were also invented, known and the House and Bain telegraphs, which would challenge the supremacy of the Morse telegraph.

O'Rielly worked diligently on completing his southern line to Pittsburgh, in western Pennsylvania, and had this line working by 26 December 1846. The first message was sent that day to U. S. President Polk concerning a dispatch of troops for the Mexican War. The line officially opened on 1 January 1847. In March, the Rochester promoters met and capitalized the line, to be called the Atlantic and Ohio Telegraph, for $300,000. Ignoring the letter from Kendall and Smith which had declared the O'Rielly contract null and void, the promoters offered the Morse patentees a one quarter interest in the line, in accordance with the original agreement which O'Rielly had made with them.

This might have been taken as an opportunity to patch up the rift which had occurred, the O'Rielly interests having shown a willingness to "forgive and forget," and go on as previously agreed. O'Rielly and his backers had incurred considerable expense and effort on behalf of the telegraph, having built lines several hundred miles across a major mountain range; this was no small feat. The Morse patentees could have realized one quarter of all the profits on this valuable line. O'Rielly and his Rochester backers made several attempts to settle the dispute with the Morse patentees; but Smith had no interest in cooperating; he wanted O'Rielly out. So Kendall and Smith refused the offer, arguing that O'Rielly had no agreement with them and could not legally use the Morse instruments.

With the opening of the line to Pittsburgh, Kendall had the justification he needed to take legal action, and he filed a motion for injunction in the Circuit Court of Pennsylvania in early 1847.

During these months, Smith was working on lines in the same general territories as O'Rielly's. In January, 1847, Smith's representative, Eliphalet Case, met in Cincinnati with several local investors and organized the Western Telegraph Company. These investors were eager to get a telegraph line into Cincinnati, and were led by Judge John C. Wright, who was chosen as chairman of the board. The purpose was to help capitalize Smith's efforts in the west. However, a few weeks after the company's organization, Kendall's movement for an injunction against O'Rielly was denied, and O'Rielly's contract upheld. This called into question the legality of Smith's agreement with the Cincinnati investors. Thus, they decided to halt any further investment or construction on their line, pending the resolution of the disagreement with O'Rielly.

Following this, at the suggestion of Judge Wright, the Cincinnati investors invited O'Rielly to come to their city and discuss a possible compromise. O'Rielly accepted the invitation, and a compromise agreement was quickly worked out. The compromise recognized the rights of O'Rielly's trunk line from Philadelphia to Pittsburgh, which had already been built, and it was agreed that O'Rielly would continue that line on to Columbus, Ohio.

The Cincinnati group would build from Columbus to Louisville, Kentucky (this line passing through Cincinnati), and at that point O'Rielly would take over again, building from Louisville west to St. Louis, Missouri. O'Rielly would also be responsible for building to the north, to Cleveland, and the Cincinnati group would be responsible for building from Louisville southward to New Orleans. This compromise would have given O'Rielly all of what he had already built and a substantial part of what he had planned for, while giving the Cincinnati group, which had the agreement with Smith, a substantial part – but not all – of the western telegraph networks. Both groups would get their telegraph connections, and both would benefit from the new telegraph networks. All that was needed for the compromise to take effect was the approval of the Morse patentees.

The compromise would have added the Cincinnati group of investors to the Rochester group, increasing the total amount of capital available for the buildout of the western telegraph network, and would have avoided the building of redundant lines. It also would have avoided the time and expense of court battles.

But neither Kendall nor Smith were interested in the compromise. Kendall's objection was that O'Rielly had set out to "mar the whole plan of the Western telegraph by severing it into many companies" instead of developing it into one powerful organization. Kendall's case was difficult to justify, since no mention of it had been made in the nullification letter sent previously, nor in other earlier correspon- dence.

O'Rielly's original plan did call for several companies, but it also called for telegraph policy to be set by the original, parent company, and neither Kendall nor Smith had objected to that plan previously. Further, addition of the Cincinnati group to the group of companies was made necessary because a Morse patentee, Smith, had initiated it; this was not the fault of O'Rielly. Not for the first time, Kendall seemed to blame O'Rielly for problems for which the Morse patentees shared at least part of the blame.

Smith's objection to the compromise, typically for him, was that he did not get a big enough part of the network. (Smith, who died broke years later, apparently never learned that a small piece of a big pie is better than all of nothing.)

The Cincinnati and O'Rielly interests made a second compromise offer to the Morse patentees three months later, which was also rejected. Public opinion turned overwhelmingly against the Morse patentees. The court had refused their injunction; they refused to compromise with O'Rielly; and their own investors, the Cincinnati group, repudiated them.

One wonders what they were thinking. They seemed more interesting in quarreling than in building a telegraph network. In the case of Smith, it is clear; his greed knew no limits, he cared for neither the other Morse patentees nor the O'Rielly group, and he imagined that he could take the whole pie. Nor was logic a part of his thinking, judging by his behavior both in this instance and others.

In the case of Kendall, the rejection is hard to excuse. Had he and Morse, the inventor who he represented, been ready to accept the compromise, it might have been possible to coerce or to force Smith to accept it.

Perhaps the inability to work out a compromise involving Smith spurred Kendall into working out a "divorce" with him. Having discussed the possibility with Morse, on 22 June 1847, the two men signed a series of four agreements, dividing the control of the patent rights. In the first three agreements, Smith was given control over the patent rights in New England, New York, and the northwest; while Kendall would control them in the rest of the country.

The agreements were not a complete divorce, however; in some cases the patent rights were retained, but the control over them was given to Smith, in the north, or to Kendall, in the south. On other lines, all patent rights were given to either Smith or Kendall. Such agreements assume that the party in control will act honorably and reasonably in the interest of all patent holders. In the case of Smith, this was not a valid assumption.

The fourth agreement placed the O'Rielly controversy entirely in Smith's hands. The agreement stated that he would settle the dispute "amicably or judicially, as soon as may be," and to secure Morse and Vail against all patent claims brought by O'Rielly.

Shortly after the "divorce" was signed, or probably even before it, Smith determined that it was not his own interest to resolve the O'Rielly dispute amicably – as the agreement said – but to destroy O'Rielly and the Rochester group. He does not seem to have given much thought as to what it would take to do this; or, if O'Rielly and his backers would fight back; or, that he himself might lose out in the process.

His logic was that the Morse patentees would receive one-fourth interest of any part of the O'Rielly network, and he himself would only receive one-fourth of that, or one-sixteenth of the whole. Instead, better to destroy O'Rielly and build his own network, in which he would have a greater share. Thus, while pretending for several months to negotiate with O'Rielly, and assuring Kendall that he was doing so, he made his own plans for building a rival network.

For Smith to legally build in the Ohio Valley area, however, he would have to recover the patent rights from the Cincinnati group of investors, which still had them. Smith was surprised to learn that Judge Wright and his Cincinnati associates would not hand the rights back for nothing. They offered him two alternatives. They would fund and build out the network as originally agreed, pending a resolution of the dispute with O'Rielly; or, they would reconvey the rights to Smith, after receipt of funds to reimburse them for the embarrassments which had been caused them.

Not uncharacteristically, Smith reacted to their offer with anger. In a letter to Kendall, in September 1847, he wrote that, to have to pay one cent to Wright would be "like paying the man who filches your property while in your employ." An agreement was needed urgently, however, because O'Rielly was steadily building his line down the Ohio River. In October, Smith attempted to negotiate, and again no agreement was made; the Cincinnati investors held firmly to their position.

Smith was in the position of having to make an agreement with them or giving up on the Pittsburgh-Cincinnati-New Orleans project. His inability or refusal to settle with them was also of concern to Kendall. Smith wrote to Kendall that "Wright is one of the most unmeasured rascals that is yet unhung, in my judgment – a janus-faced scorpion. I would not consent to pay him a farthing to save me from anything short of endless punishment."

In December, Smith again went to Cincinnati to negotiate, but this time Kendall went with him. After hours of fruitless discussion, Kendall, seeing that the negotiations were again about to fall apart, made a payment of $500 to Wright in recognition of the patentees debt, after which Wright dissolved the Cincinnati trusteeship. Thus, and not for the first time, Kendall paid an obligation which should have been settled by Smith. Kendall expected that this would free Smith to take action against O'Rielly.

Chapter 10
Explosive Growth, Destructive Competition: 1847-52

*Whenever you can get enough money raised to get a line up, start it
. . . I want no pusillaminous, or doubting movements made – but
dash on with all the battery and thunder and lightning and you
all can command.*
–F.O.J. Smith

The unwillingness of the Morse patentees to settle their dispute with
O'Rielly and the treachery of Smith set the stage for a battle between
two bitterly opposed groups for telegraph domination in the United
States. O'Rielly, who had started out as a friend of the patentees, now
became a bitter enemy. As a result, instead of an orderly buildout of a
telegraph network as Kendall had dreamed, redundant lines were built
by the opposing groups, which competed with each other for the capital
available while under construction, and, when in operation, for the
business. Both thus starved for both capital and income.

This finally shattered the dream – for a while – which Kendall and Morse
had of a profitable national telegraph empire based on Morse's patent.
This battle occurred in the northwest, from the Great Lakes to the Ohio
Valley, southwards to New Orleans and eastward to the coast, from New
York north to Boston and Canada. It handicapped both groups, and it
cost both groups dearly, eventually making it possible for new investors
to come in and take over their telegraph companies.

Once Smith had his "divorce" from Kendall, in June 1847, he began
carrying out his plans to attack O'Rielly by building duplicate lines in
the Great Lakes and Ohio Valley areas. Although his agreement with
Kendall called for him to attempt to reach an "amicable" settlement
with O'Rielly, Smith in fact had no intention of doing so. He reasoned

that such an agreement would require him to share the wealth of the telegraph empire with O'Rielly and the other Morse patentees, and Smith wanted it all to himself. Smith intended to put O'Rielly out of business, leaving the area all to himself. His plan also called for minimizing the income which would go to other Morse patentees, for his own benefit.

Smith's plan was to build a main line along the south shore of Lake Erie, then westward to Chicago. This line would be in the same area as O'Rielly's northern main line, already under construction. Rather than building a main southern line, or using O'Rielly's which was already completed to Pittsburgh and under construction farther westward, Smith would run long feeder lines to the south, into the Ohio Valley, from his northern line.

He expected to serve the Ohio Valley area in this way, and his plan was to starve O'Rielly's lines serving the same areas. Why he thought customers would use his lines rather than O'Rielly's is not clear. He probably thought he would reduce prices, put O'Rielly's line out of business, then raise prices. But to do this requires the financial strength – cash – to hold on without profits for a time, and Smith had little or no more capital than O'Rielly.

Logically, this network of lines serving the northeast would connect to the east coast from Buffalo, which was the western terminal of the line Faxton had built from New York. But Smith had no intention of sharing his revenue with Faxton, any more than with O'Rielly or the other Morse patentees. To avoid connecting to Faxton's line, he planned to construct another line from New York City westward, through southern New York state, to connect to his own northern line along Lake Erie.

The construction of this new trunk line was a violation of his agreement with Kendall and the other patentees. Even if it had been legal, it was foolhardy, as events would prove. The agreement allowed him to construct "feeder lines," shorter lines to connect to the main trunks, but no other major trunk lines. It also meant depriving other Morse contractors and patentees of revenue, to the benefit of Smith.

In a letter to Cornell, dated 15 August 1847, Smith wrote:

> I don't want to be humbugged anymore. Out with the plan of our
> campaign. Show that our Lake lines are to be the great receptacles of
> the Western intercourse with the Atlantic, and that the connecting
> lines are open to the people of the West, almost without money and
> without price, to accomplish this end.

> Our course is simple plain, straight forward, and only requires energy.
> You, Speed, Livingston and Wells and associates, have enough of this
> if set at work. Let the law, in the meantime, commence its slow work
> between both parties.

> Whenever you can get enough money raised to get a line up, start
> it, and Patentees will not hurry for their part, and your share of
> the benefits shall be made satisfactory. I want no pusillaminous, or
> doubting movements made – but dash on with all the battery and
> thunder and lightning and you all can command.

> Time saved is everything now. The West are as yet possessed of the
> proposals and views of the O'Rielly interest only. Give them ours
> in good earnest, and do, as well as say. We will determine whether
> we or the other party make the best lightning. Again I urge you,
> don't hesitate – go ahead – and open your fire everywhere – set all
> the West in a light blaze with your proposals, and keep boldly in
> view the cheapness of the lines offered and the magnificance of the
> main arteries.

> –F. O. J. Smith

Thus, Speed set to work on Smith's northern line in the fall of 1847.
O'Rielly's line had been started several months earlier, and had made
steady progress, getting subscriptions from investors more or less on
schedule. But once Smith's crew went to work, both lines were seeking
out capital from the same sources, and the confusion as to which line
was the legal one discouraged investors from putting money in either.
The Rochester group, which was obligated to support O'Rielly's line in
the event that local subscriptions were insufficient, was also not able
to provide as much support as needed, due to an economic crises in
the country. Thus both lines experienced serious delays in completion.

O'Rielly's line was finally completed in March, 1848. Smith's was not completed until January, 1849. Once in operation, both lines struggled to meet expenses. Their operation was poor at first, but this gradually improved and business picked up in volume, but due to the competition between the lines over the same routes, they both had to cut prices to lure customers, which resulted in barely meeting expenses or losing money.

In the Ohio Valley, through which O'Rielly's southern east-west trunk line was to pass, a similar situation occurred. O'Rielly had completed the first part of his line, from Philadelphia via Harrisburg to Pittsburgh, at the end of 1846. For the first five months of 1847, O'Rielly did   no work on extending this line from Pittsburgh, as negotiations were proceeding with Smith, as discussed in the previous section. In June, 1847, when it became clear that the negotiations were going nowhere, O'Rielly began building out from Pittsburgh towards the west – to Columbus and Cincinnati in Ohio, towards the ultimate destination of St. Louis, Missouri, on the Mississippi River.

Public subscriptions were not sufficient to fund the building, however. Due to the patent controversy and the rivalry with Smith, O'Rielly had a difficult time raising capital here, as he had in the Great Lakes area. In August, however, he completed the line as far as Cincinnati, and a feeder line northwards to Cleveland.

Smith was unable to build in the Ohio Valley during these months, due to the disagreements with his Cincinnati investors. Smith's attempts   to halt O'Rielly with legal action also failed, but he used negative publicity, and also tried to get all Morse lines to refuse connections with O'Rielly's network. Some of them complied. These actions discouraged investors from supporting O'Rielly.

On September 22, O'Rielly sent a telegraph to the prominent scientist, Joseph Henry, using the House telegraph. The House telegraph had been developed recently. That O'Rielly was using a different telegraph from the Morse one revealed a new strategy, that he was planning to free himself from dependence on the Morse telegraph patents. Without dependence on the Morse patents, he would not be obligated to pay them any royalties nor be limited to the contract he had signed with them. O'Rielly was also trying to get Henry on his side in the battle for public support.

Despite the lack of capital, O'Rielly pushed on towards St. Louis, using his own personal credit to continue. He ignored warnings from his investors to hold back building on sections which had too few subscribers. Up until mid-1847, his building had stayed within what could be reasonably financed. Now, stung by the rejection of the Morse patentees, he seems to have been overcome by a passion to beat them, whatever the cost. He might have been successful, had he been prudent in his use of capital and in his building of the lines. But, unfortunately, he was neither, and this would eventually lead to his failure.

He reached St. Louis in December, 1847. That city was jubilant, connected to the east coast electronically for the first time. A local newspaper announced that O'Rielly's accomplishment "marked a new era in the history of St. Louis." A public dinner celebration was given in his honor. One can imagine the feeling of pride such attention must have brought to the poor immigrant boy from Ireland. Unfortunately, such public honors only encouraged O'Rielly to continue on with his hasty and reckless building, oblivious to the lack of funding for them, to the hasty and poor construction, and the mountain of debt he was creating.

O'Rielly's planned connector lines – the north-south lines which were to connect the two great east-west trunks – also encountered difficulties. Two agents he hired to build the Dayton, Ohio to Chicago line disappeared before it was completed, stealing investor money and leaving debts. They were replaced with William J. Delano, whose reputation for integrity and hard work got construction going again. But agents of Smith, Cornell and Speed soon appeared, soliciting funds for a rival line on the same route, and bringing the patent dispute into the open. As elsewhere, this discouraged investors from providing capital to either line.

The Illinois & Mississippi line, which was to connect Chicago and St. Louis, encountered similar financing difficulties. This line was to crisscross Illinois, and three feeder lines were planned. Main line and feeders together would have a total length of seven hundred miles. This western connector line was a huge project in itself, but the work suffered from lack of competent leadership. O'Rielly himself was occupied in building other lines. His agent in St. Louis was expected to find agents to build this line. Charles Oslere was hired as foreman of construction, and he found himself always struggling for funds with which to build the line. In September, 1848 he wrote O'Rielly:

> I am now doged in every place and in the worst kind of scrape that I have seen yet . . . 18 men was laid up here without funds to move and in debt some eight hundred dollars and I with three dollars in my pocket cannot collect one cent here until line is finished to Chicago had to borrow here of friends five hundred dollars to get men out of this . . . if I can get wire and insulators will finish to Chicago in fifteen days and hope to raise money enough to pay them off . . . it makes me so nervous that I can scarcely write or think about anything will go through with it somehow.

"Somehow," the determined foreman managed to get the main line to Chicago completed by the end of October, 1848, and the feeder lines by the end of the year. Formal organization of the important Chicago-St. Louis line had to wait until April, 1849, however, because O'Rielly was occupied in building other lines in the east and in efforts to assist Alexander Bain in getting a patent for his electro-chemical telegraph.

Once built, the Chicago-St. Louis line was expected to make money to pay the investors a return. Unfortunately, although there was plenty of potential business, the line was poorly constructed. Outages were common. Flooding washed out a large number of poles along the Mississippi River, and the line came close to bankruptcy. However, in this case a leader came along, a judge in the Illinois Supreme Court, John Dean Caton.

Realizing the great potential of the line, Caton organized the directors, got the line recapitalized, and repaired or rebuilt to an efficient working state. Caton mortgaged his own property to help raise capital. It took him several years, but the Chicago-St. Louis line emerged in the 1850's as one of the most successful telegraph companies.

There was a still more feverish race, if that is possible, to connect the nation's major southern economic and communications port, New Orleans. O'Rielly and Smith both raced to build lines from the north, along the general route of the Mississippi River, while Kendall worked to build a line down the east coast and across the Gulf coast, through Virginia, the Carolinas, to Mobile, and finally New Orleans. O'Rielly had no agreement with the Morse patentees for building in this area, and his efforts were eventually nullified by court injunctions. He planned to use another telegraph patent, but this was also ruled illegal. Smith's and Kendall's lines were poorly constructed and functioned badly when completed, needing more capital and better management.

Other lines were built in other areas. The telegraph arrived in California, and plans were soon being made for a transcontinental line. Further competing lines were built along the east coast connecting New York and Boston, using other telegraph patents. Most of the lines were poorly constructed and managed, but some were well done; and the need and usefulness of the telegraph gradually became clear, so businessmen gradually began taking over the poor lines as they became bankrupt, investing the money to get them into good condition, and installing better management controls. The good lines prospered, and these eventually took over the bankrupt ones, where there was potential for profit.

The public has been slow to learn how disastrous opposition to the Western Union Telegraph Company has been. Competitive lines cannot make a go of it, and they may as well stop trying.
–Erastus Wiman, Western Union director, 1884

Chapter 11
The First Great American Monopoly: 1852-66

In the six years following Morse's initial telegraph line, tremendous progress was made in the buildout of the telegraph network. At the beginning of 1846, the 44-mile Baltimore-Washington link was practically the only line in existence (though others were already under construction). By early 1848, 2,000 miles had been built; by 1850, 12,000 miles; and by 1852, 23,000 miles of telegraph lines had been built. Of this, around 18,500 used the Morse telegraph patent, and the remainder used others.

A large number of "inventors" developed instruments for sending Telegraph signals following Morse. In 1846, Royal E. House, in Vermont, had developed a telegraph which was similar to that of Cooke and Wheatstone in England. It printed the letters which were sent, making it much easier for the operator. Also in 1846, Alexander Bain, in Edinburgh, Scotland, developed a chemical telegraph.

As of 1852, the House telegraph was in use on about 2,400 miles in the U.S., and the Bain telegraph about 2,000 miles. Both of these instruments were in some ways more sophisticated and easier to operate than the Morse telegraph. The advantage of the Morse instrument, however, was in its simplicity and flexibility, and that it could function even with poor quality wire.

The telegraph lines generally made a good profit in the first two or three years of their existence – at least those which were reasonably well-built, such as the Buffalo-New York and New York-Washington lines. In

September, 1846, the Albany, New York newspaper, the Knickerbocker, remarked:

> The Magnetic telegraph line between this city and New York, and in fact, between here and Buffalo, is coining money. They have more business than they can well attend to, just now. We told Albanians a year ago that this enterprise would pay well and begged some of them to go into it, but like donkeys as they have proved, they wouldn't take our choice.

In 1848, in a court deposition, Amos Kendall stated that the New York-Washington line was earning a twenty percent profit on capital used, of which half went to the Morse patentees.

However, as soon as other competing lines were built, the profits shrank considerably, often to almost nothing. The competition in the west between O'Rielly and Smith led to duplicate, unprofitable lines in numerous areas. Dissatisfaction with Smith's poor service along the Boston- New York corridor led to the construction of competing lines, using other telegraph patents.

Along the New York-Washington corridor, service was better, but was still expensive. Kendall and Morse often tried to maximize profit by high prices. Dissatisfaction with high prices led to the construction of other lines along the New York –Washington corridor as well, using the Bain or House telegraph patents. When this happened, that line, the Magnetic Company, saw its profits shrink also. In 1850-51, for example, the dividends on the New York-Washington line had shrunk to just two percent.

Wherever the telegraph reached, however, it was very welcome, and its potential soon became clear to a handful of shrewd investors. Businesses which fail to make a decent profit, or which lose money, soon find themselves either bankrupt, or – if the service they offer has value – the target of takeovers. This is exactly what happened to the poorly planned and hastily constructed lines of the Morse system over the next several years.

In 1855, a group of investors from New York which included Peter Cooper and Cyrus Field – these were deeply involved with Atlantic Telegraph Cable – combined with D. H. Craig to buy the New England lines which were based on the House patent. D. H. Craig also controlled a House line from Boston to New York, which had been built as a competitor to Fog (F.O.J.) Smith's Morse line, and this was included in the deal.

Field and Cooper were interested in establishing or controlling lines through Nova Scotia, to Newfoundland, where the projected Atlantic Cable would connect from Europe. These lines were united to form the American Telegraph Company.

Next, the new company attempted to negotiate a deal to buy or rent the existing House line from New York to Philadelphia. When that line's owners refused to deal, American strung a third line between those two cities, providing still more competition for the two lines in existence (the Morse line built by Kendall and the newer House line).

The House company, already in difficulty due to the competition with the Morse line, held out for a little more than two years, and was absorbed into the American company in February, 1859. Later that year, on November 1, the Magnetic Telegraph Company – the first telegraph company in the U.S., which Morse and Kendall had founded – finally had to yield as well, and was bought by the American for $500,000 of the American Company's stock. Its major shareholders included Kendall and Morse.

This buyout also gave American a lease on the line from Washington to New Orleans, and another line connecting to Cincinnati, Ohio. In the far northeast, American negotiated a lease with the New Brunswick company which connected it to the Nova Scotia border.

These developments gave the American company lines from Canada to New Orleans. There was still a rival line from Boston to New York, however – that of Fog Smith. As might be expected, Smith fought hard against consolidation. But after months of negotiation, he finally accepted $165,000 for his interest in the company, and $301,000 for all his proprietary rights in the Morse patent. Several other companies in the U.S. and Canada helped make this buyout, in order to end their royalty payments to Smith.

In 1860, the American company negotiated a fifty-year lease of the Nova Scotia lines, which extended its Canadian connection through that province. That company's investors also controlled the New York, Newfoundland and London Telegraph Company, which had a line running from Nova Scotia to St. John's, the capital of Newfoundland – and the projected western terminal of the trans-Atlantic cable.

The company also had rights to the Atlantic Cable, which was planned, but as of yet had not been successfully completed. In short, the American Telegraph Company, by 1860, had established itself as the major telegraph company in the eastern U.S. and Canada, with continuous lines from New Orleans all the way to Newfoundland. If and when the cable across the Atlantic was completed – three attempts had already failed, and many thought such a cable an impossibility – it would have links to Europe, as well.

The American Telegraph Company managed to absorb one more major company, but not until after the Civil War ended in 1865. This was the Southwestern, a company which had been built using some of O'Rielly's line to New Orleans. As noted earlier, O'Rielly had built a line from St. Louis along the Mississippi River to New Orleans. He had no patent rights on this, and was eventually forced to abandon it. In 1853, control of the bankrupt line passed to his competitors.

They also struggled for lack of capital and problems with maintenance, and in 1856 was taken over by a group of leasees, which included Dr. Norvin Green. Under their management, as the Southwestern Telegraph Company, the lines were extended into Louisiana, Arkansas, and Texas, and became prosperous. Although it suffered extensive damage during the war, this company still had valuable lines and was taken over by American shortly after the end of the war.

There were still a large number – thousands of miles, in fact – of lines which American did not yet control. It attempted unsuccessfully to get control of the lucrative New York-Buffalo line. There was another company, however, which prevented that. That company was eventually known as Western Union, and would eventually become the first major monopoly in American history.

Western Union's roots came from a group of investors in Rochester, New York. One of these was Hiram Sibley (1807-88), who in 1841 traveled to Washington, D.C. to attend the inauguration of William Henry Harrison as President. While in Washington, he met Morse, and was very impressed with his telegraph instruments. Later, he was also one of the original investors in the New York, Albany and Buffalo telegraph line.

Another Rochester investor was a judge, Samuel L. Selden. When the House telegraph was patented, Selden bought out its rights for the northwestern territories, and suggested to Sibley that they establish a new telegraph company, for building lines out westward from Buffalo.

Sibley, however, had other ideas. He had done some serious analysis of the telegraph industry, and realized that it was suffering from too much redundancy and competition. He saw that most of the lines were not making enough money to pay their ongoing expenses. Most of these lines, though much in demand, made little or no money because competition was driving their rates so low that they could not profit.

Lack of profits and capital to maintain and improve the lines made it difficult for them, exacerbating the problem. Sibley's idea was to buy out the weaker lines and combine or consolidate them into larger, more profitable ones. Selden agreed with Sibley, and they were joined by a third Rochester investor, Isaac Butts, and they formed the New York and Mississippi Valley Printing Telegraph Company in 1851.

At first it was slow going, as Sibley and his partners found it difficult to convince other investors that they were right. Telegraph lines everywhere were struggling to make any profits, so it is understandable that investors saw little need for investing in yet another new telegraph company. Some money was raised, but not enough, and the company was reorganized in 1854. Sibley hoped to raise more capital with the reorganization, and to begin absorbing the sickly companies which were fighting each other in western New York state and Pennsylvania.

Sibley struggled to convince other Rochester investors to join him, but he still found most of them to be short-sighted, unwilling to risk their money on his goal of consolidation. Since most telegraph companies were making little or no profit, they concluded that there was no money in it, nor ever would be. One friend who he asked to invest said to him, "If I do invest in it, Sibley, promise me it shall be a secret between us forever. I'll loan you $5,000 – that means give it to you, for you'll lose it, of course – but you are never to tell that I was such a fool. I believe in you, Sibley, but I don't believe in this telegraphy."

In desperation, Sibley called for a meeting of the Rochestor business-men at his office one evening. He presented his plan for consolidation of the telegraph networks to them, and asked them participate with him in the raising the capital. One conservative investor, Aristarchus Champion, asked Sibley if he would not admit that the telegraph busi-ness in general, and the individual companies, in particular, were not a financial loss. When Sibley admitted that to be the case, Champion replied, "Then how is this consolidation of failures to escape failure? If there is nothing in the result which is not in the cause, where is the element of success to come in?"

Another investor present, Judge Addison Gardiner, asked, "Admitting all that you have said, Mr. Sibley, admitting that this organization, by the investment proposed, may reap a certain and increasing success, is it at all probable that you or I or any one here present will live long enough to see your prophecy fulfilled, to reap the benefit of faith in your seership?"

Sibley would make no promise of this, only that a return would come to the present generation or the following one. Judge Gardiner decided to take a chance, however, and signed for $10,000. His signature was the first.

Another investor present was George H. Mumford. "It looks to me like a nest of boxes," he said. "We must open a great many before coming to the one that holds the treasure, and we may find nothing, after all. We must buy up line after line – the purchase of each the sequence of a preceding purchase."

The next three investors said, in rapid succession, "I agree with Mr. Champion."

Another investor, Don Alonzo Watson, stalled for time. "I'll tell you in the morning," he said. He did take $5,000 worth, though he expected to lose it eventually. Sibley later commented on that fateful meeting:

> The $90,000 subscribed at that meeting was all the money ever paid. The balance was money loaned on bonds of the company, and individual loans. Isaac Butts promised the other $10,000 and paid it in stock of other lines. That $100,000, with what was gained by the consolidation with the House lines outside of the State of New York, constituted the property of the Western Union Telegraph Com- pany, and soon exceeded in value the whole assessed value of the property, real and personal in the city of Rochester.

Finally, having raised some working capital, Sibley arranged the lease of the wires of the Lake Erie Telegraph Company, one of O'Rielly's lines. This was a T-shaped line, with one line running from Pittsburgh to Cleveland, and the cross line from Buffalo to Detroit. Some of the stock of this company was bought out for practically nothing.

Next, Sibley set his sights on the Erie & Michigan line, which paralleled the just-leased line from Buffalo to Detroit and then continued on to Chicago, Illinois and Milwaukee, Minnesota. This company had a number of valuable contracts with connecting lines running south and west to the Ohio and Mississippi river valleys, and also owned stock in most of them. Sibley proposed a consolidation with this company, to form a new company with capital stock valued at $500,000.

Ezra Cornell was the most powerful shareholders at the Erie & Michigan, and in agreeing to the consolidation he stipulated that the new company should be known as the Western Union Telegraph Company. He liked the name, and in giving it to the new company, he specified a name which would become the most noted in all business history – at least, that is, until the twentieth century.

In addition to Cornell – who had helped with the first Morse line between Baltimore and Washington – two other major investors at the Erie

& Michigan were J. J. Speed and Jeptha H. Wade. All Morse patents held by these three were included in the deal, which led eventually to the elimination of the House lines. The deal also included stocks in companies which fed into that network, lines which led to numerous points along the Mississippi and Ohio rivers.

The Western Union Telegraph Company was officially established by an act of the New York state legislature on April 4, 1856. During the next few years, it would make Sibley and all the investors who stayed with it rich beyond their wildest dreams. Not all of those investors had the vision to hold on, however. Many dumped their stock at the first opportunity, often at a loss. The only four original investors to hold on to their stock were Sibley, H. S. Potter, Joseph Medbury, and D. A. Watson.

The consolidations soon began to bear fruit. The company paid its first dividend on December 1, 1857, of 8.5 percent. Further dividends were paid the following year, and continued thereafter.

To continue expansion, Western Union needed lines into the major cities of New York and Philadelphia. The Atlantic & Ohio company owned a line from Philadelphia to Pittsburgh, originally built by O'Rielly, which was quite profitable. They had no desire or intention of selling out to Western Union, so the company applied what may be called "monopoly tactics."

One of its major investors, Jephtha Wade – who had a reputation as a tough negotiator – began talking with the officials of the Pennsylvania Railroad. The railroad company had a telegraph wire strung along its railway for railroad use only. Wade made a deal with them, which allowed him to string two more wires on their poles. He would provide the railroad company with new telegraph equipment for the offices of its executives – chief and divisional. In exchange, the company would allow Western Union to use its poles, and also provide transportation for the personnel and wires along the way. Thus, Western Union managed to establish a rival line for a minimal cost.

Faced with the pressure the new line brought, the Atlantic & Ohio soon agreed to merge with Western Union, in exchange for stock. Facing similar pressure, the New York, Albany and Buffalo line soon agreed to merge with Western Union, which provided it with a good line across the state to New York City. Thus, prior to the outbreak of the Civil War, Western Union controlled telegraph networks from the Atlantic coast to the Mississippi River, and from the Great Lakes southward to the Ohio valley.

In 1861, the two U.S. coasts were united with the completion of the transcontinental telegraph. For the first time in history, virtually instant communications was possible between California and the east coast. That same year saw the outbreak of the Civil War, and the telegraph would play a major role in it, facilitating the communication and coordination between armies and commanders hundreds of miles apart, in a way never before possible.

The war which was so devastating for many was very profitable for Western Union. Since it had no lines in the south or in areas where the war was fought, it suffered little damage, but many of its rivals did, and it further benefited by a huge increase in telegraph traffic due to the war. It paid rich dividends to its investors. By 1864, Western Union was valued at more then ten million dollars, and by 1865, more than twenty million.

By 1866, there were only two other large telegraph companies remaining. The United States Telegraph Company had been organized in 1864, combining the lines of three smaller companies, and had built additional lines as well. It had a total of about 16,000 miles of telegraph lines. Its financial position was relatively weak, however, so Western Union had little difficulty in absorbing it on April 1, 1866, for some 3.8 million dollars in stock.

The other remaining major telegraph company was the American Telegraph Company, which controlled lines from New Orleans to Nova Sco- tia. On June 12, 1866, it was acquired by Western Union for another twelve million dollars in stock. This gave Western Union a practical monopoly on telegraph in the entire United States, making it the coun- try's largest and richest company.

By 1867, the company was valued at $41,000,000. Ten years earlier, in 1857, its value had been $369,700. This is an increase of 11,000 per cent. Put another way, each dollar invested in Western Union in 1857 was worth $110 in 1867. Earlier investors – Sibley and the original ones who held on – saw even greater increases in their capital.

The early investors thus all became millionaires, each many times richer than the inventor, Morse. During the 1860's, they had already began to give away their money. Ezra Cornell gave $500,000 to found Cornell University in his hometown of Ithaca, New York. He later gave it more, and land as well. Sibley donated buildings to Cornell University and also to the University of Rochester. Amos Kendall built a $120,000 church building for the Baptist congregation in Washington where he was a member. When, a few years later, that building burned down, he replaced it.

Morse's simple telegraph had now led to the creation of a great in- dustrial empire. From his conception of the telegraph in 1832, it had taken him twelve years to get the first true line built, the Baltimore-Washington line, in 1844. Much of that twelve years had been spent searching for capital. Now, just twenty-two years later, it had grown into a great industrial empire, the biggest corporation in the United States. More, it had already made huge changes in the life of people all over the United States and in much of the world.

Little birds sit on the slender lines,
And the news of the world runs under their feet;
How value rises and how declines,
How kings with their armies in battle meet
And all the while, 'mid the soundless signs,
They chirp their gossipings, foolish-sweet.
–Mrs. Adelina D. T. Whitney

Chapter 12
Impact of Telegraph:
The Press

The invention and development of the telegraph in the United States and in England made a tremendous and lasting impact on the world. Some areas in which it had a major impact were in the press, or news organizations; in making the railroad systems safe and efficient; in connecting the financial systems of the world; and in the conduct of war.

To understand the impact which the telegraph made, one must understand the world as it was before, for it was that world which changed drastically as a result, and which has never returned. At the beginning of the nineteenth century, there was no well organized news organization. Around 1827, newspapers in New York began working together to get news. In 1828, the owners of a Journal of Commerce in New York City, named Hale and Hallock, began sending a yacht out twenty or thirty miles to sea, to meet with expected incoming ships from Europe. They also set up a semaphore station on the coast to help in getting the news quickly. For a time, they organized a pony express from New York to Philadelphia with eight changes of horses, to carry to news quickly to that city. They later extended the service to Washington.

Another New York newspaper editor, James Gordon Bennett of the *Herald*, also had horse riders organized to carry news to and from Philadelphia and Washington, and he also employed carrier pigeons to bring the news from Albany, the state capitol, to New York City. In fact, there was a lively competition between newspapers throughout the country to be the first with the news. Carrier pigeons were widely used as a means to carry messages from one city to another. Reporters often rowed out to sea in small boats to get news from incoming ships. They would then write the news on sheets of thin paper and attach a sheet to each leg of the bird, who would then fly to New York with the news. As the telegraph was established, this news would then be sent on to Boston, Philadelphia, Washington and New Orleans.

The New York association of newspapers, which became known as the New York Associated Press, was probably the first news agency to use the telegraph in an organized way, but newspapers in other cities were also soon working together. Newspapers would often share the cost of sending or receiving news from distant cities. It is not surprising that in the early days of the telegraph, there were many complaints about the service and its cost. For example, on January 17, 1846, the Lancaster, Pennsylvania *American* printed the following:

> Telegraphic Correspondence – Late from Harrisburg Expressly for the AMERICAN
>
> We this morning lay before our readers the proceedings of the Legislature up to the hour of going to press – by means of the Telegraph now in successful operation between this city and Harrisburg. In reply to our inquiry of "What have the Legislature done today?" We received in answer, quick as thought –
>
> "I will inquire."
>
> After a lapse of about three minutes – while a messenger ran to the capitol and back, we received in reply—
>
> "Nothing of any consequence."
>
> "As usual," said someone present. And we are sorry to admit that a large portion of the people are willing to believe that at the close of the session, the same may in truth be said of their proceedings.

> For this information we were charged fifty cents – the office is open
> at all hours of the day, and for the same price, any person can be
> gratified to the same extent.

The newspapers quickly became major customers for the telegraphs,
and the telegraph operators themselves often became news sources.
When some newspapers tried to save money by sharing expenses, the
Magnetic Telegraph Company retaliated by adding an extra charge for
other newspapers which used the information. This practice did not foster
good relations between the line and its customers, and helps explain
why newspapers were eager to encourage the building of additional,
competitive lines.

For their part, another way the newspapers would try to reduce the cost of
a telegram was by the use of ciphers. Whole phases were compressed into
single words, resulting in such interesting words as *caserovingedsable,*
hoveesness, rehairoringed, and *rehoeingedaqbleness.*

Fog Smith, who controlled the Boston-New York Morse line, had no
intention of letting the New York newspapers cheat him with this cipher
scheme. After giving the matter some deep thought, he issued a decree
stating that the average word length in the English language was five
letters; so for all future telegraph messages, the total number of letters
would be divided by five, giving the correct number of words, for which
the sender would charged.

O'Rielly took a different policy towards his customers than did Morse
and Kendall, or Smith. From the start, he charged fifty cents for ten
words between Pittsburgh and Louisville, which was a greater distance
than the others; or forty cents on shorter links. Even these rates were
high for the western newspapers, so they also worked together to pay
costs; but unlike Kendall and Smith, O'Rielly did not object. He was
content with a modest or reasonable profit for his service, while Kendall
and Smith were intent on squeezing as much profit per message out of
their lines as possible. For this and other reasons also, O'Rielly was
much more popular with the press and other customers.

In the early years there were many complaints with poor, expensive
service. In 1847, the Utica *Daily Gazette* wrote:

The telegraph is in complete order today, but after dancing attendance for hours, we can only get from New York the gratifying intelligence, "No report this A.M." So it goes. When there is any news, the telegraph is down; when it is in order, there is no report, or "it can't be sent," or it slips through without being taken. We pay ruinously, are as vigilant as possible, but get little for our pains but vexation of spirit. The Telegraph has great capabilities, but its particular province seems to be to tantalize those who depend upon it.

In 1849, the editors of the Ohio *Statesman*, in Columbus, described their frustration with the telegraph service in their area:

We believe the Telegraph Company could be made to pay heavy damages for these shameful derelictions of duty, and they will not be submitted to any longer. The way the thing now works is a disgrace to the whole system – ruinous to the publishers and discreditable to our city, that the foreign news can now be read in St. Louis and the whole West, and circulated among the people hours before the people of the Capitol of Ohio know what is going on!

And what is the excuse set up by the Telegrapher here? Why, HE WAS AT HIS DINNER WHEN THE NOTICE WAS GIVEN THAT FOREIGN NEWS WOULD BE SENT

THROUGH! Do other Telegraphers here never EAT DINNER! Yes, and supper too, we would presume, but they notified other officials of the hours when they would be performing that operation . . . It is just as easy for them to have their HOURS, as Railroads theirs, and their stopping places. . .

Under the leadership of D. H. Craig, the New York Associated Press eventually expanded into a national organization, transmitting news throughout the country to all its members. It became a near monopoly organization as well, using monopoly tactics to force non-members into submission. When the Western Union Telegraph Company became a national one, the Associated Press and it agreed to cooperate, each complementing the other and avoiding actions which would damage the other. It did not take long for the press to become very dependent on the telegraph, and thus one of its best customers. In time, the telegraph operators realized the wisdom of granting reasonable or bulk rates to the press and other high usage customers. Thanks to the telegraph, newspapers in New York were soon carrying the news from Washington, Boston, San Francisco – and, after 1866 – from Europe, a day or so after their occurrence.

We bring glad news to inland homes
Of ships upon the sea.
We hurry along the murderer's trail,
His Nemesis are we.
We watch all night the roaring trains
When the sleepless needle clicks;
A caution for Number 7 fast
To wait for Number 6.
–"Allid," 1870

Chapter 13
Impact of Telegraph:
The Railroad

Another industry which soon became very dependent on the telegraph – and on which the telegraph depended heavily also – was the railroads. The first Morse telegraph line between Baltimore and Washington had been laid along the railroad between those two cities, and the relationship would continue. The railroads provided a logical right of way for the telegraph lines to be laid, and also had the capability to provide transportation for the poles, wires, workers and operators. This advantage was quickly recognized by the telegraph companies.

The telegraph also soon became imperative for the railroads as well. In England, the interdependence between the two was recognized much earlier than in the U.S. Cooke and Wheatstone's telegraph (see Chapter 4) had been in operation on the Great Western Railway as early as 1839, and its capabilities severely tested, according to C. A. Saunders, secretary of the railway company. In 1842, Cooke had published a book on the use of the telegraph in railway switching, and in 1844, his method was adapted by the Yarmouth & Norwich Railway company. Through the use of his method with the telegraph, railway officials claimed to have reduced railway accidents to zero, despite the fact that it was a single track road.

American railroad leaders were much slower in recognizing the advantages which the telegraph offered them in preventing accidents and in improving the efficiency of their business. In 1854, a reporter for the London Quarterly Review wrote, "The telegraph is rarely seen in America running beside the railway, for what reason we do not know; the consequence, however, is that locomotion is vastly more dangerous in the United States than in England."

It was not until 1851 that the railroaders in the U.S. began to realize that the telegraph could be of use to them. In those days, trains using the same railroad tracks were coordinated by a protocol. When two trains were scheduled to run in opposite directions on the same track, on the same day, one was designated as "leading train." The leading train had an hour's priority over the other as it passed through a specified meeting point, where double tracks permitted both to pass. If the leading train was more than an hour late, it lost its priority and would have to wait for the other to pass.

Hours could easily be lost in this way. A train at a meeting point could also go ahead out of turn by sending a man ahead, jogging along the track, with a red flag. After a fifteen or twenty minute wait, the train would follow along. On catching up to him, the runner was taken aboard to rest, and another sent ahead with the flag while the train waited another fifteen or twenty minutes. In a history of the Erie railroad by Edward Mott, it is said that a train once flagged its way for thirty-four miles.

In 1849-50, Ezra Cornell was constructing a telegraph line in New York State. It ran from New York City to Buffalo, following country roads, but roughly in parallel with the New York & Erie Railroad. Frequently it was in sight of the railroad. All the while, Charles Minot, the visionary superintendent of that railroad, was watching the construction, and it occurred to him that the telegraph might be of use for his business.

Minot was certainly well aware of the lost time and danger on the railroads, and the need for a better system of coordinating trains. After studying Cornell's lines, he calculated that he could construct a telegraph line of his own along the railway, for the use of the line. He talked

with Cornell, who agreed to supply him with the Morse Telegraph
instruments. Cornell had no authority to do this, and it angered the
Morse patentees. Minot offered to pay them for the right to use of
instruments, but Smith refused, trying to induce Minot into investing
in his telegraph company. Minot refused, and continued to string wire
along his railroad. Some believed that he had a secret agreement with
Cornell from the beginning.

Minot succeeded in getting the wire strung along the line, but it took
a while for the operators to learn to use it to schedule and coordinate
the trains. The operators were very suspicious of the wire, and had to
be convinced of its value. The turning point came in June, 1851, when
Superintendent Minot was traveling westward on the line, on Train No.1.
The schedule called for it to pass the No. 2, traveling in the opposite
direction, at a village called Turner's. After waiting for an hour at
Turner's, Minot directed the operator to telegraph Goshen, the next
village, and inquire whether the No. 2 had passed. When the negative
reply came back, Minot sent the following telegraph to Goshen:

> To the agent at Goshen Dear Sir:
> Hold all eastbound trains until I arrive. Chas. Minot, Supt.

Once Goshen acknowledged receipt, Minot telegraphed Goshen again,
"Do you understand?" and received back the reply, "I understand that
I am to hold all eastbound trains until you arrive and will do so."
Following this, Minot wrote out an official order:

> To Conductor and Engineer, Day Express
> Run to Goshen, regardless of opposing train. Chas. Minot, Supt.

He handed the order to the conductor, a man named Stewart, whose
eyes widened in surprise. Stewart gave the order to the engineer. Stewart
described what then happened to the Erie's historian:

> I took the order, showed it to the engineer, Isaac Lewis, and told him
> to go ahead. The surprised engineer read the order, and handing it
> back to me, exclaimed: "Do you take me for a damned fool? I won't
> run by that thing."

I reported to the Superintendent, who went forward and used his verbal authority to the engineer, but without effect. Minot then climbed on the engine and took charge of it himself. Engineer Lewis jumped off and got in the rear seat of the rear car.

Lewis wanted to get as far away as possible from the collision he expected. Superintendent Minot drove the train to Goshen, without collision, and inquired if the No. 2 Train had passed Middletown, the next stop. On learning that it had not, he sent a similar telegraph to Middletown, and continued to that stop. There he repeated the process, and continued on to Port Jervis, where he arrived just as the No. 2 was pulling into the station. An hour or more of time had been saved, and the usefulness of the telegraph was proven.

It took time to work out a system, or set of protocols, for the dispatching of trains, but this was eventually done and the Erie became the first railroad line in the U.S. to use the telegraph extensively. It took several years before its use spread to other U.S. railroads; it seems most railroad executives were very conservative, slow to notice and adapt to new ideas. Newspapers took note, and one wrote:

We invoke the attention of all Railroad Companies to the propriety of speedily supplying themselves with lightning . . . so as to prevent those awful accidents which too frequently make sad inroads upon the limbs and lives of passengers, as well as upon the credit and cash of too many companies.

In defense of the slowness of the railroad companies to use the telegraph, in the early years it was not very reliable, and it took time to get enough competent operators. Referring to this, a veteran railroad worker said in 1898:

With the old telegraph register then used in receiving, it took 30 minutes or more to make meeting points by wire. The train orders were written on any kind of paper and rewritten several times, being sent to one office at a time. Each would in many cases get a different wording, and frequent were the collisions from a lap order. During the prevalence of the single order, the dispatcher spent about a third of his time checking up his orders to see if he was going to have a collision, and at about what point on the line it would occur. The

Standard Code, later adopted by the American Railway Association's
Train Rule Committee made the service more efficient, and took
away the terrific strain on the mind, of the old system.

Even into the 1860's, some railroads were still not using the telegraph
for their switching needs. One day General Anson Stager of Western
Union put on a spectacular demonstration which gained considerable
positive publicity for the telegraph. He was a passenger on the Pittsburgh, Ft. Wayne and Chicago Railroad when the engine broke down.
After waiting a while, he asked the conductor if he could call for another locomotive if the request were sent by wire. When the conductor
agreed, Stager cut a nearby commercial telegraph wire, a piece of it was
thrust into the ground, and Stager sent the message by tapping the end
of the line wire against it. He received the reply by holding the line wire
against his tongue.

By the late 1860's, the railroad companies and the telegraph companies – soon to be just one telegraph company, Western Union – realized
their complementary nature, and made agreements to reciprocate.
The telegraph company would provide the wire and the poles, and
the Telegraph equipment; the railroad companies would provide
transportation for these and for telegraph personnel. Each would allow
the other the use of its facilities when working on company business.

Another interesting technical development seems to have occurred on
the Erie Railroad, though it quite likely occurred in other places as well.
This was in the receipt of telegraph messages by sound.

In the early days, the telegraph was connected to a pen and paper
which wrote dots and dashes in accordance with the Morse code signals
received, and the operator would then write out the message by hand,
translating the Morse code into letters and words. One day in Addison,
New York, a railroad operator was waiting for an order coming through
the telegraph. He noticed that the telegraph operator, Charles Douglas,
was writing down the message as the message come in, by listening to
click-click of the instruments, and not even looking at the paper tape
where the dots and dashes were written. The conductor was taken aback
that the operator had not looked at the tape, and refused to accept the

order until the operator had rewritten the message from the dots and dashes on the tape.

The train conductor reported the incident to the Division Superintendent, named Tillotson, who was shocked with such recklessness with the lives of train passengers. He called Douglas to his office, in Elmira, to receive a reprimand. Douglas insisted that messages could be received just as accurately by sound as by reading a tape, and that there were probably many other operators doing it as well.

He offered to take any test the superintendent wished to prove it, and spent the afternoon reading by ear all the messages which Tillotson and the Elmira operator could devise. Passing these tests, Tillotson ordered Douglas back to Addison, where he was sent a long message as rapidly as the Elmira operator could tap it out. Douglas received it by sound, in the presence of witnesses, and sent it back without error. From that day on, reception by sound was officially permitted on the Erie Railroad line. In later years, receipt by sound became the standard.

As time went on, nearly all telegraph lines were run alongside the railroads, and the two industries complemented each other immensely.

With the channels of thought and of commerce thus owned and controlled by one man or by a few men, what is to restrain corporate power or fix a limit to its exactions upon the people?
–Senator William Windom, 1881

Chapter 14
The Fight for
Government Control

THE CONSTITUTION confides the carrying of intelligence to the Federal Government. . . It is, therefore, the positive duty of Congress to provide for the use of the telegraph as part of the postal service.
–Frank Parsons, in *The Telegraph Monopoly*, 1899

A number of new telegraph companies were started following the Civil War, which competed, or attempted to compete, with Western Union. Many were started with the intention of getting bought out by it. Many of these companies were poorly capitalized, unable to meet their own expenses, and expired on their own before the "giant" bought them. Others built new lines where they were needed, and succeeded in selling themselves at a profit to the Western Union.

Of one of the new startup companies, the Rock Island Daily Argus wrote on February 20, 1869:

> A year or two ago a few sharks in St. Louis organized what they pompously called the "Mississippi Valley National Telegraph Company" – probably for the purpose of covering certain territory and then inducing the Western Union to buy them out. They put up a few poles, and opened here and there an office in some garret with a $2.50 table and one chair for furniture, and employed such boys as they could get for about half wages.

However, neither the Mississippi Valley National Telegraph Company or any other stood much of a chance of competing with Western Union after the consolidations of 1866. The huge telegraph company now had deep pockets and a national telegraph network, and was able to easily buy out any newly built networks which complemented it, and any others usually soon went out of business.

The company was able to and did charge very high rates for its service because of its monopoly position, and this quickly made the company's directors and major shareholders rich. It also made the general public resentful. Prices were so high that the general public had difficulty in affording the service. There were a great many calls for the government to nationalize the company in the interest of providing an affordable telegraph service.

The Washburn Committee of the House of Representatives declared in 1870 that the telegraph rates in Europe averaged less than half those in America. In England, the committee declared, they were less than one-third the U.S. rate, in France less than one-fourth.

In England, the telegraph was nationalized in 1870. In that country the telegraph was not a single ubiquitous monopoly as in the U.S., but several different companies. But in general there was only a single company in an area, and the companies worked together in maintaining high rates. Further, there were a number of rural areas, villages and hamlets, which had no service at all, because no telegraph company believed it profitable to provide a line to those areas.

In the countries of Europe, such as Belgium, Switzerland and France, where the telegraph was already a government monopoly, rates were much lower and usage much higher. When the industry was national-ized in Britain, the British government calculated a fair market value for the lines and paid off the companies for their property. Afterwards, English rates dropped to much lower levels, and lines were built out to many of the small towns which previously had no service. Yet, even before the British telegraph was nationalized, rates were considerably lower there than what was being charged by Western Union in the U.S.

In 1866, a bill was introduced into the House of Representatives which would have established a separate, rival telegraph company. The company would have had special privileges, thus providing some competition to Western Union. However, the bill was never passed. Instead, that same year, the U.S. government made Western Union's monopoly position even stronger.

During the Civil War, around 14,000 miles of telegraph lines had been built by the military throughout the country in support of its operations, as well as another two hundred miles of underwater cable. This was all turned over to the Western Union Company, or to companies which were about to fall under its control. Supposedly, this was done to compensate the companies for the losses they had had during the war.

The irony in this, of course, is that the war had hurt Western Union not at all; in fact, the war helped it by hurting those other companies which might have been able to offer it some competition, and by giving it a great deal of extra revenue. Critics charged that this turnover of valuable property, paid for by the government, was done at the behest of General T. T. Eckert, who soon thereafter became a Western Union official.

The attacks against the Western Union monopoly were accompanied by attacks against its partner, the Associated Press. The two were firm allies. The president of the news organization testified before Congress that it was under an agreement with Western Union to use its wires exclusively, and that all papers in the Associated Press were forbidden from using any other telegraph line. There were many complaints of refusal to give news service by the combined monopolists.

The telegraph company held the upper hand in the arrangement, however, and the result was that all the papers in the organization – which meant the great majority of papers in the U.S. – were forbidden from reporting anything negative about Western Union. This included the writing of negative comments in editorials by local newspapers. A Congressional Committee reported that "The Associated Press has notified all newspapers that they would withhold the news from all papers that criticized such dispatches. This power was exercised in the case of the Petersburg Index."

Another Congressional report told of newspapers which had expressed approval of the idea of a Government telegraph, which then lost their news or telegraph service, or had their rates raised so much that they could not afford to pay. Another report stated that "The understanding between the telegraph company and the press association secures to the latter low rates and the power of excluding new papers from the field, and the former a strong influence upon press dispatches, the support of the papers in such association, and the right to transmit and sell market quotations."

In 1873, Postmaster General Creswell pointed out the absurdity and injustice of many of the Western Union rates. Some examples: a ten word telegram from Washington to Boston cost $0.55, but from Boston to Waltham, just ten miles away, the charge was $1.75. From Washington to Chicago the charge was $1.75, but to Genever, just forty miles from Chicago, it was $3.00.

Congressman Charles A. Sumner of California worked for the establishment of a government or postal telegraph. On October 12, 1875 he gave a speech in San Francisco which attacked the Western Union monopoly vehemently. In it, he said that

> The Western Union has a twin connection with another incorporated thief and highway robber known as the Associated Press. They are banded together in the strong bond of mutual plunder and rapacity against the people . . . I know prominent men in this city against whom today there are pending in Massachusetts indictments of getting money under false pretenses through the very machinery I have described.

In 1894, the International Typographical Union testified to the Henderson Committee that "there was a tremendous bar in the way of starting newspapers, it being practically impossible to launch a daily without the consent of the Western Union Company and the Associated Press."

There is no doubt that there was a great deal of frustration and resentment felt by many Americans who found the services of the Western Union Telegraph company to be excessively high. A very similar feeling of frustration also was felt in England, prior to 1870, when in that country the telegraph was nationalized. Yet, despite a large number of investigations and committee reports, Congress never took action either to nationalize Western Union or to support the development of a competitive telegraph network, which through competition might have brought more competitive rates.

One of the reasons action was never taken was quite likely that the Congressmen did not feel the pain of the ordinary citizen: Western Union used its wealth liberally, and made sure that all politicians had plenty of free passes for the use of the telegraph. This practice was quite widespread and took place over many years, and amounted to thousands of free telegraphs per year for the lawmakers and other influential politicians. Not only the Congress, but state and local politicians were included. In 1873, Western Union President Orton referred to this practice in his annual report to the directors:

> The franks [free passes] issued to government officials constitute nearly a third of the total complimentary business. The wires of the company extend into thirty-seven states and nine Territories within the limits of the United States, and into four of the British Provinces. In all of them our property is more or less subject to the action of the National, State and municipal authorities; and the judicious use of complimentary franks among them has been the means of saving to the company many times the money value of the free service performed.

It is probable that more of the free franks went to the Republican Party, but the Democrats also got their share. Even in smaller elections and pre-election fights, books of franks were given out to both candidates and party bosses, often on both sides.

Western Union was accused of helping the Republican candidates in the elections of 1876 and 1884. Following the election of 1876, at the behest of the Democrats, thousands of political telegrams were seized from Western Union offices. These revealed the buying of an elector in Oregon and some other relatively minor skullduggery on the part of the Republicans, but revealed even more scheming on the part of the Democrats.

For example, there was a telegram message from a Democratic negotiator to the party headquarters in New York, saying that the Florida canvassing board and Governor's signature could be bought for $200,000, and a reply back from headquarters that the quantity was too high. Another telegram from a scout on South Carolina reported that "Majority of Board have been secured. Cost is $80,000." The same telegram went on to describe how the money be distributed, in parcels of $1,000 and $500 bills. After the telegrams revealed more conniving on the part of the Democrats than the Republicans, furious Democratic newspaper editors accused Western Union President William Orton, that "unscrupulous Republican Partisan," of hiding from Congress some of the most incriminating Republican telegrams. John Bigelow, who wrote a biography of Democratic Presidential candidate Tilden, makes this accusation in his book. It seems quite possible that the accusations were correct.

Efforts to have the government take over the telegraph continued throughout the last two decades of the nineteenth century. Between 1845 and 1899, there were nineteen committees in the Senate, House, or both, which studied the telegraph monopoly and made recommendations. Seventeen of these were in favor of government ownership, two against it. John Wanamaker, Postmaster General from 1889-93, was the last to make a real effort to bring the telegraph under the control of the Post Office, and it was said that financier Jay Gould – discussed in the next chapter – spent $250,000 to defeat his effort.

After the turn of the twentieth century, the efforts died out. Competition was looming by then for the Western Union, from MacKay's Postal Telegraph, and also from a pair of new technologies. One of these allowed people to actually speak to one another over a wire, and the other allowed communications at a distance without wires.

To conclude this discussion on monopoly, the Western Union monopoly – as have been other monopolies before and since – was undoubtedly abusive of its financial power, and was less of a force for economic improvement and welfare for the country than it might have been. On the other hand, governments are also known for corruption and abuse, and there is no guarantee that things would have been better. In the end, it was competition from other companies that ended the monopoly.

For Vanderbilt and Company, 'tis indeed a gilded age,
But poverty increases, and 'tis thus that tramps are made.
Shall it, will it be continued when the people's votes are weighed?
As we go marching on.
No! We'll hang Jay Gould on a sour apple tree,
And bring to grief the plotters of a base monopoly;
From the heartless ghouls of booty we're determined to go free,
As we go marching on.
−Anti-monopoly Song, 1880

Chapter 15
The Nation's Telecom Network

Following 1866, Western Union dominated the telegraph for a number of years. It made excellent profits. Its detractors, and there were many, often called these exorbitant. There were numerous instances in which new telegraph companies were started, which attempted to compete with "the giant," as it was often called. The most serious of these cases occurred near the end of the 1870's.

Jay Gould was one of the leading capitalists in the U.S., and controlled a great deal of the nation's railroads. Deep pocketed, he started a new telegraph company, the Atlantic & Pacific. By 1877, it had 36,000 miles of telegraph lines. Besides the Morse instruments, much of his network also used a newer telegraph invented by Thomas Edison. Edison's improvements made possible the sending of messages at a much faster rate than before. In one case, for example, Sir William Thomson reported that he saw 1,500 words received in Philadelphia, from New York, in fifty-seven seconds.

In the early months of 1877, Western Union began to move aggressively against the Atlantic & Pacific, which had now become its chief rival. Telegraph rates were cut, key small telegraph lines were acquired, and the Atlantic & Pacific was forced to react in kind. This brief "war" between the companies soon came to an end.

At the end of the year, a peace treaty was signed which "permitted" Western Union to acquire some 72,502 shares of A&P stock at a price of $25. For this $912,550 was paid in cash, and the rest with 12,500 shares of Western Union stock. Nearly all of this payment went to Gould. Thus, Western Union got control of the A&P, and Gould made nearly a million dollars in cash and acquired a sizeable amount of Western Union stock. The agreement stipulated that seven-eighths of the company's revenue would go to Western Union, and the remaining eighth to the Atlantic & Pacific. Though now a shareholder in Western Union, Gould was not done competing with it.

On May 15, 1879, Gould organized yet another telegraph company which he called the American Union Telegraph Company, with a capital of ten million dollars. He furnished practically all the capital himself. In January of the next year, Gould brought in General T. T. Eckert as president of the new company. Under Gould's able leadership, the company soon reached a dominant position. Smaller telegraph lines were acquired, and key alliances with railroads were made. Some quantities of shares of the company were sold to finance new construction, and a number of new lines were built.

Among these arrangements, the Dominion Telegraph Company was leased, and its directors were permitted to invest in the new telegraph company. President Garret, of the Baltimore and Ohio Railroad, was invited to become an investor, and ally, and he did so. An agreement for foreign business was made with a French cable company. Telegraph rates were cut, and more than 5,000 men were put to work building out major new telegraph lines which would compete with the Western Union lines. In short, a new war was now well underway for the dominance of the telegraph industry in the U.S.

Western Union had a telegraph line along the B&O Railroad, through its subsidiary, the Atlantic & Pacific (which had recently been taken over from Gould). In 1877 its lease expired, and the B&O ordered it to vacate. The B&O thus took over its own telegraph lines for a while.

These were soon leased to Gould's new company, the American Union. Gould then stepped up his campaign to take over the Western Union. His campaign was described by Alvin Harlow in his 1936 book:

> Next the company seized the wires on the Union Pacific and Kansas Pacific, being aided thereto by Gould's domination of those roads. Whenever and wherever there was resistance to the seizures, force was used . . . It was a battle of giants. Bills, injunctions, subpoenas, search warrants, con- tempt citations and other legal instruments flew about like hail; and there were more illegal than legal actions. Many a warrior was knocked cold and carried away on a shutter.
>
> President Garrett of the B&O was among the numerous citizens arrested for contempt.

By the end of 1880, the American Union Telegraph had two thousand offices and nearly fifty thousand miles of wire. It also had critical contracts with a number of the major railroad lines. Western Union felt the pressure of the competition. At the end of 1880, its revenues had fallen significantly, and its stock price was at its lowest point since the 1850's. On January 9, 1881, Gould received a brief letter from Western Union's largest shareholder:

> Dear Sir: I would like to see you a few moments, at 9 o'clock, if convenient to you, at my house.
> Yours very truly,
> W. H. Vanderbilt

Vanderbilt wanted to discuss a possible merger with Gould's company. The competition between the two was cutting into the profits of both; a consolidation would make it possible to reduce expenses and raise prices back to a profitable level. Negotiations proceeded rapidly, and just over a month later – on February 15 – it was approved by the Western Union board of directors.

Under the agreement, the two companies were combined and the capitalization of Western Union – the name that would be kept – was raised to $80,000,000. Jay Gould and three of his fellow directors were made directors of Western Union. Gould became the most powerful director of the new company. Harlow described the public reaction to the merger:

When the terms of the deal reached the public prints, one of those summer heat-lightning storms of indignation common to the American people burst over the land. The Evil One at last had possession of the monopoly. "The cormorant of the past has been swallowed up," said The Operator [a telegraph trade journal], "and the Western Union of today is only the Western Union in name, and the American Union in fact"; by which it meant that Jay Gould was now telegraph dictator of the continent, and such was the fact. Dr. Green [Western Union president] thenceforth had to play second fiddle.

Several Western Union stockholders brought suit, trying to prevent the merger, but to no avail. The Anti-Monopoly League held a meeting two weeks after the consolidation, and many speeches protesting the merger were made. The anti-monopoly song, part of which appears at the beginning of this chapter, was sung by a glee club. Mention of Jay Gould, who anti-monopolists considered to be the "Evil One," provoked cries of "Hang him!" and "Cut his throat!" None of the protestors carried out these threats, however: Gould died peacefully in 1892. The Republican Party, considered a friend of the monopoly, was widely condemned. But since it seemed that nothing legal could be done about it, the rally ended and the protestors went home.

The consolidation of 1881 by no means marked the end of the telegraph wars, though it was the biggest one. Other telegraph companies were started, but these were usually soon bought out by Western Union, or went out of business. These continued to operate in small areas, but were not a threat to the profits or existence of the giant. As late as 1886, there were still 214 telegraph companies in the U.S., but 210 of these were very small companies, perhaps only a single line connecting small towns, or different parts of a city. The Western Union company was one of the most lucrative businesses in existence, and continued to be so for many years afterward.

Dr. Norton Green, who was president of the company during and after the consolidation of 1881, died in 1893. He was succeeded by T. T. Eckert, now sixty-eight years old, who had come in as a director with Jay Gould. Eckert remained at the helm until 1900, when he resigned. At the time of his resignation, the company had a capitalization of

$99,800,000. The company admitted to having taken in $515 million in revenue, of which $180 million was profit, during the four plus decades of its existence. Some outside financial analysts claimed that these numbers were too low. The company would continue to be profitable for several more decades, but the richest days were already over. Competition was already arriving in the form of the telephone, patented in 1876, and in wireless, which was just getting started in 1900.

Similarly, the telegraph is not to be regarded as the work of any one mind, but of many, and during a long course of years. . . All who have extended our knowledge of electricity, or devised a telegraph, and familiarised the public mind with the advantages of it, are deserving of our praise and gratitude, as well as he who has entered into their labours, and by genius and perseverance won the honours of being the first to introduce it.
–John Munro, *Heroes of the Telegraph*

Chapter 16
Decline and Conclusions

As late as 1936, Western Union was still a large telegraph company, though no longer the dominant telecom power. Competition from the AT&T – telephone and the teletype – and wireless had long since been felt. Western Union still owned almost two million miles of land wires and thirty-thousand miles of submarine cable, and the telegraph continued throughout the Second World War as an important means of communication. The underseas cables were still particularly important, for AT&T had yet to lay an undersea telephone cable.

Alfred Vail, who had assisted Morse in the construction of his telegraph and also helped to improve it, died in 1859, at the age of fifty-two, in relative poverty. He had been forced to sell off most of his telegraph stock to support his family. His contributions were not highly appreciated or recognized during his lifetime. Kendall said of him:

> If justice be done, the name of Alfred Vail will forever stand associated with that of Samuel F. B. Morse in the history of the invention and introduction into public use of the Electro-Magnetic Telegraph . . . Mr. Vail was one of the most honest and scrupulously conscientious men it has ever been my fortune to meet.

Vail's legacy was remembered and appreciated by his family, however. A younger cousin of his, who grew up hearing about him and even worked in telegraph offices, would make a major impact on telecommunications history in the U.S. Theodore N. Vail carried out a major role as leader of the next telecom giant, AT&T.

When Morse heard of Vail's death, his comments were less generous: "his intentions were good, and his faults were the result more of ill- health, a dispeptic habit than of his heart." Morse paid Vail's widow, Amanda, $5,000 as Vail's share in an indemnity payment Morse had received.

Amos Kendall, the former Postmaster General who had become Morse's legal and financial partner, and probably dearest friend, passed away in 1869. Kendall was one of the few who had never attempted to manipulate Morse, or take advantage of him. Morse missed him deeply. Kendall had become wealthy from the telegraph stock he owned, but died a sad and lonely man. He had worked for years on a biography of his hero, Andrew Jackson, but never finished it. Most of his loved ones had died before him. One son had been murdered. His nine siblings were all dead. The two wives had both passed away. His five sons were all dead, and of nine daughters, only four still lived.

Morse wrote that to Kendall, "I owe (under God) the comparative comfort which a kind Providence has permitted me to enjoy in my advanced age."

Morse's last few years were a mix of honors and recognition, on the one hand, accompanied by jealousy and bitterness, on the other. Financially he was comfortable, even mildly wealthy, from the dividends from the telegraph stock he owned, and from some substantial financial awards; but his wealth was quite small in comparison with that achieved by the directors of the Western Union company. He was honored by a fabulous dinner given by Western Union, which he seemed to appreciate; but this was slightly marred by rumors that the dinner was more politically motivated than by a sincere desire to honor him.

There were movements to nationalize the telegraph industry, and Western Union wanted to get Morse's support on this issue. In Europe he was honored by a dinner and a large financial award, but his old enemy Fog Smith sued him successfully for a share of it. Amanda Vail, Smith, and Henry O'Rielly continued to espouse their theory that Morse was not really the inventor of the telegraph; rather, it had been the scientist Joseph Henry and Alfred Vail. Their charges received considerable publicity, and tormented Morse for the rest of his days.

Morse died at home, accompanied by wife Sarah, April 2, 1872, weeks before his eighty-first birthday.

Should the reader still harbor any doubt of the magnitude of the impact which the telegraph made on life in America and the world, the recognition which the world and the nation gave to its inventor upon his death should be considered.

The nation's newspapers printed front-page obituaries in his honor, reviewing his long life. "If it is legitimate to measure a man by the magnitude of his achievements, the greatest man of the nineteenth century is dead," said the Louisville *Courier-Journal.*

The New York *Herald* said, "Morse was, perhaps, the most illustrious American of his age." Another paper, the *Patent Right Gazette*, reported that "The first inventor of his age and century is dead!"

He was mourned as are only the greatest and most widely recognized. Flags were flown at half-mast, and telegraph operators throughout the nation draped their instruments in black. Artists gathered in recognition of his contributions to American art. In view of Morse's admiration of Washington, one speaker in Poughkeepsie gave him the ultimate tribute: "Never since Washington died has such sympathetic unanimity been witnessed."

Few people in the history of the nation have been so honored as Morse was by the U.S. government. On April 16, a ceremony was held at the U.S. House of Representatives. The ceremony was described by Kenneth Silverman in his biography of Morse:

> The most imposing ceremony took place on April 16 at the House of Representatives. From its gallery hung an evergreen-wreathed portrait of Morse. Members of his fam- ily sat in the semicircle facing the Speaker's desk, along with President Grant, his Cabinet, and justices of the United States Supreme Court. Throughout the

memorial, receivers clicked off messages coming in from simultaneous meetings around the world – from telegraphers in London and in Java, Brigham Young in Salt Lake City, ex-President Millard Fillmore in Buffalo, the aldermen of Galveston, Texas. Typical was the telegram sent from a San Francisco gather- ing led by the city's mayor: "Resolved. That, on behalf of the citizens of San Francisco and the people of California, we recognize the inestimable services of Professor Samuel F. B. Morse . . . His vast conception of enlisting electricity in the work of civilization was the grandest thought of time." The collected telegrams and speeches, later published by the Government Printing Office, made a volume of 359 pages.

F.O.J. Smith, often called "Fog Smith," who had met Morse as a member of the House of Representatives, and helped Morse get his initial $30,000 grant, but had tormented him throughout the rest of his life, outlived the inventor by four years; he died in 1876. Even after Morse's death, Smith continued to defame him.

Henry O'Rielly, who had worked so energetically for the telegraph but reaped so few of its rewards, passed away an invalid in 1886 at the age of eighty.

Ezra Cornell, who had helped Morse lay that initial Baltimore-Washington line, had reaped the rewards. As mentioned earlier, he had also given from those rewards to others, giving land and money to help found the university that still bears his name. He died two years later, in 1874.

William Fothergill Cooke, who invented the telegraph in England with the help of Charles Wheatstone, was awarded the Albert Gold Medal in 1867, and was honored with knighthood in 1869. He died in 1879. Wheatstone was awarded knighthood in 1868. He died in 1875.

In May, 1944, the United States and most of the world was embroiled in the biggest war in modern history. Allied forces were preparing for the D-Day invasion of Europe, which would be launched the following month. Yet, on May 15, Congress took time to recognize the one-hundredth anniversary of the first message which Morse had sent, on completion of the Baltimore-Washington line. As may be recalled, Morse, sitting in the chamber of the Supreme Court, had tapped out

the message to Alfred Vail, "What hath God wrought!" The event was
re-enacted, with telegraph operators sitting in the same places as Morse
and Vail had sat. The event was broadcast nationally by NBC and CBS
broadcasting companies, and the messages were picked up by the U.S.
Army Signal Corps and transmitted around the world.

In 1944, the telegraph was still in wide use; there were still some two
hundred million messages per year being sent in the U.S. But the biggest
part of communications had already been taken over by the telephone,
the teletype, and the radio. Soon after the end of the war in 1945, the
telegraph faded as an important means of communications, and the last
telegraph by Western Union was sent in 1960.

Numerous trans-Atlantic telegraph cables were laid after Cyrus Field
first proved it possible. (This is the subject of Part 2). The last of these
was abandoned in 1966, having been replaced by telephone cables and
optical-fiber ones, with a nearly immeasurably greater capacity.

Morse code was still widely used by the U.S. military and Coast Guard
until the 1990's, when it was phased out. All students at the U.S. Naval
Academy were required to learn Morse code until 1990. In 1966, a U.S.
Naval officer, Jeremiah Denton, used the code to communicate with
U.S. intelligence by blinking his eyes during a television broadcast.
Denton was a pilot who had been shot down, and suffered numerous
injuries and abuse as a prisoner of war in Vietnam. A graduate of the
U.S. Naval Academy, Denton was a POW for eight years, and he was
forced to appear on television by his captors. Using Morse code, which
his captors did not know, he blinked out the message TORTURE with
his eyes. Denton later served as a U.S. Senator from Alabama.

The code is still used by amateur radio operators, and has been considered as a means of communication for persons who are unable to move,
or who are unable to speak or use sign language.

Part 2

The Atlantic Telegraph Cable

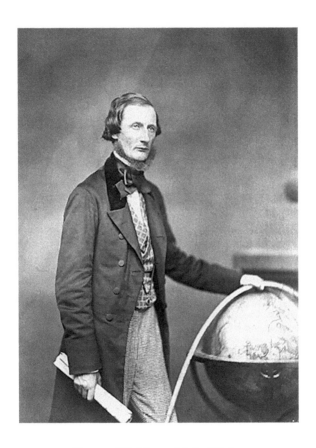

Cyrus Field and his Globe

Nothing in the world can take the place of Persistence. Talent will not; nothing is more common than unsuccessful men with talent. Genius will not; unrewarded genius is almost a proverb. Education will not; the world is full of educated derelicts. Persistence and determination alone are omnipotent.
– Calvin Coolidge (1872-1933), thirtieth president of the U.S.

Chapter 1
Birth of a Grand Plan

In late 1850, the local newspaper in St. John's, Newfoundland published a letter from the Roman Catholic bishop of that British colony, J. T. Mullock:

Sir:

I regret to find that, in every plan for transatlantic com- munications, Halifax is always mentioned, and the natural capabilities of Newfoundland entirely overlooked. This has been deeply impressed on my mind by the communication I read in your paper of Saturday last, regarding telegraphic communication between England and Ireland, in which it is said that the nearest telegraphic station on the American side is Halifax, twenty-one hundred and fifty-five miles from the west of Ireland.

Now would it not be well to call the attention of England and America to the extraordinary capabilities of St. John's, as the nearest telegraphic point? It is an Atlantic port lying, I may say, in the track of the ocean steamers, and by establishing it as the American telegraphic station, news could be communicated to the whole American continent forty-eight hours, at least, sooner than by any other route.

But how will this be accomplished? Just look at the map of Newfoundland and Cape Breton. From St. John's to Cape Ray there is no difficulty in establishing a line passing near Holy-Rood along the neck of land connecting Trinity and Placentia Bays, and thence in a direction due west to the Cape. You have then about forty-one to forty-five miles of sea to St. Paul's Island, with deep soundings of one-hundred fathoms, so that the electric cable will be perfectly safe from icebergs. Thence to Cape North, in Cape Breton, is little more than twelve miles. Thus it is not only practicable to bring America two days nearer to Europe by this route, but should the telegraphic communication between England and Ireland, sixty-two miles, be realized, it presents not the least difficulty. . .

–J. T. Mullock, St. John's, November 8, 1850.

The bishop's knowledge of geography was excellent, and his suggestion was as well.

Newfoundland is a large island just off the eastern coast of Canada, northeast of Nova Scotia. It is the most eastern part, not only of Canada, but of North America. It is separated from mainland Canada in the northwest by the Strait of Belle Isle, a narrow strait about 80 miles long and averaging about 11 miles wide. On the southwest, Newfoundland is separated from Nova Scotia, and mainland Canada, by the Cabot Strait, about 70 nautical miles across. The Gulf of St. Lawrence is to the west, between Newfoundland (New Found Land), Nova Scotia – a peninsula – and the mainland.

With an area of about 42,000 square miles, Newfoundland is the fourth largest island in Canada, the sixteenth largest in the world, and about one-third larger than Ireland. Its eastern coast, where the port city of St. John's lies, contains one of the nearest points in North America   to Europe; this distance was measured at 1610 nautical miles. The absolute nearest point to Ireland is Cape Charles, on the eastern coast of the Labrador mainland; it is about ten miles nearer to the Irish coast, at a total distance of 1600 nautical miles; but it is also several hundred miles farther to the north, making the total telegraphic distance to New York much longer.

St. John's also lies about 1200 miles, or about one-third the total distance, nearer to Britain than New York City. It is also about 500 miles northeast of and nearer to Britain than Halifax, Nova Scotia. As of 1851, the telegraph had reached Halifax, but no further north.

By 1850, the electric telegraph had taken root firmly in the U.S., Canada, Britain, and Europe, and was rapidly spreading. To the lead-

ing businessmen and engineers of the day, it was clear that rapid communication across entire continents was imminent. But communication
between the U.S. and Europe was still limited by the speed of a

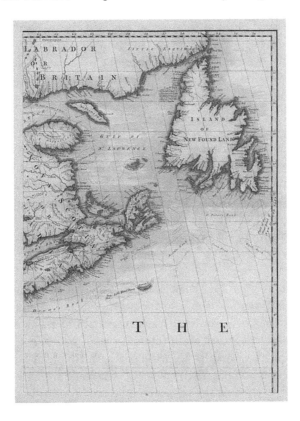

Newfoundland and Nova Scotia

In 1620, the *Mayflower*, carrying a load of pilgrims, had sailed from Plymouth on September 16, and reached the eastern coast of Massachusetts
on November 9. That time of almost two months was considered to
be a good one then, and, at the beginning of the nineteenth century,
two months was still a good time. The invention of the steam engine
improved this. By the middle of the nineteenth century, the time to cross
the Atlantic had been cut to as little as ten days.

In 1850, for news to get to New York, America's financial capital, from
London, the world's financial capital, a ship had to sail from the port of
London, east through the Thames River to the North Sea, then south
through the Dover Strait into the English Channel, south through the
English Channel, around the south coast of Britain, then across the
Atlantic to Nova Scotia, where the telegraph could send it the rest of
the way. Thus, by connecting London to the west coast of Ireland, and
St. John's to Halifax, the time of communication from London to New
York could be cut from ten days to about seven or eight.

At about the same time, the idea of shortening the communication time
between New York and London also occurred to Frederic Gisborne. It
seems to have occurred to him independently from the bishop. Gis-
bourne was a telegraph operator who had been born in England, and
emigrated to Canada. He soon became an engineer, learning on the job,
and advanced from an operator to a builder of telegraph lines which
connected Montreal with New Brunswick and Nova Scotia. He rose to
become head of the Nova Scotia Telegraph Company.

It was in this position that he noticed the possibility of connecting with
Newfoundland, the big island to the northeast, and the geographical
advantage it has over Halifax. In the spring of 1851, he went to the
Newfoundland legislature and proposed that a 400-mile line be built
from St. John's to Cape Ray, on the southern tip of the island. From
there, connections via carrier pigeons or ship could be made across the
Cabot Strait to the existing telegraph lines in Nova Scotia. Eventually,
a submarine cable might be built. The legislature voted to allocate £500
to an exploratory survey.

The engineering and science of submarine telegraph cables was still a
largely unexplored discipline in 1851. As early as 1842, Samuel Morse
had experimented with underwater cables, and considerable difficulties
were encountered when an underwater cable was needed to cross the
Hudson River, to connect New York with the lines leading to the south.

In 1845, John and Jacob Brett, two English brothers, sought permission to lay a submarine cable across the English Channel, twenty-two
miles at the narrowest point, to the coast of France. Finally getting

permission from both governments, in 1850 they bought twenty-five miles of light weight insulated wire, and using a small steam-powered tugboat, laid it across the channel in a single day.

London, North Sea, English Channel, and Ireland

The wire was so light it would not sink, so weights were attached at intervals to force it to the bottom. When they reached Dover, on the other side, they tried to transmit a message, but only got gibberish. By the next day the line was dead. As it turned out, the line had been found by a fisherman's anchor, whose owner hauled it up and cut it, thinking that the copper in the wire might be gold.

The next year, however, a new attempt was made with better insulated wire, and it succeeded. For the first time, London could communicate instantaneously with Europe, a major communications milestone. By 1854, submarine cables had been put in place connecting England with Ireland and Holland, and from Italy to Sardinia and Corsica. These were all short-distance connections, however, and un- der shallow seas.

Gisborne carried out the survey of the Newfoundland southeast coast, which took him three months. It was very difficult, because that coast of Newfoundland is extremely rugged, with numerous mountains and canyons, with streams and rivers rushing down through them to the fiords and the sea. The weather is also extreme; the island is covered with snow several months each year. In a letter reporting the expedi- tion, he wrote: "On the fourth day of December, I accomplished the survey through three hundred and fifty miles of wood and wilderness. It was an arduous undertaking. My original party, consisting of six white men, were exchanged for four Indians; of the latter party, two deserted, one died a few days after my return, and the other, 'Joe Paul,' has ever since proclaimed himself an ailing man."

Despite the hardships of the survey, Gisborne reported to the legislature that the project was feasible, and it authorized him to build the line, giving the company which he organized exclusive rights to the telegraph in Newfoundland for many years. The legislature did not provide capital for the project, however; so, for that he took a steamship to New York. He found investors who agreed – according to his understanding – to support him. He returned to Newfoundland, and began construction of the line. He had constructed about thirty miles of the line when his investors unexpectedly refused to honor his bills. He had to stop construction, and thus fell into debt. He was arrested and his property in Newfoundland was confiscated to partially pay the debt.

Gisborne returned to New York in January of 1854, seeking investors to help him carry on with the project. Staying in the Astor House Hotel, he met Matthew D. Field, a civil engineer who had built railroads and suspension bridges in the south and west. Gisborne told Field about his plans for the telegraph in Newfoundland, who listened with great interest. He suggested that Gisborne meet his brother, Cyrus Field, to discuss his plans.

Cyrus West Field was born November 30, 1819, in Stockbridge, Massachusetts. He was the eighth child, and the seventh of eight sons of David Dudley Field, a well-known New England minister. The Reverend Field was a strict but loving father, who educated his children in the Bible, Greek, Latin, and English literature. He taught his sons a line from John Bunyan's book, *The Pilgrim's Progress*: "To know is a thing which pleaseth talkers and boasters; but to do is that which pleaseth God." In a biography of Field, Philip MacDonald describes the early family life:

> Life among the hills of Massachusetts during Cyrus' childhood was still cast in the puritanical tradition. Every morning and evening the family came together for a religious service, each member with a Bible to read from. The father long prayers at these gatherings made a deep impression on the kneeling children although they did not always understand the obscure theological terms. There is something peculiarly moving in this picture of the devout family bowed down in the bare sitting room listening to the Old Testament phraseology with its big words.
>
> Of the several boys who knelt down at this parsonage among the hills, one was to become a leading figure at the American bar, one was to build bridges and railroads, one was to supply knowledge of the West to the highest court in the land, one was to conquer the Atlantic for the transmission of intelligence, and one was to exert an influence for a more liberal interpretation of religion.

The lessons of the minister took hold. His oldest son, David D. Field, Jr., (1805-94) became a successful lawyer, one of the most highly paid in the country, and was influential in reforming the codification of common law in the United States and Europe. Stephen J. Field, born in 1816, also became a lawyer, and in 1863 was appointed to the U.S. Supreme Court by President Abraham Lincoln.

Henry M. Field, the youngest, born in 1822, became a minister and a writer. Among others, he wrote a book which is one of the sources for part of this book. Matthew Field, who introduced Gisborne to Cyrus, became a civil engineer responsible for building a number of railroads and bridges throughout the U.S.

Cyrus Field left home for New York City with his father's permission when only fifteen years old. There was not enough money available from the minister's small salary for a college education. He convinced his father to allow him to seek his fortune in business, and would someday become a successful entrepreneur.

On April 19, 1835, he left home, with eight dollars in his pocket, which his father had given him from the meager family purse. The trip to New York cost him two of the eight dollars, and took twenty-four hours. Letters home during his first months there show considerable homesickness. The fifteen year old was brave and determined to behave like a man, but he still missed home.

New York was in the midst of a major economic boom, and thus represented an opportunity for tremendous economic growth. His older brother, David, had preceded him to New York, and was already a successful and wealthy lawyer. When Cyrus arrived in New York in 1835, David helped him get his first job, as an apprentice at A. T. Stewart's store on Broadway. Stewart's was the largest dry goods store in New York at the time. Stewart built a huge business based on the department store concept, and eventually amassed a huge fortune, more that forty million dollars at his death in 1876.

Cyrus did well in his three years as an apprentice, impressing both his fellow clerks and his bosses with his friendly, outgoing personality and his attention to business details. He learned the business well, asking questions when he failed to understand something, and also took night courses in bookkeeping to expand his knowledge. When the financial crash of 1837 occurred, he had a firsthand view of the results: well-financed and well-run businesses survived it, and the others went bankrupt. He learned his lessons well.

When his three year apprenticeship ended, Stewart offered Cyrus a good job, but the young man wanted to strike out on his own. His brother Matthew, who had invested in some paper mills, gave him a job for $250 a year, plus room and board, doing bookkeeping and helping with the management. His outgoing personality got him out on the road, selling paper to wholesalers in New England and New York, at which he excelled.

During one of his business trips, he met Mary Stone, who he had known as a child. The pair fell in love and were married in 1840, when he was just twenty-one years old. The marriage was a long and happy one, which would last a half-century, and because his new bride wanted to live in New York City, Cyrus accepted a junior partnership with the paper wholesaling firm of E. Root & Company.

E. Root & Company, however, had not been very well managed, and was suffering badly from the collapse of 1837 and the depression which followed it. The firm soon fell into bankruptcy. The entrepreneurial Field, however, turned this to his advantage. He struck a deal with its creditors to pay them thirty cents on the dollar for its debts, and took over the old company. In 1840 he was in business as Cyrus W. Field & Company. He soon turned it into one of the leading paper and printing supplies wholesalers in the country.

During the next ten years he built up the business, and by 1850, at the age of thirty-one, appeared on the New York Sun's list of richest New Yorkers, with a net worth of over $200,000. In 1852, his business had total revenues of more than $800,000.

Field then did something very unusual, then or now. He paid off the remaining 70% of the debt which had been owed by the E. Root company, which he had taken over ten years earlier, with interest. He had no legal obligation to do so. Perhaps he felt a moral obligation to his former creditors. There is no doubt that the act enhanced his reputation for honesty; one of the creditors wrote Field to thank him, expressing "our thanks for the sum enclosed, not so much for the value thereof in currency as for the proof it affords that 'honesty still dwells among men.' "

Having achieved financial independence, Field traveled extensively, including a tour of South America. This trip was taken with a friend, Frederick Church, a great landscape painter. The pair arrived in Colombia, and took an overland journey by mule from Bogotá to Guayaquil, Ecuador. This overland journey of more than six hundred miles crossed the Andes, passing through tropical zones and through mountains well above the snow line. On reaching the coast of Ecuador, Field took a ship back to New York, as planned. The trip took four months.

One of the motives behind the trip to South America was to search for a lost brother. Timothy Field had enlisted in the Navy and sailed from New Orleans in a ship in 1835, which had never been heard from. The family had heard rumors that he was living in South America. Cyrus found no sign of him, however, and the family finally gave him up as lost. So, when his brother Matthew brought Gisborne to see him in 1854, Cyrus, thirty-four years old, was also widely traveled, as well as wealthy.

Gisborne explained his plan for building the telegraph across Newfoundland to shorten the communications time between New York and London. Field certainly understood the importance of rapid communication with London, but was not overly impressed with the plan as Gisborne explained it.

It would mean investing a considerable amount of capital to build a telegraph line four hundred miles across a frigid and mountainous island, and then, through either an underwater link or the use of boats or carrier pigeons, crossing the 75-mile strait to Nova Scotia, and finally another 140-mile telegraph line to the nearest telegraph stations, all to shorten the time to London by a couple of days. Its merit seemed doubtful to Field.

But after Gisborne left his home, Field looked at the globe in his library, and it occurred to him that if a trans-Atlantic telegraph cable could be laid, the communication time could be shortened from ten days to just minutes. This was something which excited him; it would truly change the world. And for such a cable, Newfoundland, as the nearest point to Britain, was the sensible choice of termination point, so Gisborne's line would be a critical part of the connection with London.

Before committing himself to Gisborne, Field wrote to a pair of well-known technical experts, Samuel F. B. Morse and Lieutenant Matthew Maury. Morse was the inventor of the American telegraph, and he had already considered the possibility of a trans-Atlantic cable. Ten years earlier he had written a letter predicting that such a cable would be built. Though Morse was correct in his prediction of a trans-oceanic cable, he greatly underestimated the tremendous difficulties and expenses that the successful laying of such a cable would eventually entail. Morse came to see Field a few days later, and the two got along well. Morse conveyed his opinion that such a cable was certainly possible, and he was quite enthusiastic with the project.

Matthew F. Maury (1806-73) was an officer in the U.S. Navy, and was very interested in navigation and oceanography. In 1834, he had written A *New and Practical Treatise on Navigation*. He was appointed head of the U.S. Naval Observatory in 1844, and devoted the rest of his career to charting the winds and currents of the world's oceans, and gathering data for meteorology. In 1855 he published *The Physical Geography of the Sea*, the first American textbook on oceanography, which made him famous internationally, and became one of the best selling scientific books of the nineteenth century. Maury is considered by many to be the father of oceanography.

Field's letter to Maury asked if he considered the laying of a cable practical from an oceanographic point of view. Coincidentally, Maury had already considered the subject. He replied to Field, "singularly enough, just as I have received your letter, I was closing one to the Secretary of the Navy on the subject." The letter contained exactly the information which Field was seeking, and Maury enclosed a copy. The letter is quite lengthy, but as it addresses exactly the issues Field was interested in, it is shown here in its entirety:

National Observatory, Washington, February 22, 1854

Sir:

The United States brig *Dolphin*, with Lieutenant Commanding O. H. Berryman, was employed last summer upon special service connected with the researches that are carried on at this office concerning the winds and currents of the sea. Her observations were confined principally to that part of the ocean which the merchantmen, as they pass to and fro upon the business of trade between Europe and the United States, use as their great thoroughfare. Lieutenant Berryman availed himself of this opportunity to carry along also   a line of deep-sea soundings, from the shores of Newfound- land to those

of Ireland. The result is highly interesting, in so far as the bottom
of the sea is concerned, upon the question of a submarine telegraph
across the Atlantic; and I therefore beg leave to make it the subject
of a special report.

This line of deep-sea soundings seems to be decisive of the question
as to the practicability of a submarine telegraph between the two
continents, in so far as the bottom of the deep sea is concerned. From
Newfoundland to Ireland, the distance between the nearest points
is about sixteen- hundred miles; and the bottom of the sea between
the two places is a plateau, which seems to have been placed there
especially for the purpose of holding a submarine telegraph, and of
keeping them out of harm's way. It is neither too deep nor too shallow;
yet is so deep that the wires but once landed, will remain for ever
beyond the reach of vessels' anchors, icebergs, and drifts of any kind,
and so shallow, that the wires may be readily lodged upon the bottom.
The depth of this plateau is quite regular, gradually increasing from
the shores of Newfoundland to the depth of from fifteen hundred to
two thousand fathoms, as you approach the other side. The distance
between Cape St. Charles, or Cape St. Lewis, in Labrador, is somewhat
less than the distance from any point of Ireland to the nearest point
of Newfoundland. But whether it would be better to lead the wires
from Newfoundland or Labrador is not now the question; nor do I
pretend to consider the question as to the possibility of finding a time
calm enough, the sea smooth enough, a wire long enough, a ship big
enough, to lay a coil of wire sixteen-hundred miles in length; though I
have no fear but that the enterprise and ingenuity of the age, whenever
called on with these problems, will be ready with a satisfactory and
practical solution of them.

I simply address myself at this time to the question in so far as the
bottom of the sea is concerned, and as far as that, the greatest practical
difficulties will, I apprehend, be found after reaching soundings at
either end of the line, and not in the deep sea. . .

A wire laid across from either of the above-named places on this side
will pass to the north of the Grand Banks, and rest on that beautiful
plateau to which I have alluded, and where the waters of the sea appear
to be as quiet and as completely at rest as it is at the bottom of a mill-
pond. It is proper that the reasons should be stated for the infer- ence
that there are no perceptible currents, and no abrading agents at work
at the bottom of the sea upon this Telegraphic plateau. I derive this

inference from a study of a physical fact, which I little deemed, when
I sought it, had any such bearings.

Lieutenant Berryman brought up with Brooke's deep- sea sounding
apparatus specimens of the bottom from this plateau. I sent them to
Professor Bailey, of West Point, for examination under his microscope.
This he kindly gave, and that eminent microscopist was quite as
much surprised to find, as I was to learn, that all those specimens of
deep- sea soundings are filled with microscopic shells; to use his own
words, 'not a particle of sand or gravel exists in them.' These little
shells, therefore suggest the fact that there are   no currents at the
bottom of the sea whence they came; Brooke's lead found them where
they were deposited in their burial-place after having lived and died
on the surface, and by gradually sinking were lodged on the bottom.
Had there been currents at the bottom, these would have swept and
abraded and mingled up with these microscopic remains the debris of
the bottom of the sea, such as ooze, sand, gravel, and other matter;
but not a particle of sand   or gravel was found among them. Hence
the inference that these depths of the sea are not disturbed either by
waves or currents. Consequently a telegraph wire once laid there, there
it would remain, as completely beyond the reach of accident as it would
be if buried in air-tight cases. Therefore, as far as the bottom of the
deep sea between Newfoundland, or the North Cape, at the mouth
of the St. Lawrence, and Ireland, is concerned, the practicability of a
submarine telegraph across the Atlantic is proved. . .

In this view of the subject, and for the purpose of hastening the
completion of such a line, I take the liberty of suggesting for your
consideration the propriety of an offer from the proper source, of a
prize to the company through whose telegraphic wire the first message
shall be passed across the Atlantic.

I have the honor to be, respectfully, etc.,
M. F. Maury, Lieutenant, United States Navy. Hon. J. C. Dobbin,
Secretary of the Navy.

The letter noted that specimens of the bottom had been taken up by
"Brooke's deep-sea sounding apparatus." For centuries, seamen have taken
measurements of the depths of the seas by dropping weighted, measured
lines from ships. But it was only in recent times that J. M. Brooke, another
U.S. Naval officer, invented a way to take up samples of the ocean floor.

To do this, a heavy weight such as a cannon ball is attached to the end of a line. A hollow tube was also attached. The end of the tube is open, but with a door, or valve, closed by a spring when the apparatus hits bottom. The weight of the cannon ball drives the tube into the bottom, and then drops off; the valve closes, with a small amount of sediment from the bottom inside it. Since the weight was discarded, the tube could be easily pulled back up. Thus, the bottoms of the world's oceans have been littered with hundreds of weights from sounding equipment.

So, the depths of the Atlantic between Ireland and Newfoundland had already been explored, and seemed to be ideal for the laying of a Telegraph wire. The maximum depth was stated as about 2,000 fathoms, or 12,000 feet. The distance from Ireland to Newfoundland was given as 1,600 (nautical) miles.

Having received positive encouragement from both Morse and Maury, Field also sought out the advice of a leading attorney: his older brother David, who had helped him get started in New York, and who conveniently lived next door to him in New York City.

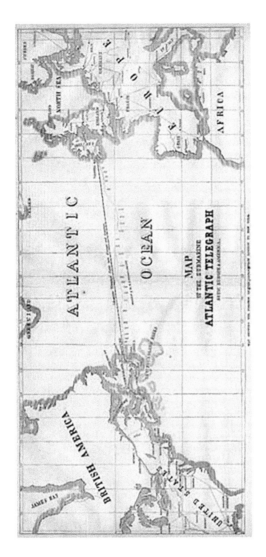

Atlantic Cable Route

Based on the advice and positive encouragement he had been given
by Morse, Maury, and his brother, Field made the decision that, if he
could get a sufficient number of capitalists to join with him, he would
go forward on the project. Not Gisborne's relatively simple project of
building a line across Newfoundland, but a much grander one, which

would for the first time in history link the old world with the new, a trans-Atlantic telegraph cable.

As he later said, and this story will show, he had no idea of the magnitude of the project which he was about to undertake.

Chapter 2
The Plan: Raising Capital, Forming the Company

Some see private enterprise as a predatory target to be shot, others
as a cow to be milked, but few are those who see it as a sturdy
horse pulling the wagon.
–Sir Winston Churchill (1874-1965)

A successful businessman, Field well knew that a critical part of his plan must be to obtain the support a number of other capitalists to help him provide the money and share in the risk. The first investor he went to see was Peter Cooper, who, conveniently, lived next door to him.

Born into a relatively poor family, Cooper had managed to save up $2,000 as a young man and with it bought a glue factory. Improving its operations, he earned $10,000 in the first year, and within a few years, was making an income of $100,000 a year, a very large income in those days. He later invested in iron and railroads, and eventually became one of the wealthiest businessmen in New York. He was several years older than Field, and had no need or desire to go into a new and risky venture, but when he saw the great benefit which a trans- Atlantic telegraph would have for the world, he agreed to invest on the condition that Field find several other investors to participate. Cooper was one of the best known businessmen in New York City, and was highly respected. His agreement to participate added a great deal of momentum to the project, helping Field enlist the support of other investors.

Field next visited Moses Taylor, another well-known capitalist of the city. Field did not know him previously, but after sending a letter of introduction from an acquaintance, Taylor agreed to see Field in his home. Of his interview with Taylor, Field later said, "I shall never forget how Mr. Taylor received me. He fixed on me his keen eye, as if he would look through me: and then, sitting down, he listened to me for nearly an hour without saying a word." Taylor was clearly impressed with what

Field told him, as he agreed to participate in the project, also subject to the condition that other investors join in.

Taylor also brought in a friend of his as another investor, Marshall O. Roberts. Roberts was another of the leading businessmen of New York. Years earlier, he had taken interest in the Erie Canal, and during the California gold rush, had run steamers from New York to the isthmus of Panama. He was thus quite familiar with the importance of shortening the distance between financial centers.

The next investor which Field visited was Chandler White. Like the others, he was also a successful businessman, with no need of a new project, but the enthusiasm of Field and the grandness of the idea excited him as well, so he agreed to participate, under the same conditions.

Field had initially intended to find ten investors, but once he had five (including himself), Cooper suggested that was enough, and the others agreed. A date was set for a meeting to discuss and formalize the plan. The first meeting was held at the Clarendon Hotel, and then for four subsequent nights the group met at Cyrus Field's house.

The meetings were also attended by Gisborne, Samuel Morse, and Cyrus's brother David, who agreed to support the project with legal counsel. On March 10, 1854, the group agreed to take over Gisborne's bankrupt company, including its debts of about $50,000, and form a new company, which would be called the New York, Newfoundland and London Telegraph Company. The agreement was subject to the condition that the government of Newfoundland grant a charter more favorable than the charter which had been given to Gisborne's company.

The two Field brothers, White, and Gisborne agreed to leave at once on a trip to Newfoundland, to present the proposal to the Newfoundland government. They left New York on March 14, 1854.

Travel in 1854 was not like travel today. The group took a day to get to Boston, and then took a steamship from Boston for Halifax, Nova Scotia. Four days after beginning the trip, on the night of March 18, the group left Halifax in a small steamer for St. John's, Newfoundland a distance of some five hundred miles. Of that last part of the trip, Matthew Field wrote:

> Three more disagreeable days, voyagers scarcely ever passed, than we spent in that smallest of steamers. It seemed as if all the storms of winter had been reserved for the first month of spring. A frost-bound coast, an icy sea, rain, hail, snow and tempest, were the greetings of the telegraph adventurers in their first movement towards Europe.
>
> In the darkest night, through which no man could see the ship's length, with snow filling the air and flying into the eyes of the sailors, with ice in the water, and a heavy sea rolling and moaning about us, the captain felt his way around Cape Race with his lead, as the blind man feels his way with his staff, but as confidently and as safely as if the sky had been clear and the sea calm; and the light of morning dawned upon deck and mast and spar, coated with glittering ice, but floating securely between the mountains which form the gates of the harbor of St. John's.

On arriving in St. John's, the group was first met by Edward M. Archibald, the attorney general of Newfoundland. Bishop Mullock was also there to greet them. Archibald took a strong interest in the project, and would support it through many difficulties until its completion. He introduced the group to the governor, Kerr Bailey Hampton. He called a meeting of advisors to hear the presentation of the project, and within a few hours after hearing it the council agreed to recommend approval of the plan to the legislature.

It took a few weeks to work out the details of the new charter, to obtain the support of the public, and the approval of its legislature, but in the end a charter very favorable to the new company was approved. The charter of Gisborne's old company also had to be repealed as a part of the process. The charter began: "Whereas, it is deemed advisable, to establish a line of telegraphic communication between America and Europe, by way of Newfoundland."

It granted the company the authority to establish a line of telegraphic communication from Ireland to the coast of Newfoundland, and prohibited any other company from touching the coast of Newfoundland or its possessions, which included Labrador, for the next fifty years. It also granted the Company fifty square miles of land upon completion of the telegraph line. It provided for equality between citizens of the United States and Britain in the use of the telegraph, and allowed company meetings to be held in London, Newfoundland, or New York.

The local newspapers of St. John's reported in detail the discussion and approval of the charter, and it was widely welcomed and approved by both the public and government officials. Following its approval, the event was celebrated by a grand banquet given by the officers of the new company, for the dignitaries of the colony.

Meeting of the Investors, painting by Daniel Huntington

1.Peter Cooper 2. David Field 3. Chandler White 4. Marshall Roberts 5. S F B Morse 6. Daniel Huntington 7. Moses Taylor 8. Cyrus W. Field 9. Wilson Hunt.

Within days of the signing of the document, Chandler White drew out $50,000 from the New York investors, and paid off all the debts of Gisborne's old company. A large part of this debt was payment of wages to the workers who had constructed the first thirty miles of telegraph line, but had not been paid due to the failure of Gisborne's company. The repayment of this debt made a very favorable impression,

as shown in the following paragraph from the St. John's paper of
April 8, 1854:

> The office of the new Electric Telegraph Company has been
> surrounded the last two or three days by the men who had been
> engaged the last year on the line, and who are being paid all debts,
> dues and demands against the old association. We look upon the
> readiness with which these claims are liquidated as a substantial
> indication on the part of the new Company that they will complete to
> the letter all that they have declared to accomplish in this important
> undertaking.

By Saturday, May 6, Field and his fellow travelers had returned to New
York. Because some of the investors had plans to travel on Monday,
and they did not wish to meet on Sunday, the Sabbath, they held the
formal organization of the company at six A.M. on Monday morning,
May 8, 1854, at the home of Matthew Field. The charter was formally
accepted, the stock subscribed, and the first officers officially chosen.
Capital of $1.5 million was subscribed, as had been agreed, and the
New York, Newfoundland and London Telegraph Company was officially
established, for the purpose of establishing a trans-Atlantic telegraph
line between Europe and the United States.

Cape Spear, just south of the capital, is the easternmost point of North
America... Newfoundland is the site of the only authenticated Norse
settlement in North America... the settlement dates to about the year
1000, and the site contains the earliest-known European structures in
North America... About 500 years later, in 1497, the Italian navigator
John Cabot became the first European since the Norse settlers to set
foot on Newfoundland.
–Wikipedia, on Newfoundland

Chapter 3
The Newfoundland
Connection

The plan was to get started on the construction of the Newfoundland
link first. This link, once completed, was expected to provide a source of
revenue for the company, perhaps helping with the financing of the undersea cable. This link was comprised of (1) construction of a 400-mile
overland line from St. John's to the southern coast of Newfoundland;
(2) a marine cable across the Cabot Strait to the northern coast of Cape
Breton Island, and (3) a 140-mile line across that island, to connect to
the existing telegraph network in Nova Scotia. Cape Breton Island is
an island which is separated from the rest of Nova Scotia by a narrow
strait.

Chandler White, one of the initial investors, agreed to run the office in
St. John's, and Matthew Field was appointed as supervising engineer.
Frederick Gisborne was a consultant. Gisborne's company had already
constructed about thirty or forty miles of the link, from St. John's,
but this was over the easiest part of the way; the remaining 360 miles
was over very difficult country. It was very mountainous, with many
fast-rushing streams flowing down to the sea, and the weather was
often very foggy or rainy, with snow and freezing temperatures in
the winter.

Matthew Field recruited a construction party which numbered some six-
hundred men. The work was quite difficult, even by the standards of the

mid-nineteenth century. This was made worse by rough terrain, weather and rocky soil. The men slept on the ground, occasionally with tents or crudely built huts, but often under the open sky. The wire for this link was provided by a wire factory owned by Peter Cooper in Trenton, New Jersey. The workers food and other supplies were provided by sea, from a steamer which Cyrus Field bought in Nova Scotia. The steamer sailed back and forth between St. John's and the nearest docking point, from which the supplies had to be carried on foot up steep, rocky mountain paths.

The company's directors had rather naively assumed that this four hundred mile link could be completed in a few months, or by late 1854. Instead, it took more than a year, and consumed about $500,000, or one third of the company's initial working capital.

The wire provided by Cooper's factory was adequate for the land lines, but for a marine cable better insulation was needed, and this was only available in Britain. While the Newfoundland land line was under construction, Cyrus Field was to go to England to buy the wire for this link. A pair of personal tragedies delayed his trip.

First, his brother-in-law and business partner, Joseph Stone, passed away, forcing Cyrus to remain in New York for a time, for business reasons. Then, in August, 1854, his only son, Arthur Stone Field, four years old, died suddenly. It is probable that the boy consumed some microorganisms drinking milk, as was common in those days, which caused him to sicken and die. Sadly, in those days it was fairly common for children to get sick from milk or other foods, and young children sometimes died from these illnesses. Thus, it was not until the end of 1854 that Cyrus finally set sail for England.

The success of the Brett brothers in laying the English Channel cable in 1851 was possible largely due to a material called gutta-percha. This material had been known for centuries in its native land of Malaya (now Malaysia). It is a natural plastic, or polymer, which comes from several trees in that country. It is similar to rubber, but less flexible, and does not deteriorate when submerged in water. Soft and pliant when heated, it becomes hard at room temperature or below, and in the cold water of the deep Atlantic remains quite hard. It turned out to be ideal for the insulation of wires which were to be submerged in the sea.

In 1843, Jose d'Almeida, a Portugeese engineer, described gutta-percha and its uses to the Royal Asiatic Society in London. A few months later, some samples were sent to London by the East Asia Company, displayed at the Society of Arts, and the material soon became popular for use in boot soles, bottle stoppers, walking sticks, and many other items. It was also soon used to make golf balls.

Gutta-percha golf balls turned out to be cheaper and longer-lasting than the old style balls, made of leather stuffed with goose feathers. Balls made from gutta-percha also turned out to have another important quality: after they had been used a while, they could be driven further. This was due to the dents they received in play. Thus, it was learned that golf balls with dimples have better aerodynamic qualities than smooth ones. Further, and relevant to this story, gutta percha also extruded nicely around the wire in a continuous manufacturing process.

Werner von Siemans (1816-92), founder of the German electronics com- pany of the same name, learned that gutta-percha was a good electrical insulator. He developed a machine, similar to a macaroni-making ma- chine, that extruded a wire coated with the material. Gutta-percha quickly became the preferred material for the insulation of marine cables.

When Field arrived in England at the beginning of 1855, he immediately went to see John W. Brett, then head of the Magnetic Telegraph Company, and a recognized expert on submarine telegraph cables. Brett became a friend who would encourage Field when others did not. Brett recommended a cable made of three strands of copper wire, each insulated with gutta-percha, then bundled together, wrapped in hemp, again insulated with gutta-percha, with the whole cable sheathed in galvanized iron wire.

Field ordered eighty-five miles of the cable, enough to cross the Cabot Strait with several miles to spare. He arranged for it to be loaded, ready for laying, on the *Sarah L. Bryant*, a 500-ton brig. Once the cable was manufactured and loaded, the ship was to sail for Port aux Basques, on the south coast of Newfoundland, which was to be the Newfoundland terminus of the marine cable. Field also hired Samuel Canning, a British engineer with experience in marine cables, to oversee the project.

Having arranged for the manufacture and transport of the cable, Field returned to New York in March, 1855. He wrote a letter to his brother Matthew in Newfoundland, inquiring about the progress of the overland cable. The reply told him of the difficulties which were encountered: "Recently, in building half a mile of road we had to bridge three ravines. Why didn't we go around the ravines? Because Mr. Gisborne had explored twenty miles in both directions and found more ravines. That's why! You have no idea of the problem we face. We hope to finish the land line in '55, but wouldn't bet on it before '56 if I were you."

Though the progress of the land line was slower than expected, there was no reason not to go ahead and lay the submarine cable, as soon as preparations were complete. Once Field knew that the submarine cable was completed and on its way, he chartered the *James Adger* to meet it in Newfoundland, at a cost of $750 per day. The *James Adger* was a coastal steamer that ran regularly between Charleston, South Carolina and New York. It was needed to tow the *Sarah L. Bryant*, which was powered only by sails, as the cable was being laid out.

The *James Adger* set out from New York for Newfoundland on 7 August 1855. A large party of about fifty guests had been invited to go on the voyage and witness the laying of the first major ocean submarine cable in North America.

The party included Peter Cooper, the company's president; Reverend David Dudley Field, Cyrus' father, then seventy-four years old; Reverend Gardner Spring, another prominent minister; Samuel F. B. Morse and his wife; Henry Field, Cyrus' brother, who later wrote a book on the trans-Atlantic cable, and his wife. Several reporters from New York were also included. Two of Field's daughters also came along, but not his wife, for she had recently given birth to a second son, Edward Morse Field, and was still nursing him. His middle name was in honor of the inventor. The captain of the *James Adger* was a man named Turner, who would play an unexpected role in the laying of the cable.

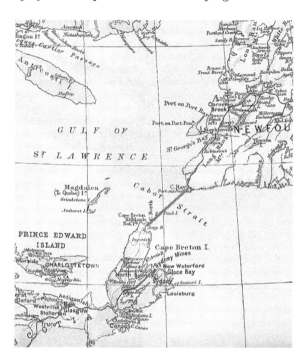

Newfoundland, Cape Breton Island and The Cabot Strait

The steamer stopped briefly in Halifax, Nova Scotia, to let off some passengers, and then continued on to Port aux Basques, on the southern coast of Newfoundland, where it was to meet the *Sarah L. Bryant*, en route from England. But on its arrival, the cable-bearing ship had not yet been sighted, so Field decided to sail up the coast to St. John's, hoping to meet it. The ship was not sighted, however, and the *James Adger* reached St. John's. Field invited officials from the city on board for a party, and the passengers were invited ashore for a ball. When the *James Adger* returned to Port aux Basques, the *Sarah L. Bryant* had finally arrived, with some damage after a rough voyage.

Once the damages to the *Bryant* had been repaired, the laying out of the cable finally got under way. As the operation started, the anchor of the *Bryant* was discovered to be foul, that is, it had become entangled. For that reason the anchor had to be slipped, or cut loose. The two ships then collided. Captain Turner of the Adger cut the tow rope and steamed away from the *Bryant*, leaving her to fend for herself. The crew had to cut the telegraph cable and hoist her sails hurriedly to avoid running aground.

Some of the passengers accused Captain Turner of deliberately ramming the *Bryant*. He appeared to have taken a rather negative attitude towards the entire project. Field had placed the Reverend Spring at the head of the ship's table, which the captain felt should have been his. Turner also appeared to resent taking orders from a passenger, Field, even though he was paying $750 per day for the use of the vessel.

When the *Bryant*'s anchors had been recovered and repairs made, the cable laying started again. A flag had been placed on shore in line with a prominent rock, to mark the course which was to be followed, in order to reach Cape Breton Island within the required distance. The captain proceeded to chart his own course, however, and the passengers soon saw that it was going well off the desired course. Peter Cooper approached him and demanded that he follow instructions. "I know how to steer my ship. I steer by my compass," he replied.

Cooper could see that they were going well off course, and that, following such a course, the cable would not be long enough to reach Cape Breton. It was only after he demanded again that the captain follow instructions, and had a company lawyer on board draw up a document stating his responsibilities, that the captain finally changed course. When he did so, he changed course so sharply that it caused a kink in the cable.

Another equally serious difficulty was that the *James Adger* was steaming more rapidly than the *Bryant* was able to lay out cable into the sea. The captain refused to slow his speed. As more and more cable was laid out, it began to act as an anchor on the stern of the *Bryant*, pulling it down towards the water.

As this continued, the weather worsened into a gale, and, to prevent the ship from sinking, Samuel Channing, the engineer in charge aboard, finally had to cut the cable. Too much of the cable had been paid out and lost to start again. The expedition thus ended as a complete and ignominious failure. The two vessels headed for Sydney, the largest port on Cape Breton Island, and the *James Adger* then sailed on back to New York. The *Sarah L. Bryant* unloaded the remaining cable.

As one would expect, the failure was a deep disappointment to Cyrus Field. Back in New York, he and the other directors met to decide what to do. One comforting fact was that the reason for the failure was clear. Peter Cooper later wrote, "We had spent so much money, and lost so much time, that it was very vexatious to have our enterprise defeated by the stupidity and obstinacy of one man."

The loss of the cable cost the company $351,000 in capital, a complete loss. With the cost of the land cable across Newfoundland, and Cape Breton, and the costs of numerous trips and other operating expenses, the original $1.5 million in capital had been almost depleted.

Another important lesson was that it was not prudent to have the cable on a ship which was not steam-powered, and so unable to control its own speed. It was decided to order a new cable from Kuper and Company, the same firm which had manufactured the first cable, but this time the company was also contracted to lay the cable, at its own risk. Field was in no mood for any more yachting parties.

The next summer, 1856, the cable was laid successfully. That year also saw the completion of the 400-mile land line across Newfoundland, and the relatively easy 140-mile land line across Cape Breton Island, with much easier terrain, and which connected the submarine cable to the existing telegraph network in Nova Scotia.

The first leg of the plan had been executed, taking two and a half years. The big part, the trans-Atlantic link, had not yet begun. It was clear that much more capital would be needed, and Cyrus Field made plans to sail once again for Britain, the financial capital of the world, and the only country where the amounts of capital which he needed could be found. This trip would last several months. Though he could not possibly have known it at the time, many more voyages would be taken and disappointments suffered before his dream would be realized.

Chapter 4
Preparing for a
Massive Project

A thing long expected takes the form of the unexpected when at last it comes.
−Mark Twain (1835-1910)

A number of issues had to be resolved before a cable could be laid across the Atlantic. A critical one was the raising of sufficient capital to pay for it and for all the work involved. The $1.5 million which had been raised was already largely exhausted by the construction of the Newfoundland link.

A second issue was the composition of the cable itself; such a cable would be by far the longest cable ever manufactured, and would be immersed in seas far deeper than ever before. In both electrical properties and physical strength, it would need to far exceed any cable previously known.

A third important issue was the cooperation of the British and U.S. governments. While the Newfoundland legislature had already been very cooperative, similar cooperation was needed by the others if the venture was to have any realistic chance of success.

A fourth question was the issue of an ocean-going ship to carry the cable, and what equipment was needed to store it on board safely and to pay it out from the ship.

Finally, the issue of exactly where to lay the cable and land it on each side of the Atlantic needed to be resolved. Maury and Berryman had already given an approximate answer, but additional measurements were needed.

With this last issue in mind, Field made a trip to Washington to request another survey by the Navy on the behalf of the company. His request was granted, and the job was again assigned to Lieutenant O. H. Berryman, who had carried out the previous series of soundings. He sailed from New York on July 18, 1856 for St. John's, and was seen off by Field, with whom he had become friends. From there he sailed on the great circle for the west coast of Ireland, which he reached about three weeks later.

A great circle is one on the surface of a sphere, with the same center as the sphere. It has an important property: the shortest distance between any two points on a sphere is along the great circle common to them. Examples on the earth are the equator and lines of longitude.

For this reason, great circles are important to navigators. Thus, Berryman was following the shortest path from Newfoundland to Ireland. The results of his survey confirmed the existence of a great plateau, running practically from the coast of Newfoundland to that of Ireland. The only important exception to this gentle plateau was about two hundred miles off the coast of Ireland, where the depth drops from 560 fathoms to about 1,750 fathoms in about a dozen miles. Even this more drastic change in elevation, however, was not so much as to present a serious difficulty for the laying of a cable.

The day after Berryman sailed from New York, July 19, Field sailed for Britain, this time accompanied by his family, to raise capital and ask for the support of the British government. He also planned to work on the questions of the cable and the ship or ships which would be needed. Up to this time, almost all of the capital had been provided by Americans. The only exception was John Brett – the same who in 1851 laid the English Channel cable with his brother – who had taken a few shares to show his support.

On arriving in England, Field immediately went to see Brett, and also wrote a letter to George Villiers, Lord Clarendon, the British foreign secretary, which outlined the project and asked for a meeting. The letter received a "prompt and courteous reply," and the meeting was quickly arranged.

Field met with Lord Clarendon for more than an hour, and was accompanied by Samuel Morse, who also was in England at the time, and whose name now had become quite well known. Clarendon showed much interest in the project, and seemed rather startled at its magnitude, and at the confidence which Field and Morse displayed. At one point in the meeting, he asked Field, "But, suppose you don't succeed? Suppose you make the attempt and fail – your cable is lost in the sea – then what will you do?"

"Charge it to profit and loss, and go to work to lay another," replied Field immediately. Lord Clarendon must have liked the answer, because he encouraged Field on the project and, without formally committing the government, promised to do what he could to help. Shortly thereafter, Field received an invitation to visit Mr. James Wilson, the British Secretary of the Treasury. Wilson invited Field to visit him at his residence near Bath, to discuss at length the proposed project and government assistance. Field accepted the invitation and made the visit. Soon after, he received a letter, part of which is quoted below:

> Treasury Chambers, Nov. 20, 1856.
> Sir:
> Having laid before the Lords Commissioners of her Majesty's Treasury your letter of the 13th ultimo, addressed to the Earl of Clarendon, requesting, on behalf of the New York, Newfoundland and London Telegraph Company, certain privileges and protection in regard to the line of telegraph which it is proposed to establish between Newfoundland and Ireland, I am directed by their lordships to acquaint you that they are prepared to enter into a contract with the said Telegraph Company, based upon the following conditions, namely:
> 1. It is understood that the capital required to lay down the line will be (£350,000) three hundred and fifty thousand pounds.

The letter also offered to make available ships for additional soundings as needed; guaranteed a payment of £14,000 per year for the use of the line by the British government when completed; and also promised additional payments, should government use of the line exceed that amount. The letter stipulated that the British Government would get priority on the use of the telegraph, with the exception that an equal priority be granted to the U. S. government, if that government entered into a supporting role on the same principles. In short, Wilson was offering Field's company an extremely favorable contract.

Field asked the British admiralty to conduct another survey of the Atlantic, which was authorized by the letter from Wilson. This was agreed to, providing for yet a third survey, independent of the first two. Though there were some relatively minor differences in the soundings taken, the British survey essentially confirmed the findings of Berryman's surveys of 1853 and 1856.

To obtain financing, Field organized a British company, chartered in London in October, 1856, called the Atlantic Telegraph Company. Its capitalization was set at £350,000, the estimated cost to manufacture the cable. Three hundred fifty shares of £1,000 each were to be sold. To raise the money, he visited a number of wealthy British capitalists, and made a tour of the country, talking to local government officials and others who showed an interest.

The entire capital of £350,000 was subscribed within a few weeks. Investors from London, Liverpool, Manchester, and Glasgow all participated in providing the capital. Field himself took eighty-eight shares, about one-fourth of the total, with the intention of selling most of them to American investors. He thought that Americans should participate in providing the capital for the cable that was to connect Britain with the U.S.

Field returned to New York in December, arriving on Christmas Day, 1856. By the new year he was off on another trip, this time to Newfoundland, to arrange for the legislature to grant the same landing privileges to the Atlantic Telegraph Company which it had already granted to the New York, Newfoundland and London company. As soon as that business was taken care of he returned to New York.

Following this, he had yet another trip, this time to Washington D.C. The U.S. Congress was not being as cooperative as the British government had been; there was serious opposition by several Congressmen to government participation in the Atlantic cable project. However, with the support of President Buchanan and several far-sighted Congress-

men, Field was finally able to get the legislation passed granting the
same rights and concessions as had the London government. The bill
was signed into law March 3, 1857. With it, among other concessions,
the U.S. government agreed to provide the use of Naval ships to help in
the laying of the cable, and for the survey that had already been carried
out by Berryman.

When Field again returned to New York and attempted to get American
investors to take some of the eighty-eight shares he held, he was only
able sell twenty-seven of them, and some of those at a loss. A financial
panic had hit the country, and this made it difficult for him to find
more investors for his shares. This left Field with sixty-one shares, at
£1,000 each, or a total of about $305,000. As he had already invested
some $200,000 of his own money in the project, the majority of his own
net worth was now invested in the cable. Field's personal fortune would
now swim or sink with the success, or failure, of the Atlantic cable.

When he was in England, Field talked with Brett and a number of
others about the technical aspects of the cable. Brett introduced Field
to Charles Bright. Bright was only twenty-four years old at the time,
and worked with the Magnetic Telegraph Company. Bright had been in
telegraphy since the age of fifteen, and at nineteen had laid a network
of telegraph wires in the city of Manchester.

Bright was hired as chief engineer for the project. Bright had also
imagined the possibility of a trans-Atlantic telegraph cable as early
as 1853, and had also explored the west coast of Ireland for a suitable
termination point. He chose Valentia Bay, in the extreme southwest part
of the island, because of its smooth, sandy shore and because it was
relatively sheltered from the strong Atlantic waves which hit much of
the western Irish coast. His choice seems to have been the right one, as
Valentia Bay became the location of all trans-Atlantic cables originating
or terminating in Ireland.

The company also hired Dr. Edward Whitehouse as electrician. Whitehouse was a medical doctor, but had done a great deal of experimenting
in electricity and telegraphy. While he seemed to have sufficient tech-

nical qualifications for the job, events would later reveal that he was often stubborn and overly confident in the correctness of his own opinions.

The company also invited a well-known physicist to join the company's board of directors. Professor William Thomson (1824-1907), of the University of Glasgow, Scotland, was very interested in undersea cables. Thomson, later honored as Lord Kelvin, would eventually be known as one of the great physicists of the 19th century, along with his colleagues James Clerk Maxwell and Michael Faraday.

Field had practically no knowledge of electric cables, so he had no choice but to follow the advice of Brett and other experts. The trans- Atlantic cable would be longer than any other undersea cable, by far, and would be placed in far deeper water. The sheer *weight* of a cable two and one-half miles long, hanging off the edge of a ship, would be enough to snap most cables then in use in shallower waters. Further, the propagation of an electrical signal through such a long distance of wire was not a very well understood issue.

After discussing the matter with Brett and other experts of the day, Field decided to order a cable with a copper core. The core was actually seven copper wires, each of a thickness of 0.028 inches, all twisted together to form a core wire of 0.083 inches in diameter. This copper core would then be covered by three separate coats of gutta-percha, for insulation. It was reasoned that any hole or flaw in one of the layers would be covered up by the other layers. The insulated wire was then wrapped in hemp soaked with tar, pitch, and wax. This entire cable was then covered with an armoring layer of 18 iron wires, each of seven strands, and then the entire cable was coated with a mixture of tar.

The finished cable was about five-eighths (5/8") inch in diameter, and weighed about one ton per mile. Submerged, its weight would be less, 1,340 pounds per mile. It was calculated that it should bear a weight of 6,500 pounds before breaking; this was equal to about five miles of its weight in water. Since the deepest point in which it would be submerged was less than two and one-half miles, this was believed to be a sufficient safety margin.

The ends of the cable, which would be landed, were given extra attention. This part of the cable, being in the shallowest water, and nearest
to the coasts, was obviously more vulnerable to damage. These were
made much heavier, with more insulation and armor. The resulting cable
weighed nine tons per mile. The end at the Irish coast was made ten
miles long, and the end for the Newfoundland coast was fifteen miles;
the bottom near Newfoundland was rougher and rockier for a greater
distance from land, so it was decided that a longer end cable was needed.

Even today, more than a century and a half later, the magnitude and
dimensions of the cable are quite amazing. For the copper core, 20,500
miles of copper wire was manufactured, and made into a core (seven
strands woven together) of 2,500 miles. The insulation required three
hundred tons of gutta-percha, which was applied to the core in three
separate layers. For the outer sheathing, 367,500 miles of iron wire had
to be drawn, made from 1,687 tons of charcoal iron. The total of copper
and iron wire manufactured was then some 340,500 miles – enough to
stretch from the earth to the moon, with almost 100,000 miles to spare.

The contract for the entire cable was £225,000; the core cost was £40
per mile, while the sheathing cost was £50 per mile. In the 1850s, one
pound (£) sterling was worth a little more than five U.S dollars ($5);
so the cost in 1850 dollars was about $1.2 million. In 2007 U.S. dollars,
this comes to more than $27.3 million.

Charles Bright and William Thomson recommended that a thicker,
heavier cable be used, but Morse and Faraday felt the measurements
given would be adequate. The cable which Bright and Thomson wanted
would have also been more expensive, and taken longer to manufacture.
The company directors, eager to get the cable laid as soon as possible,
and also wanting to minimize capital costs, decided to go with the lighter,
less expensive cable described above. Field and the other directors were
eager to get the cable laid as quickly as possible; they were hoping to
get it done in the summer of 1857.

The core of the cable and the insulation was manufactured by the
Gutta-Percha Company. It was decided to manufacture a cable 2,500
nautical miles long, which provided a surplus of several hundred miles;

the distance from Valentia Bay, Ireland to Trinity Bay, Newfoundland was about 1,640 nautical miles. The surplus provided for the irregularities in the bottom of the Atlantic, as well as for possible errors. (A nautical mile is 6,076 feet; a statute mile, or "land mile," is 5,280 feet).

At a weight of one ton per mile, the cable would have a total weight of approximately 2,500 tons. The outer sheathing of the cable was given to two different companies, in order to speed up the manufacturing process. The manufacturing of the cable began in February, 1857; and four months were allotted for this, for delivery in June, 1857.

Once he had obtained the support of the U.S. government in March, 1857, Field sailed once again for England, where preparations were well underway. In 1857, no ship in the world was large enough to be able to carry the entire cable. The largest ships could carry half of it, however, so it was decided to use two ships and splice the two halves of the cable together at the midpoint, in the middle of the Atlantic.

During one of his visits to England – it was probably in 1856 – Field met Isambard Kingdom Brunel. Brunel was the greatest engineer in Britain of the day, and had shown considerable interest in the Atlantic cable project, offering advice to Field on the cable and, later, on the equipment to be used to pay it out.

At the time, Brunel was engaged in the construction of a huge iron ship which was to be known as the *Great Eastern*. This ship would be the largest ever constructed, by far. Brunel took Field to see the ship under construction, and said to him, "There is the ship to lay the Atlantic cable." The ship was not being built to lay cable, however, nor did the company have any intention – at that time – of using it.

The problem of what ships to use was conveniently solved by the willingness of both governments to provide ships from their navies. The U.S. government provided the *Niagara* and the *Susquehanna*, which were the two finest ships in the American Navy.

The *Niagara* was probably the largest warship in the world at the time, and was chosen to carry half of the cable. She was built in 1845, and had a total displacement of 5,200 tons. Designed as a steamship, with a powerful engine and graceful curves, the *Niagara* was capable of a speed of twelve knots. She was also equipped with three masts for sails. To prepare her for the job, her armaments were cleared from the deck and her bulkheads – the walls on the interior hull of a ship – were removed to make room for the huge cable. These preparations took a few weeks, and in late April the ship set sail for England. She arrived on May 14, and cast anchor at Gravesend, about twenty-five miles below London, on the Thames River, to await the cable.

The British government provided the H.M.S. *Agamemnon*, an older vessel with a displacement of 3,500 tons. She was not as large or as fast as the *Niagara*, but had seen action in some important battles, and was judged capable of carrying the British half of the cable. While the *Niagara* was waiting in Gravesend, the *Agamemnon* sailed up the river towards London, within sight. The occasion is recalled in Henry Field's account:

> As the *Agamemnon* came up the river in grand style, she recognized the *Niagara* lying off Gravesend, and manning her yards, gave her a succession of these English hurrahs so stirring to the blood, when heard on land or sea, to which our hearts replied with lusty American cheers. It was pleasant to observe, from this time, the hearty good-will that existed between the officers and crews of the two ships, who in their exertions for the common object, were animated only by a generous rivalry.

The *Niagara* was sent to Birkenhead, near Liverpool, to load her half of the cable, 1250 nautical miles, where it was being manufactured by Newell & Company. On the way, she stopped in Portsmouth for several days, where more alterations were carried out. These were done to provide still more space for the cable, and to fit an iron cage over the screw; this was to prevent the cable from getting caught by it.

The *Agamemnon* was also equipped with such a cage over its screw. The loading of the cable took three weeks; 120 men were divided into crews of thirty men working at a time. Great care had to be taken in this, to avoid any possible damage from kinking. At the same time, the *Agamemnon* was loading her half of the cable at Greenwich, near London, where it had been manufactured by Glass, Elliot and Company.

The paying out equipment, which was for the purpose of unwinding the cable from the ship and paying it out into the ocean, was equipped with brakes which could be used to slow down the speed at which the cable paid out. The sheer weight of a cable more than two miles long could cause the cable to begin running out of the ship, getting out of control. Since this cable was longer and heavier than any used before, and would pay the cable out in water far deeper, the braking equipment on the paying out machine was made much stronger than had been on previous expeditions.

The officers and crews of both ships were treated to banquets and celebrations in Liverpool and London, as the cables were being loaded. The mayor of Liverpool gave the officers a dinner, the Chamber of Commerce another, and the Americans who were living in Liverpool gave them a banquet on the fourth of July, reportedly the first time that the U.S. independence from Britain was celebrated in that country. In London, a huge banquet was also held for the officers and men of the *Agamemnon* when the cable was loaded.

The loading of both ships was completed by late July, and each set out for Queenstown, Ireland, which had been designated as their rendezvous point. Queenstown, Ireland's major Atlantic seaport, was just a few miles from Valentia Bay, where the cable was to be landed. There, for the first time, the electricians were able to test the entire 2,500 miles of cable; the end of one was brought from one ship to the other, where they were spliced together. The cable was sound; the signal propagated through the entire length as expected, surely to the relief of all.

There had been considerable debate about whether to lay the cable from one ship, starting at the coast, to mid-ocean, and there to splice it together; or, alternatively, that the ships should meet in mid-ocean, splice the two ends together, and then simultaneously lay both ends towards the shores.

The advantage of meeting in mid-ocean was that the cable could be laid out faster, lessening the chance of running into bad weather. The advantage of starting from the coast was that a continuous communication could be maintained with land, and should a signal be lost, it would be immediately known, and easier to find the fault. In the case of both ships laying the cable simultaneously, a fault would be harder to isolate and correct.

The electricians, including Morse, preferred the first method, while the engineers preferred the second. It was decided to defer to the electricians. The cable would first be landed at Valentia Bay, and laid out in one continuous line to Newfoundland, making a splice at mid-ocean. This would allow for continuous communications between land and the ships throughout the expedition.

The expedition consisted of seven ships in all. The Niagara was escorted by the U.S.S. *Susquehanna*; these were the only U.S. vessels. The *Agamemnon* was escorted by the H.M.S. *Leopard*. Both escorts were side-wheelers. In addition, there were also three smaller British steamers, the *Advice*, the *Willing Mind*, and the *Cyclops*. The *Cyclops* was commanded by Captain Dayman, who had carried out the British survey the year before, and would carry any additional soundings which might be necessary.

As July, 1857 came to a close, preparations for the greatest engineering project in history were completed, and the job itself would soon begin.

Chapter 5
The First Attempt: 1857

It is not the critic who counts; not the man who points out how the strong man stumbles, or where the doer of deeds could have done them better. The credit belongs to the man who is actually in the arena, whose face is marred by dust and sweat and blood; who strives valiantly; who errs, who comes short again and again, because there is no effort without error and shortcoming; but who does actually strive to do the deed; who knows great enthusiasms, the great devotions; who spends himself in a worthy cause; who at the best knows in the end the triumph of high achievement, and who at the worst, if he fails, at least fails while daring greatly, so that his place shall never be with those cold and timid souls who neither know victory nor defeat.

–Theodore Roosevelt, former US President, 1920

As the ships steamed into Valentia Bay, on Tuesday afternoon, August 4, 1857, sizeable crowds of people could be seen, standing on the hills to witness the most exciting event to come to this remote corner of Ireland in decades. Though ideally suited geographically as the European terminus of a trans-Atlantic cable, Valentia Bay, in the County of Kerry, is one of the most remote parts of Ireland. In the 1850s, many of the local people still spoke Gaelic. It is also one of the most beautiful parts of the British Isles, and of Europe, with long peninsulas running out to the sea from Ireland's mountains, dropping off in cliffs hundreds of feet high.

The fleet was welcomed by George Howard, Earl of Carlisle, and Lord Lieutenant of Ireland, who had come from Dublin to witness the landing of the cable and the departure of the fleet. Sir Peter Fitzgerald, Knight of Kerry, the major local landowner, also came to welcome the ships. The Lord Lieutenant gave an inspiring speech concerning the importance of the cable, a part of which follows:

Amidst all the pride and the stirring hopes which cluster around the work of this week, we ought still to remember that we must speak with the modesty of those who begin and not of those who

close an experiment, and it behooves us to remember that the pathway
to great achievements has frequently to be hewn out amidst risks and
difficulties, and that preliminary failure is even the law and condition
of the ultimate success.

Therefore, whatever disappointments may possibly be in store, I
must yet insinuate to you that in a cause like this it would be criminal
to feel discouragement. In the very design and endeavor to establish the
Atlantic Telegraph there is almost enough of glory. It is true if it be
only an attempt there would not be quite enough of profit. I hope that
will come, too; but there is enough of public spirit, of love for science,
for our country, for the human race, almost to suffice in themselves.
However, upon this rocky frontlet of Ireland, at all events, today we
will presume upon success. We are about, either by this sundown or
by tomorrow's dawn, to establish a new material link between the Old
World and the New.

It was to be the next day, August 5, 1857, that the cable would be
landed, as the ships had arrived too late in the day to begin on the
fourth. During the night, preparations were made to begin to land the
very heavy shore link.

In the morning, the weather was too windy to work, but it lessened
in the afternoon, so work began about two-thirty. The first task was
to drag the landing cable ashore from the ship. This was not easy, as
the landing cable was very heavy, weighing nine tons per mile. In the
interest of diplomacy and good will between the two nations, it had
been agreed the American sailors would haul the landing cable ashore
on the British side, while British sailors would perform the same task
on the American side.

The effort took several hours, as the U.S. sailors dragged the cable from
the larger ship, the *Niagara*, which due to its size was anchored some
distance out from land, to smaller cable boats for pulling it ashore. Henry
Field described the scene as follows:

Valentia Bay was studded with innumerable small craft, decked
with the gayest bunting – small boats flitted hither and thither, their
occupants cheering enthusiastically as the work successfully progressed.
The cable boats were managed by the sailors of the *Niagara* and the

Susquehanna, and it was a well-designed compliment, and indicative of the future fraternization of the nations, that the shore rope was arranged to be presented at this side of the Atlantic to the representative of the Queen, by the officers and men of the United States Navy, and that at the other side British officers and sailors should made a similar presentation to the President of the Great Republic.

It took them until seven-thirty that evening to get the cable ashore. Captain Pennock of the *Niagara* formally presented it to the Lord Lieutenant, who had been standing on the beach patiently throughout the afternoon. A ceremony took place in which a prayer was offered, and the Lord Lieutenant gave another inspiring discourse, in which he referred to the tragedy which had occurred recently in Ireland, the potato famine, in which two million people, one-fourth of the population, had either died from starvation or disease, or emigrated to escape them. His speech included the following:

> I believe that the great work so happily begun will accomplish many great and noble purposes of trade, of national policy, and of empire. But there is only one view in which I will present it to those whom I have the pleasure to address. You are aware – you must know, some of you, from your own experience – that many of your dear friends and near relatives have left their native land to receive hospitable shelter in America. Well, then, I do not expect that all of you can understand the wondrous mechanism by which this great undertaking is to be carried on.

> But this, I think, you all of you understand. If you wished to communicate some piece of intelligence straightway to your relatives across the wide world of waters – if you wished to tell those whom you know it would interest in their heart of hearts, of a birth, or a marriage, or, alas, a death, among you, the little cord, which we have now hauled up to the shore, will impart that tidings quicker than the flash of the lightning. Let us indeed hope, let us pray that the hopes of those who have set on foot this great design, may be rewarded by its entire success..

At the end of his speech, the he called for cheers for the project and all those involved, which resulted in "loud and protracted cheering." Next there were calls for Field to speak. His reply was the following:

> I have no words to express the feelings which fill my heart tonight – it beats with love and affection for every man, woman, and child

who hears me. I may say, however, that, if ever at the other side of the
waters now before us, any one of you shall present yourselves at my
door and say that you took hand or part, even by an approving smile,
in our work here today, you shall have a true American welcome. I
cannot bind myself to more, and shall merely say: 'What God hath
joined together, let not man put asunder.'

As the landing had taken place late in the evening, Wednesday, August
5, expedition of laying it out from the ships was set to begin the next
morning. At dawn, the expedition got started, the cable running out
from the U.S.S. *Niagara*, going very slowly, about two knots. At about
five miles from shore, however, the heavy shore cable got caught in the
machinery and broke. The *Willing Mind* returned to shore, where a
hawser (a very heavy ship rope) was run under the cable there, and the
ship worked its way back pulling up the cable to the surface until the
broken end was reached. It was then spliced to the remaining shore cable.

The *Niagara* then continued on its way, still moving very slowly and
carefully as the remaining five miles of shore cable was paid out. When
the end of the shore cable was reached, it was spliced onto the lighter
ocean cable, and the ship continued on her way. The speed of the ship and
the paying out were allowed to increase slightly, up to about five knots.

The next few days passed as hoped for, the cable steadily paying out.
Saturday, August 8 was a beautiful day and spirits were high. By
midnight of that day, eighty-five miles of cable had been paid out, and
the electrical signal continued to function perfectly.

On Monday, August 10, the ship reached the point where the sea bottom began its plunge from 500 fathoms to 1,750 fathoms in about eight
to twelve miles. (Bright's log indicated that the drop occurs in eight
miles, while earlier soundings had indicated twelve miles; both could
have been correct, as the route of the cable-laying ships were not on
exactly the same course as the soundings expeditions.)

The paying out machinery continued to function, but the cable was
thrown off its runners several times, and had to be manually put back
in place. Tar from the cable also tended to build up in the grooves, and

hardened, causing difficulties. Occasionally the ship would have to stop while these were cleaned.

Paying Out Cable from the *USS Niagara*
From the *Illustrated Times* of London, 15 August 1857 and the
Atlantic-Cable.com Website

As the cable plunged into deeper and deeper water, it became necessary to apply the brakes of the machinery to keep it from running out too fast. By noon on Monday, the depth had reached two thousand fathoms – more than two miles – and 255 miles of cable had been paid out. The ship was 214 miles from the coast. The waves began to increase in size, and the pressure which was being applied on the brakes was increased several times, reaching two thousand pounds.

About nine o'clock Monday night, the electricity on the cable went dead. The cable was intact, and nothing obvious pointed to the reason. Morse, who was on board, and who had been suffering from seasickness, was roused from his bed, and he tried the instruments but could not find the cause. Nor could the electricians on board. When, after two or three hours of trying, no one could fix it, the engineers were preparing to cut the cable, and to begin hauling it back in an attempt to find the cause, the electricity suddenly started to work again.

The return of the signal brought back the high spirits on board. The cause of this temporary outage was never definitely determined. Morse theorized that perhaps there been a break in the insulation, which, when the cable reached the bottom, somehow was resealed by the cold water or its position on the bottom.

The operation of paying out the cable was resumed and continued. All evening the speed of the paying out of the cable had been increasing, making necessary increased pressure on the brakes. At one point, the paying out was going at about six miles per hour, while the speed of the ship was only advancing at about four. Supposedly this was due to the great depth of the water and a current as well. To control the speed, the brake had to be applied constantly. At nine in the evening, the pressure had been increased to twenty-five hundred pounds.

Charles Bright, the chief engineer, was monitoring the paying out equipment personally. At two A.M., he had to increase the pressure to three thousand pounds. The ship was passing over waves, which would lift the stern and then drop it. As this occurred, Bright adjusted the brakes to compensate for the raising and lowering of the stern. Then, as the first light was beginning to show itself on the horizon, at about a quarter to four in the morning, it happened. In Bright's words:

> I had up to this attended personally to the regulation of the brakes, but finding that all was going well, and on it being necessary that I should be temporarily away from the machine – to ascertain the rate of the ship, to see how the cable was coming out of the hold, and also to visit the electrician's room – the machine was for the moment left in charge of a mechanic who had been engaged from the first in its construction and fitting, and was acquainted with its operation.

In proceeding towards the fore part of the ship I heard the machine stop. I immediately called out to relieve the brakes, but when I reached the spot the cable was broken. On examining the machine – which was in otherwise perfect working order – I found that the brakes had not been released, and to this, or to the hand wheel of the brake being turned the wrong way, may be attributed the stoppage and subsequent fracture of the cable.

Just before the break, the stern of the ship, where the cable was paying out, had been in the trough of a wave. As it rose into the peak of the next wave, the brakes should have been eased to compensate, as Bright had been doing; but the mechanic he had left in charge failed to do so. The resulting pressure was too much and the cable snapped, cracking like a pistol shot, and disappeared into the sea, two and one-half miles below. In a letter to his family, Field described it from his viewpoint:

I retired to my state room a little after midnight Monday, all going on well, and at a quarter before four o'clock in Tuesday morning, the eleventh instant, I was awoke from my sleep by the cry of 'Stop her, back her!' and in a moment Mr. Bright was in my room, with the sad intelligence that the cable was broken. In as short a time as possible I was dressed, and on deck; and Captain Hudson at once signaled the other steamers that the cable had parted, and in a few moments Captain Wainwright, of the *Leopard*, and Captain Sands, of the *Susquehanna*, were on board the *Niagara*.

Naturally the setback must have been very disappointing, but, to his credit, Field showed no discouragement. His letter which reported the incident began, "The successful laying of the Atlantic Telegraph Cable is put off for a short time, but its final triumph has been fully proved, by the experience we have had since we left Valentia. My confidence was never so strong as at the present time, and I feel sure, that with God's blessing, we shall connect Europe and America with the electric cord."

Bright's report stated clearly the cause, and he also showed no thought of giving up: "The origin of the accident was, no doubt, the amount of retarding strain put on the cable, but had the machine been properly manipulated at the time, it could not possibly have happened."

At the time of the break, 380 miles of cable had been paid out, of the 2,500 miles of total cable; so more than 80% of the cable was still intact.

Evidently, no one considered the possibility of attempting to recover the lost cable, splicing it, and continuing. It is doubtful that the ships were equipped with tools or sufficient rope for "cable fishing," particularly at the depth of more than twelve thousand feet. The remaining 2,100 miles of cable was still, perhaps, enough to make a connection – the distance from Valentia Bay to Newfoundland being 1,640 miles – but it might not have provided enough slack, allowing for the greater distance at the bottom of the sea as compared to the surface.

Field instructed the two cable ships to remain at the sight for a few days, to do some testing and practice splicing of the cable, and the Cylops to take soundings. He boarded the *Leopard* and started for Portsmouth right away, where he would call a special meeting with the directors of the company.

The directors decided that it was too late in the year to make another attempt; winter weather would be coming soon to the North Atlantic, and time was needed to manufacture the nearly four hundred miles of cable that had been lost. Also, some lessons had been learned which, if applied, would increase probability of success the next summer.

For one, the paying out equipment needed improvement, especially the braking part. Some method was needed to automatically release the brakes should the pressure suddenly increase, as happened with the rising of the ship with a wave. Secondly, the crews needed better training. These could both be accomplished in time. There was also a need for practice in the handling of the ships working together.

The *Niagara* and the *Agamemnon* returned to Plymouth, and unloaded their cable into tanks, for storage until the next year, so that they could return to duty with their respective navies. In October, the engineer- in-chief, Charles Bright, went to Valentia Bay to attempt to salvage some of the lost cable. The heavy shore end, ten miles long, was picked up and the end buoyed, and about fifty miles of the cable was recovered for use the following year. This reduced the amount of lost cable from about 380 miles to about 330 miles.

Field, Bright, the directors, and all closely involved with the project remained quite optimistic. Much had been learned, the cable had been manufactured and proven to work in deep water, and the cause of the accident was clearly understood. Fortunately, sufficient capital remained for the manufacturing of the lost cable, and the preparations for a successful expedition the following year were started. As might be expected, however, the press and those who had insisted that the cable was impossible began to turn public opinion. A parody of "Pop Goes the Weasel" was often heard:

> Pay it out, oh pay it out As long as you are able;
> For if you put the damned brake on, Pop goes the cable!

Chapter 6
The First Expedition of 1858

The lamplight falls on blackened walls,
And streams through narrow perforations;
The long beam trails
o'er pasteboard scales,
With slow, decaying oscillations;
Flow, current, flow!
Set the quick light spot flying!
Flow, current, answer, light-spot!
Flashing, quivering, dying.
–James Clerk Maxwell (1831-79)

The directors decided, after the failure of 1857, to make another attempt in the summer of 1858. Several things needed to be accomplished in the intervening months: additional cable had to be manufactured, to replace the cable that had been lost; the paying-out equipment needed to be improved, if possible; and additional training for the crews of the ships was needed. In addition, Professor Thomson, having observed the first expedition, returned to his laboratory and went to work.

Field returned to New York, and then went to Washington to ask for the use of the same two ships in the attempt of the next summer, and further, that William Everett be released from his duties as a Naval officer to work on the project.

Everett was the engineering officer of the Niagara, and had helped design its engines. He had been along on the 1857 expedition, and had observed the performance of the paying out equipment first-hand. Everett had some ideas about how to improve it, and Field wanted him to be able to put them into practice on the next attempt. The government was cooperative – no act of Congress was necessary this time – and gave Field the use of both the ships and Everett. Secretary of the Navy Isaac Touch gave Field a letter, saying to Field, "There, I have given you all you asked."

The letter was dated December 30, and on January 6, 1858, Field and Everett boarded a ship, the *Persia*, for England. It was a recently built Cunard liner, the fastest transatlantic steamer of the time, capable of crossing that ocean in just over nine days. When they got back to England, the directors made Field the general manager of the company, and offered him a salary of £1,000 per year. Field accepted the position but declined the salary, preferring to let the company conserve its capital. He made Everett the chief engineer of the company, and Everett went to work immediately on the design of a new paying-out machine. He worked on this for the next few months at the engineering firm of Eston and Amos, across the Thames River from London.

The new equipment which Everett designed, and which was built with the help of the engineering firm, improved considerably on the previous machinery. It was much lighter, only one-fourth the weight of the previous machinery, and only took about one-third the space on the deck. Obviously both space and weight were at a premium.

But the biggest improvement was in the braking system. Everett based it in a design by J. G. Appold, an amateur – but competent – mechanic. The brakes could be set with a maximum braking pressure, depending on the condition, and would automatically release if the pressure reached the limit. Such a feature would, in all likelihood, have prevented the rupture of the previous year.

Once Everett had a model of the new paying-out equipment complete, he invited the best known engineers in London, both in and out of the company, and its officers as well, to see it. These included Isambard Kingdom Brunel, who was building the huge ship, *Great Eastern*; Charles Bright, the engineer of the company, his assistants; Field, and several others.

The operation of the machine was demonstrated, and it was immediately clear to all that it made a great improvement. In addition to the smaller weight and size, it was also simpler and easier to operate. But the automatic release feature of the brakes was clearly the most important improvement.

The issue of the cable composition and quality was also still open. True, the signal had been propagated through twenty-five hundred miles of cable, including when it was immersed in very deep water. But the signal had also been lost for some hours, and no one could give a definite explanation. Thomson worked on ways to improve this situation, and came up with a major improvement in the measurement of electrical current.

After passing through more than two thousand miles of cable, an electrical signal is very weak. Signals attenuate, or weaken, as they travel through space or a wire, much as the sound waves from a human voice attenuate as they travel through the air. Thomson looked for a way to measure very weak current.

He used a tiny magnet, with an equally small mirror attached to it. Magnet and mirror weighed about a grain, or about one four-hundredth of an ounce. These were hung from a silk thread in the middle of a coil of very thin, insulated copper wire. As Michael Faraday had learned, a changing electric current flowing in a wire induces a magnetic field around it. The magnetic field would exert a force on the magnet, causing it to move slightly, in proportion to the strength of the field.

A light was shone on the mirror from a lamp, which was reflected onto a scale. As the current flowed in the dots, dashes and spaces of the Morse code, the movement of the mirror was shown and greatly amplified in the light it reflected onto the scale. This greatly improved the speed of transmission which was possible through the cable.

Additional detail about the instrument, known as a "mirror galvanometer," was provided by Bernard Finn:

> The mirror galvanometer had several (usually five) thin short magnetic wires glued to the back of a small mirror suspended by a thread inside a coil of wire. The signal from the cable was fed through the coil, producing a magnetic field, which acted on the magnets causing the mirror to twist (current going one way pro- duced a twist in one direction, other way in the other direction). After each twist, the thread (which was taught, tied down at both ends) automatically turned back to the original position). A beam of light (from an oil lamp) reflected onto a marked- off scale so that the operator saw not only the direction (indicating the polarity of the pulse) but also the distance (indicating its strength).

Thomson's invention was lauded throughout the engineering and science world as brilliant. His colleague, James Clerk Maxwell, wrote a poem about it, part of which appears at the beginning of this chapter.

Since the bulk of the cable was already manufactured, there was little which could be done to improve it. An additional seven-hundred miles of cable was ordered, to allow a substantial surplus. At Thomson's behest, the newer wire was thoroughly tested for the quality of the copper and its conductivity. Thus, on the next attempt, the ships would start out with nearly three thousand miles of cable on board, half on each one.

The *Niagara* sailed from New York for London March 30, arriving in Plymouth to be reloaded in mid-April. The *Susquehanna*, which had been promised as her escort, suffered an outbreak of yellow fever and had to be quarantined, so she would not be available. This left Field in a difficult position. He immediately called on Sir John Packington, the first Lord of the Admiralty, who had shown much interest in the Atlantic cable.

Galvanometer Used on the *Niagara*

Packington agreed to see Field immediately, who frankly explained the situation to him and asked if he could help. Packington replied that the

British Navy had no ships to spare at the moment; that it was itself chartering vessels to use, but that he would nonetheless see what he could do. Within hours he had sent word to the company's office that the H.M.S. *Valorous* had been ordered to replace the *Susquehanna* in the expedition.

The reloading of the cable onto the ships was done throughout most of April and early May. On Saturday, May 29, the ships sailed from Plymouth towards the south, in order to carry out some practice operations, on the splicing of the cable, the testing its physical strength, and electrical conductivity. This also provided opportunity to give the crews of the ships some practice in using the new paying-out equipment. The ships returned to Plymouth a few days later, for final preparations.

Field decided to follow the advice of the engineers on this expedition, and sail first to mid-ocean, where the cable would be spliced together, and paid out by both ships simultaneously. The cable fleet of four ships set sail from Plymouth on Thursday, June 10. They were to converge at latitude 53° 2' N, longitude 33° 18' W. The weather was very mild, and it was supposed that June was one of the best months of the year for fair weather in the North Atlantic.

According to Henry Field's account, as the expedition began, "...the sea was so still, that one could scarcely perceive, by the motion of the ship, when they passed beyond the breakwater into Plymouth channel, or into the open sea. At night, it was almost a dead calm. The second day was like the first. There was scarcely enough wind to swell the sails."

Much had been learned from the experience of the previous year. The machinery for paying out the cable was greatly improved, the crews were better trained, and the instruments for detecting signals were also much better. Had the weather had cooperated, the ships might have easily succeeded in paying out the cable, and thus greatly improving the world communications network, within the month.

The third day, Saturday, was also calm. But on Sunday, June 13, the barometer began to fall, and the wind began to pick up: indications   of an approaching storm. And, unfortunately, this was no ordinary storm.

The frightening account of the next seven days was recorded   in great detail, for there was a reporter from the *Times* of London, Nicholas Woods, aboard the *Agamemnon*, which, as the smaller of the two cable-bearing vessels, had the most difficult time. Parts of his description are repeated below. Woods' account begins on the first day of the storm:

> Our ship, the *Agamemnon*, rolling many degrees – not every one can imagine how she went at it that night – was laboring so heavily that she looked like breaking up. The massive beams under her upper-deck coil cracked and snapped with a noise resembling that of small artillery ... Those in the impoverished cabins on the main deck had little sleep that night, for the upper-deck planks above them were "working themselves free" as sailors say...

> The sea, too, kept striking with dull, heavy violence against the vessel's bows, forcing its way through hawse- holes and ill-closed ports with a heavy slush; and thence, hissing and winding aft, it roused the occupants of the cabins aforesaid to a knowledge that their floors were under water... Such was Sunday night, and such was a fair average of all the nights throughout the week, varying only from bad to worse. On Monday things became desperate.

So passed the first day and night of the storm; but it was just beginning. The coming week, things would only get worse. The heavy load of the cable – particularly its position in the ship – made conditions more precarious for both ships, but especially for the *Agamemnon*, the smaller vessel. On Monday afternoon the wind picked up even more, to a fierce gust that drowned out everything else, and making matters seem desperate. The storm continued throughout the week, doing extensive damage to the ship, and causing numerous injuries to the crew. The account continues:

> Tuesday the gale continued with almost unabated force, though the barometer had risen to 29.30, and there was sufficient sun to take a clear observation, which showed our distance from the rendezvous to be 563 miles. During this afternoon the *Niagara* joined company, and the wind going more ahead, the *Agamemnon* took to violent pitching, plunging steadily into the trough of the sea as if she meant to break her back and lay the Atlantic cable in a heap. This change in her motion strained and taxed every inch of timber near the coils to the very utmost. It was curious to see how they worked and bent

as the *Agamemnon* went at everything she met head first. One time she pitched so heavily as to break one of the main beams of the lower deck, which had to be shored with screw-jacks forthwith.

Throughout the week the ship and its crew struggled to stay afloat, and alive. The heavy load of cable might have to be jettisoned, but only as a last resort to save the ship from sinking. We continue the reporter's account the following Saturday:

Saturday, the 19th of June, things looked a little better. But alas! appearances are as deceitful in the Atlantic as elsewhere; and during a comparative calm that afternoon the glass fell lower, while a thick line of black haze to windward seemed to grow up into the sky, until it covered the heavens with a somber darkness, and warned us that, after all, the worst was yet to come.

There was much heavy rain that evening, and then the wind began, not violently, or in gusts, but with a steadily increasing force, as if the gale was determined to do its work slowly but do it well ...By and by, however, it grew more dangerous, and Captain Preedy himself remained on deck throughout the middle watch, for the wind was hourly getting worse and worse, and the *Agamemnon*, rolling thirty degrees each way, was straining to a dangerous extent . . .

At about half-past ten o'clock three or four giant waves were seen approaching the ship, coming slowly on through the mist nearer and nearer, rolling on like hills of green water, with a crown of foam that seemed to double their height. The *Agamemnon* rose heavily to the first, and then went down quickly into the deep trough of the sea, falling over as she did so, so as almost to capsize completely on the port side. There was a fearful crashing as she lay over this way, for everything broke adrift, whether secured or not, and the uproar and confusion were terrific for a minute, then back she came again on the starboard beam in the same manner only quicker, and still deeper than before. Again there was the same noise and crashing...

Here, for an instant, the scene almost defies description. Amid loud shouts and efforts to save themselves, a confused mass of sailors, boys, and marines, with deck-buckets, ropes, ladders, and everything that could get loose, and which had fallen back again to the port side, were being hurled again in a mass across the ship to starboard. Dimly, and only for an instant could this be seen, with groups of men clinging to

the beams with all their might, with a mass of water, which had forced
its way in through ports and decks, surging about, and then, with a
tremendous crash, as the ship fell still deeper . . .

Matters now became serious, for it was evident that two or three more
lurches and the masts would go like reeds, while half the crew might
be maimed or killed below.

In an effort to survive, on Monday, June 21, Captain Preedy ordered
the ship to increase its steam power and run with the storm. Amazingly,
the ship survived without capsizing or having to jettison the cable, and
no one was killed; but there were many injuries, including broken arms
and legs, and one sailor who suffered from temporary insanity. At one
point, the lurch of the ship reached forty-five degrees.

The storm finally abated late Monday, and on Tuesday morning, June
22, the ship again set its course for the rendezvous point – but now some
two hundred miles farther away than it had been nine days earlier, when
the storm began. It was Friday, June 25, fifteen days after the voyage
began, that the ships finally arrived at the rendezvous point.

By Saturday afternoon, the ships were ready to splice the cable and
start laying it out. The two ships were maneuvered together, stern to
stern, tied together with a hawser, and the end of the *Niagara*'s cable
was brought over to the *Agamemnon*, where the splicing operation was
done. But as soon as the two ships began to move apart, the cable broke.
Captain Hudson of the *Niagara* wrote, "The cable, being hauled in the
wrong direction through the excitement and carelessness of one of the
men, caught and parted in the *Niagara*'s machinery."

The two halves were respliced and the ships again began to move apart.
Throughout the evening all went well, but at about three the next
morning, Professor Thomson, who was monitoring the electrical current
from the *Agamemnon*, announced that the line had gone dead. Each
ship had laid out about forty miles of cable.

At the same moment, Field and C. V. de Sauty, the electrician on board
the *Niagara*, also detected the fault. Neither ship had detected any
break in the cable, so each assumed that a break must have occurred

at the other. Following Field's instructions, both ships returned to the rendezvous point. Since the break had not occurred at either ship, and it was estimated that it was at least ten miles from each, the break must have occurred at the bottom of the Atlantic.

This was a matter of concern: might there be rocks or other matter at the bottom which could fracture the cable? But the true cause was never determined with certainty.

For a third time, the two ships maneuvered together, and the cable was again spliced. The eighty miles of cable which had already been laid was lost, but there was still more than enough left. Field gave the order that, should any break occur, the ships would return to the rendezvous if less than one hundred miles had been laid out; but otherwise, to return to Queenstown.

Once again, the ships began move apart, the *Agamemnon* towards Ireland, the *Niagara* towards Newfoundland. Field estimated than each could reach its destination – a distance of about eight hundred nautical miles – in five days. Finally, the operation seemed to be getting underway in earnest. On both ships, the hundred mile mark was reached and passed, and all still went well, the electrical signal still passing between them.

On Tuesday evening, on board the *Agamemnon*, after 146 miles of cable had been paid out, the end of the coil stored on the deck was reached, and making necessary the transfer to the main coil below. The maneuver had been rehearsed during the practice runs, and no problem was anticipated. The ship and the paying-out machinery were both slowed in anticipation of the move. Near midnight, with only about a ton of pressure showing on the dynamometer, the cable snapped and vanished into the water.

The part of the cable which was paying out had been stored on deck throughout the storm. The lowest part of this cable, which had been lying directly on the deck, had been damaged. The storm had been unable to destroy the *Agamemnon* or force its captain and crew to turn back, but in the end – apparently – it had succeeded in doing just enough damage to cause a break in the cable.

Since just over a hundred miles of the cable had been paid out, Captain Preedy opted to return the *Agamemnon* to the rendezvous point, in case Field wanted to try again. There was still enough cable on board the two ships for one more attempt. He waited there, in mid-ocean, for several days. When none of the other ships were sighted, he returned to Queenstown, as had been previously agreed, arriving on Tuesday, July 12.

The break was detected immediately by the *Niagara*. Field waited some hours, hoping that the signal would magically return, as it had the previous year. When that did not happen, he reluctantly ordered the ship to return to Queenstown, since both ships had exceeded the one-hundred mile limit. Rather that just cutting the cable, however, he decided to conduct some testing on its strength. The cable had been designed to bear a pressure of three tons, and the paying out machinery was designed to release the cable at a pressure of half this. The paying out equipment was locked, to see if the cable would break. Captain Hudson's log recorded the result: "Although the wind was quite fresh, the cable held the ship for one hour and forty minutes before breaking, and notwithstanding a strain of four tons."

Chapter 7
The Second Expedition
of 1858

A man who becomes conscious of the responsibility he bears
. . . to an unfinished work, will never be able to throw away his
life. He knows the "why" for his existence, and will be able to bear
almost any "how."
–Victor Frankl (1905-97)

Field returned to England with the *Niagara*, arriving on July 5, and
the *Agamemnon* arrived a week later. Field, Bright and Thomson then
went to a meeting of the board of directors, to report on the expedition
and decide what to do next. Of course, news of the failure had already
reached them, and the atmosphere was one of profound discouragement.
Henry Field, Cyrus' brother, wrote of the meeting of the board:

> Now it met, as a council of war is summoned after a terrible defeat,
> to decide whether to surrender or to try once more the chances of
> battle. When the Directors came together, the feeling – to call it by
> the mildest name – was one of extreme discouragement. They looked
> blankly in each other's faces. With some the feeling was one almost of
> despair. Sir William Brown, of Liverpool, the first chairman, wrote,
> advising them to sell the cable. Mr. Brooking, the Vice-Chairman,
> who had given more time to it than any other Director, when he saw
> that his colleagues were disposed to make still another trial, left the
> room, and the next day sent in his resignation, determined to take
> no further part in an undertaking which had been proven hopeless.

Field remained optimistic, but found it difficult to convince the directors that another attempt should be made. There was still enough
cable remaining for another attempt. Bright and Thomson also sided
with Field, pointing out that enough cable remained, and that all had
learned from their experiences, making success more likely on the next
attempt. Considering all this, the remaining directors went along in
authorizing another attempt.

The ships were both loaded; all that needed to be done was reload them with fuel and provisions. All this was accomplished in a matter of days, and once again the fleet of four ships sailed on Saturday, July 17, 1858.

In great contrast to the first attempt, there were no cheering crowds. Nicholas Woods, the *Times* reporter, wrote, "As the ships left the harbor, there was apparently no notice taken of their departure by those on shore or in the vessels anchored around them." Many had already given up on the great hopes for a trans-Atlantic telegraph cable.

This time, the ships all sailed to the mid-point independently, and all reached it safely with no major problems. The *Niagara* reached the rendezvous point on July 23, and the *Agamemnon*, on Wednesday, July 28. The next day the weather was good, so the splice was made. Cyrus Field described it in his journal:

> Thursday, July 29, latitude fifty-two degrees nine minutes north, longitude thirty-two degrees twenty-seven minutes west. Telegraph fleet all in sight; sea smooth; light wind from S.E. to S.S.E., cloudy. Splice made at one P.M. Signals through the whole length of cable on board both ships perfect. Depth of water fifteen hundred fathoms; distance to the entrance of Valentia harbor eight hundred and thirteen nautical miles, and from there to the telegraph-house the shore end of the cable is laid. Distance to the entrance of Trinity Bay, Newfoundland, eight hundred and twenty-two nautical miles, and from there to the telegraph-house at the head of the bay of Bull's Arm, sixty miles, making in all eight hundred and eighty two nautical miles. The *Niagara* has sixty miles further to run than the *Agamemnon*. The *Niagara* and *Agamemnon* have each about eleven hundred miles of cable on board, about the same quantity as last year.

The splice, weighted with a thirty-two pound cannon ball, was lowered from the stern of the *Agamemnon*, and two ships began their respective journeys, in opposite directions. At first the ships moved very slowly, but after a few hours without mishap, the speed was increased to about five knots, with the cable paying out at about six knots, on both ships.

Shortly after the speed of the ships was increased, about four P.M., the *Agamemnon* had a scare. A large whale was approaching the starboard side of the ship, and appeared to be on a course to collide with the cable as it paid out. Fortunately, the animal passed by the cable without doing it any harm.

The Niagara, HMS Valorous, HMS Gorgon and Agamemnon laying the cable at mid-ocean, 1858

A few hours later, at about eight P.M., a more serious crisis occurred. A part of the cable was found to be damaged, only a mile or two from what was being paid out. Engineers worked to repair it before it would pay out, but then the electricity suddenly stopped. The engineers immediately assumed it was due to the damaged cable, and decided to cut it out and resplice the cable, then and there. The scene was an anxious one, as described by Woods:

> The main hold presented an extraordinary scene. Nearly all the officers of the ship and of those connected with the expedition stood in groups about the coil, watching with intense anxiety the cable as it slowly unwound itself nearer and nearer the joint, while the

workmen worked at the splice as only men could work who felt that the life and the death of the expedition depended upon their rapidity. But all their speed was to no purpose, as the cable was unwinding within a hundred fathoms; and, as a last and desperate resource, the cable was stopped altogether, and for a few minutes, as the strain was continually rising above two tons and it would not hold much longer. When the splice was finished the signal was made to loose the stoppers, and it passed overboard in safety.

But the signal did not return. On both ships, the fault was immediately detected. On the *Agamemnon*, as noted above, it was thought to be a problem with the faulty cable; but this was not the case. But of course, the *Niagara*'s crew knew nothing of this. For a while, both crews waited, and just as had occurred the year before, the signal returned. This time, however, it was determined that there had been a problem with one of the batteries on the *Niagara*. Once repaired, the signal returned.

The next morning a crisis occurred on the *Niagara*, when a sextant reading showed that the ship was seriously off course. This far off course, the ship would run out of cable before reaching Newfoundland. The problem turned out to have a simple solution, however. There was so much iron on board the *Niagara* – the armor in the cable – that the ship's own magnets were being deflected from the earth's magnetic field. The simple solution was to have the companion ship, the H.M.S. *Gorgo*n, run ahead of it, far enough away that its compass would not be affected, and plotting the course from its compass.

As the paying out progressed, there was concern on the *Agamemnon* that the ship might run out of fuel before reaching the coast. She had used more fuel than expected en route to the rendezvous, because of headwinds, and as the return began, still more headwinds were encountered. It must have seemed to those on board that, whatever direction the ship took, the wind would shift to oppose it. But luckily, after the first few days the winds shifted to a favorable direction, allowing sufficient use of sails to complete the mission.

Other than the signal loss of the first day, the *Niagara*'s trip was fairly smooth. Field's journal records steady progress. By Saturday, July 31, over three-hundred miles of cable had been paid out from both ships. Now, they were well beyond the point of no return.

Field's journal entry for Monday, August 2 records: "The *Niagara*, getting very light, and rolling very much; it was not considered safe to carry sail to steady ship, for in case of accident it might be necessary to stop the vessel as soon as possible." Most of the cable was now on the bottom of the Atlantic.

On Tuesday, August 3, at about three A.M., all on board the *Agamemnon* were awakened by the loud booming of a gun. All rushed to the deck of the ship, fearing that the cable had broken again. This was not the case, but another threat to the cable was seen: an American bark was on a course which would take it just behind the *Agamemnon*, where the cable was being paid out. The H.M.S. *Valorous* had rounded to and was firing shot after shot across her bow. This soon got the Americans attention, and they put their sails back, waiting until the cable expedition had passed. Nicholas Woods wrote of this incident, "Whether those on board considered that we were engaged in some filibustering expedition, or regarded our proceedings as another outrage upon the American flag, it is impossible to say."

Later that same day, in another part of the same ocean, another American ship, the *Niagara*, sighted icebergs; some of them were more than a hundred feet high. The icebergs were an indication that she was nearing the Grand Banks, the great fishing ground off the coast of Newfoundland. Field's journal records:

> Tuesday August third. At a quarter past eleven, ship's time, received signals from on board the *Agamemnon*, that they had paid out from her seven hundred and eighty miles of cable. In the afternoon and evening passed several icebergs. At ten minutes past nine P.M., ship's time, received signal from the *Agamemnon* that she was in water of two hundred fathoms. At twenty minutes past ten P.M., *Niagara* in water of two hundred fathoms, and informed the *Agamemnon* of the same.

Both ships had reached continental shelves: the *Agamemnon*, that of Europe, and the *Niagara*, that of North America. With a far shorter length of cable now hanging off the ends of each ship, the danger of it suddenly snapping was now greatly reduced. With the signal still coming through clearly, the chances of a successful conclusion now seemed excellent.

On Wednesday, August 4, the *Niagara* made landfall at Newfoundland. Field wrote, "Made land off entrance to Trinity Bay at eight A.M. Entered Trinity Bay at half-past twelve . . . At five P.M. we saw Her Majesty's steamer *Porcupine* coming to us."

The *Porcupine* was the British steamer which had been assigned the task of guiding the *Niagara* the last few miles, up Trinity Bay. Captain Otter of that vessel came on board to act as pilot. At one forty-five A.M., local time, Thursday morning, August 5, 1858, the ships anchored.

Field immediately had himself rowed to shore, even though it was in the middle of the night. He went ashore looking for the nearest telegraph house. Once he found it, he awoke the men in the house, shouting, "The cable is laid!" The men were maintenance personnel, however, not telegraph operators, so Field sent messengers to the next closest station, about fifteen miles away. He sent messages to his wife, his father, and to Peter Cooper, informing them that the cable had arrived successfully. The message to his wife read, "Arrived here yesterday. All well. The Atlantic cable successfully laid. Please telegraph me here immediately." He also sent a telegraph to President Buchanan, advising him of the success, and that he could soon expect a message from the reigning queen of England, Queen Victoria.

Shortly after five o'clock that morning, the cable was brought ashore. By six, its end was in the telegraph house, and was receiving messages from the *Agamemnon*.

At daylight on Thursday, August 5, those on board the *Agamemnon* had sighted land, the rocky mountains around Valentia Bay, Ireland. The H.M.S. *Valorous* steamed ahead and fired a gun to signal the population of the arrival of the telegraph fleet. Reporter Woods wrote that, "As soon as the inhabitants became aware of our approach, there was a general desertion of the place, and hundreds of boats crowded around us."

As the crew of the *Agamemnon* was preparing to land the cable, a message was received from the *Niagara*, that they were landing and had paid out 1,030 nautical miles of cable. The *Agamemnon* had paid 1,020 miles, making the total length paid out of 2,050 miles.

Buoying Out the Cable from the *Niagara*
Bay Bull's Arm, Newfoundland
Frank Leslie's Illustrated Newspaper, Sept. 11, 1858

The end of the cable was brought to boats and then ashore. It took a while, as the weather was windy. The knight of Kerry was across the bay, and soon arrived in a Royal Navy gunboat.

As soon as he landed at Valentia, Charles Bright sent a cable, dated August 5, to the board of directors in London, which was immediately passed on to the press: "The *Agamemnon* has arrived in Valentia, and we are about to land the cable. The *Niagara* is in Trinity Bay, Newfoundland. There are good signals between the ships."

At about noon that same day, local time, the following message was received in New York City:

United States Frigate Niagara
Trinity Bay, Newfoundland, August 5, 1858,
To the Associated Press, New York:

The Atlantic Telegraph fleet sailed from Queenstown, Ireland, Saturday, July seventeenth and met at mid-ocean on July twenty-eighth. Made the splice at one P.M., Thursday, the twenty-ninth, and separated – the *Agamemnon* and *Valorous*, bound to Valentia, Ireland; the *Niagara* and *Gorgon*, for this place, where they arrived yesterday, and this morning the end of the cable will be landed The cable had been paid out from the *Agamemnon* at about the same speed as from the *Niagara*. The electric signals sent and received through the whole cable are perfect . . .

Cyrus W. Field.

The impact which this message had on New York, and on the western world, is difficult to imagine. An event which truly changed the world had taken place; and, thanks to the event itself, as well as the proliferation of telegraph lines in Europe and the United States in the previous fifteen years, the entire western world learned of it almost si- multaneously. There were celebrations and elation on both sides of the Atlantic.

George Templeton Strong, a diarist who was a neighbor of Field in New York City, wrote on August 5:

. . . all Wall Street stirred up into excitement this morning, in spite of the sultry weather, by the screeching newsboys with their extras. The *Niagara* has arrived at Trinity Bay with her end of the telegraph cable in perfect working order. But the *Agamemnon* has not yet linked her end at Valentia ... The transmission of a single message from shore to shore will be memorable in the world's history for though I dare say this cable will give out before long, it will be the first successful experiment in binding the two continents together, and the communication will soon be permanently established.

The very fact that, on August 5, 1858, in New York City – twelve hundred miles from St. John's, Newfoundland, and nearly three thousand from Ireland – he could know those details about the two ships was historic.

Field's brother David, the lawyer, wired him: "Your family is all at Stockbridge and well. The joyful news arrived here Thursday, and almost overwhelmed your wife. Father rejoiced like a boy. Mother was wild with delight. Brothers, sisters, all were overjoyed. Bells were rung, guns were fired; children let out of school, shouted, 'The cable is laid! The cable is laid!' The village was in a tumult of joy. My dear brother, I congratulate you. God Bless you."

The excitement was just as great, if not more so, in Britain. The following appeared in London's paper, The *Times*, the day after the cable was landed in Valentia (emphasis added): "Mr. Bright, having landed the Atlantic cable at Valentia, has brought to a successful termination his anxious and difficult task of linking the Old World with the New, thereby annihilating space. *Since the discovery of Columbus*, nothing has been done in any degree comparable to the vast enlargement which has thus been given to the sphere of human activity. "

Another indication of the impact of the event was that, only days after the successful landing of the cable, Queen Victoria conferred a knighthood on Charles Bright, who was only twenty-six years old. He was the first to be knighted for engineering or science. It was said that she would have also knighted Cyrus Field if he had been a British subject. Since she was abroad, the knighthood was conferred on Bright by the Earl of Carlisle, Lord Lieutenant of Ireland – the same who had made the arousing speech the year before.

A series of celebratory banquets were given on both sides of the Atlantic. Field was honored in New York, Bright and Thomson in Britain. In Dublin, Ireland's capital, a banquet was given by the mayor and civic authorities on September 1, in honor of Bright. Eloquent speeches were given, comparing the laying of the cable to the discovery of the New World by Columbus. In one of the speeches it was pointed out that Columbus had sailed from Spain on August 5, the same date that the cable was landed in Valentia Bay.

On August 16, the following message was received over the Atlantic cable:

> To the President of the United States, Washington:
> The Queen desires to congratulate the President upon the successful
> completion of the great international work, in which the Queen has

taken the deepest interest. The Queen is convinced that the President will join with her in fervently hoping that the electric cable which now connects Britain with the United States will prove an additional link between the nations, whose friendship is founded upon their common interest and reciprocal esteem. The Queen has   much pleasure in this communicating with the President, and renewing to him her wishes for the prosperity of the United States.

President Buchanan replied to her the same day, with an equally cordial and appropriate message. The following day, August 17, there were numerous celebrations in New York, featuring the firing of cannons and other guns. There were so many fireworks, that the cupola of the City Hall caught on fire. Fortunately it was controlled before the building was destroyed. The following day Cyrus Field returned to New York from Newfoundland on board the *Niagara*.

On Wednesday, September 1, Field was given an official hero's welcome by the city. There was a service at Trinity Church, and a parade in which he rode in a carriage with the mayor, drawn by six white horses. The next night, he was honored with a banquet at New York's best hotel, the Metropolitan.

The utility of the trans-Atlantic telegraph cable was quickly confirmed by a number of messages which passed over it in the first few weeks of operation. In addition to the messages exchanged by Queen Victoria and President Buchanan, Peter Cooper sent a long, congratulatory message to the directors of the company in London. The mayor of New York sent a lengthy message to the mayor of London, who replied in acknowledgment. There was a collision of two great Cunard mailsteamers on August 14. As soon as the news reached New York, it was telegraphed to London. This was the first public news message. Following this, news messages were transmitted between continents on a daily basis.

On August 31, a pair of messages from the British government were transmitted. Previously, orders had been sent by mail to two British regiments in Canada, ordering them return to England; this was due to a mutiny which was in progress in India. The mutiny had been controlled after these orders had been mailed. The telegraph message of August

31 cancelled these orders, and it saved the British government the cost of transporting these regiments, estimated to be £50,000 to £60,000. The original price of the cable had been £225,000.

But all was not well with the cable. In fact, there were serious problems. The message from the queen had taken sixteen hours to transmit, or about ten words per minute. The signals had been coming through very weakly, and were quickly getting weaker as time passed. The day of the banquet, Field had been told by the electrician, de Sauty, that the signals were nearly unintelligible. At the banquet, a cable was delivered to Field, most of which was blank. The cable was sick, and weakening rapidly.

For a few weeks the company tried to conceal the problem, doing tests and trying to resolve it. But there was little more that could be done. The company was finally forced to admit that the cable no longer functioned. Its last signal was sent on October 23; a total of 732 messages had been sent in the three months of its operation. The cable was dead, for good.

The same press that had exalted Field and his company as heroes now ridiculed them. The Boston Courier wrote that the whole thing had been a deception, a stock swindle to allow Field to unload his worthless shares. (In fact, Field sold one share during the month of August, at a loss of $500.) There were claims that the whole undertaking had been a fraud, and that Queen Victoria's message had been sent by ship. C. V. de Sauty, the electrician on board the *Niagara* – who had missed out on all the celebrations because he had remained behind in St. John's to operate the Atlantic terminus of the cable – was ridiculed in poetry:

> Thou operator, silent and glum,
> Why wilt thou act so naughty?
> Do tell us what your name is – come!
> De Santy or De Sauty?
> Don't think to humbug any more,
> Shut up there in your shanty,
> But solve the problem once for all—
> De Sauty or De Santy.

By the end of 1858, when all hope of reviving the dead cable had faded, many of Field's old friends and partners were avoiding him. But Peter Cooper – his neighbor and friend who had been the first to invest, remained by Field's side. "We will go on," he said to Field.

An investment of several hundred thousand pounds – or millions of dollars – now lay useless at the bottom of the Atlantic. But the enterprise had proven that a two-thousand mile cable could be successfully laid across a deep and wide ocean, that telegraph messages could be transmitted across it, and the messages sent during its short life – particularly the one which saved the British government the cost of transporting two regiments from Canada to England – had proven the hypothesis that such a cable would be very, *very* useful.

Chapter 8
The Inquest

Most of the important things in the world have been accomplished by people who have kept on trying when there seemedto be no hope at all.
–Dale Carnegie (1888-1955)

The measurements of the current when the cable was spliced at mid-ocean on July 29, as described in Bright's account, were "72 degrees of deflection... on the *Agamemnon*, from 75 cells of a sawdust (Daniell's) battery on board the *Niagara*." These units of measurement are unfamiliar today, but it is simple enough to read them for comparison purposes.

On August 5, at six-thirty A.M., in Valentia Bay, when the ships had reached their respective coastline destinations, the same instruments gave measurements of "68 degrees, while the sending-battery power on the *Niagara* had fallen off at entry to 62 1/2 degrees." The battery had apparently lost a considerable amount of its power, but the receiving instruments were still getting almost as much as power as before.

In Bright's words, "These figures show that the insulation of the cable had considerably improved by submersion, and when the engineers had accomplished their part of the undertaking, on August 5th, the cable was handed over in perfect condition to Mr. Whitehouse and his electrical assistant."

This does seem to be the case; other than a few momentary problems, the signal had been sent and received successfully throughout the voyages and when the cables were first landed in Ireland and Newfoundland. The cold temperatures of the water at the bottom of the ocean have a tendency to cause gutta-percha, the insulation material, to harden; so the conclusion that the insulation was better on the ocean floor than when coiled up on the ships was a reasonable one.

What, then, caused the cable to die?

Once the cable was landed on August 5, the operation of the telegraph station in Valentia was put under the control of the company's electrician, Dr. Edward Whitehouse. Whitehouse believed that use of high-powered signals, as much power as possible, were best for signaling over a long distance cable. He attached high-powered coils to the cable, much higher powered than had been available on board the ships, and began using them. According to Bright, the insulation of the cable was not able to bear these higher powered signals and slowly began to fail.

The next year, 1859, an undersea cable was laid in the Red Sea, which was to be a link in a telegraph cable to India from Britain. It was a different type of project, consisting of several different sections of undersea cable. The British government supported it, because of its eagerness for a communication link with India. This cable also failed to operate; it never operated successfully as a whole, but only in sections, and every section along the way soon failed.

By 1861, over eleven thousand miles of undersea cable had been laid, of which only about three thousand miles was still in service. The Indian cable failure had cost the British government a huge amount of money, as it had guaranteed the interest on the capital for the next twenty years.

These two great cable failures caused a demand for a an inquiry into their causes, and one was soon set up. In 1859, a commission of eight members was appointed to study the problem. The commission included Captain Douglas Galton, of the Royal Engineers, who represented the British government; Charles Wheatstone, one of the inventors of the British telegraph; George Parker Bidder, one of the out- standing engineers of the day, who was famous for performing mathe- matical calculations in his head; William Fairbairn, former president of the British Association for the Advancement of Science; C. F. Varley, considered the best telegraph electrician in England; Latimer Clark and Edwin Clark, both engineers experienced with telegraphy; and George Saward, Secretary of the Atlantic Telegraph Company.

The committee met on twenty-two different occasions, over a period of nearly two years, and questioned the people who had been involved in both cable projects, as well as other experts. Charles Bright, William

Thomson, and Edward Whitehouse were among those questioned. A number of experiments were also carried out, testing the effect of high powered electrical currents on insulation. Some of these were carried out on the dead line from Valentia; others on cables set aside for experimental use.

One experiment was described by C. F. Varley, one of the committee members, which he carried out in conjunction with Charles Bright:

> We attached to the cable a piece of gutta-percha-covered wire, having first made a slight incision, by a needle-prick, in the gutta-percha to let the water reach the conductor. The wire was then bent, so as to close up the defect. The defective wire was then placed in a jar of sea water, and the latter connected with the earth. After a few momentary signals had been sent from the five-foot induction cable coils into the cable, and, consequently into the testwire, the intense current burst through the excessively minute perforation, rapidly burning a hole nearly one-tenth of an inch in diameter, afterward increased to half an inch in length when passing the current through the faulty branch only. The burned gutta-percha then came floating up to the sur- face of the water, while the jar was one complete glow of light.

> It was determined from the tests that there was a leak in the insulation, nearer the Valentia side, thought to be about three hundred miles from Valentia. No break was found in the copper conductor itself; there seemed to be a leak only in the gutta-percha insulation.

Sir William Thomson, Lord Kelvin

In 1860, Professor Thomson, later honored Lord Kelvin, wrote an article for the Encyclopedia Britannica, stating his professional opinion:

> It is quite certain that, with a properly adjusted mirror galvanometer as receiving instrument at each end, twenty cells of Daniell's battery would have done the work required, and at even a higher speed if worked by a key devised for diminishing inductive embarrassment; and the writer – with the knowledge derived from disastrous experience – has now little doubt but that, if such had been the arrangement from the beginning, if induction-coil and no battery-power exceeding twenty Daniell cells had ever been applied to the cable since the landing of its ends, imperfect as it then was, it would be now in full work day and night, with no prospect or probability of failure.

The report which resulted from the inquest filled a large volume, was published in 1863, and led to significant improvements in submarine telegraph cable engineering and in electrical engineering. One of the problems which the report brought out was the lack of agreement on standard units for measuring fundamental electrical quantities such a current and resistance. This soon led to the formation of committees dedicated to resolving that problem, leading eventually to standard units

such and the watt, volt, ohm, and ampere. These units were named
after famous pioneers in the study of electricity and magnetism.

But the reason for the failure of the Atlantic cable, which was functioning well on August 5, 1858, but gradually died over the next several
weeks, was generally accepted to be the application of excessive power
by the company's electrician, Dr. Edward Whitehouse. The company
had already fired him. The directors wrote a letter explaining his dis-
missal, part of which follows:

> Mr. Whitehouse has been engaged some eighteen months in
> investigations which have cost some £12,000 to the company and now,
> when we have laid our cable and the whole world is looking on with
> impatience . . . [W]e are, after all, only saved from being a laughing-
> stock because the directors are fortunate enough to have an illustrious
> colleague [Professor Thomson] . . . whose inventions produced in
> his own study – at small expense – and from his own resources are
> available to supercede the useless apparatus prepared   at great labor
> and enormous cost . . . Mr. Whitehouse has run counter to the wishes
> of the directors on a great many occasions – disobeyed time after time
> their positive instructions – thrown obstacles in the way of everyone,
> and acted in every way as if his own fame and self-imposed importance
> were the only points of consequence to be considered.

On an earlier occasion, when the cable crossing the strait from Newfoundland to Nova Scotia had been lost due to the stubbornness of a
ship captain, Peter Cooper had written, "We had spent so much money,
and lost so much time, that it was very vexatious to have our enterprise
defeated by the stupidity and obstinacy of one man." The words seem
even more applicable to the 1858 cable failure, than the occasion for
which he first wrote them.

Yet, the eight members of the committee, having thoroughly investi-
gated the causes of the failures of the Atlantic and other submarine
cables, ended their investigation on a positive note, and unanimously
signed the following statement summing up their investigation:

> London, 13th July, 1863
> We, the undersigned, members of the committee, who were appointed
> by the Board of Trade, in 1859, to investigate the question of submarine

telegraphy, and whose investigation continued from that time to April, 1861, do hereby state, as the result of our deliberations, that a well-insulated cable, properly protected, of suitable specific gravity, made with care, and tested under water throughout its progress with the best known apparatus, and paid into the ocean with the most improved machinery, possesses every prospect of not only being successfully laid in the first instance, but may reasonably be relied upon to continue for many years in an efficient state for the transmission of signals.

The Atlantic Cables of 1857-58 had been great disappointments, and had lost a lot of money for their investors. But the lessons which had been learned, when taken to heart, would one day lead to success.

Chapter 9
The Little Giant and
the Great Eastern

They are up early and looking eastward to see the day break, when a ship is seen in the offing. She is far down on the horizon. Spyglasses are turned toward her. She comes nearer – and look there is another and another. And now the hull of the Great Eastern *looms up all-glorious in that morning sky. They are coming!*
–Henry M. Field (1822-1907), *History of the Atlantic Telegraph*

At the same time that Cyrus Field was making plans, organizing companies, raising capital, and finally manufacturing and laying the Atlantic cables, in the unsuccessful attempts of 1857-58, another grand engineering project was taking place in England. This was the conception, design, construction, and launching of – by far – the largest ocean-going ship the world had ever seen, or would see, prior to the twentieth century. The ship was the S.S. *Great Eastern*, and its designer was Isambard Kingdom Brunel.

Isambard Brunel was born in 1806 in Portsmouth, on the southern coast of England. His father, Marc Brunel, a great engineer and entrepreneur himself, was born in 1769 in Normandy, France. Marc Brunel had the rare distinction, which he shared with Thomas Paine, of being a legal citizen of France, the United States, and Great Britain.

Rather than serve in the church, as his birth order would have dictated, Marc Brunel left home and joined the French Navy. After six years he left the navy, and found himself in a Royalist stronghold, as the French Revolution was raging in Paris. There he met Sophia Kingdom, an English girl who had come to work on her French.

As the political situation of the French Revolution grew worse, Marc Brunel emigrated to New York, where he lived for six years and became an American citizen.

212

His engineering talents resulted in his becoming the chief engineer for the city's port. In 1798, at a dinner with Alexander Hamilton, he learned about ships blocks. Ships blocks are wooden or metal casings which hold the pulleys for the sails of ships. Both the American and Royal Navies spent large sums of money on these. Not only an engineer but also an entrepreneur, Brunel saw that, if he could devise a better and cheaper way to make them, he might make himself rich.

Seizing the opportunity, Brunel devised better machinery for making ships blocks, and sailed for England, where there was a larger market for his invention. There he sought out and married Sophia Kingdom, became a British citizen, and presented his ideas to the British admiralty. His ideas led to great success, saving the Royal Navy substantial costs, and it paid him £17,500. Brunel quickly became one of the most successful and best-known engineers in England. His British wife Sophia gave birth to his only son, Isambard Kingdom, in 1806.

Isambard followed in his father's footsteps. He showed a great talent for engineering, and his father saw to it that he received an excellent education in mathematics and engineering, sending him for some years to the Lycée Henri-Quatre, a school in France which was known for its excellent mathematics instruction.

At the age of twenty, he was already working on one of his father's greatest projects, a tunnel under the Thames River. He nearly lost his life in that project when the collapse of a wall nearly drowned him; he luckily caught a wave which carried him up a shaft to safety.

Isambard Brunel eventually became the most celebrated civil engineer of the middle nineteenth century. He was short in stature, and was known as "The Little Giant." He built bridges, tunnels, railroads, drydocks, and steamships. All of his projects were big and innovative.

In 1838, at the age of thirty-two, he designed the first steamship which could cross the Atlantic under its own power, the *Great Western*. On her first voyage, the ship shattered the record for a trans-Atlantic voyage, making the crossing in fifteen days, nine hours. In 1843, he launched the *Great Britain*, a 322-foot steamer, the first iron-built ocean ship, and the first to rely entirely on a propeller.

Brunel also built twenty-five railroads in four countries; five suspension bridges, and 125 railway bridges. He designed a 1,500 bed military pre-fabricated hospital, the parts of which were manufactured in England, then transported to Turkey, and the hospital was constructed there. He designed it so that every part could be carried by two men.

Having designed two steamships, Brunel was very knowledgeable of the problems of sea transportation. The *Great Western* could cross the Atlantic entirely on steam power, but then would have to reload its tanks with coal for the return voyage. In 1850, Britain and America were the only two countries which mined coal in large amounts.   When a steamship went to India, cargo ships under sail would have to go ahead, leaving coal for refueling along the way.

Brunel dreamed of building a ship large enough to carry enough fuel to make a 22,000 mile round trip. This would be enough to go to Britain's farthest port and return, without refueling; almost enough to go around the globe. With the help of a colleague, another great engineer of the day, John Russell, a Scot, he designed a ship which would be known as the "iron leviathan." It was to be five times larger than any ship the world had ever seen.

The dimensions of the ship are impressive, even today, a century and a half later. The ship was 693 feet long, 120 feet wide, and had a displacement of 22,500 tons. She was the longest ship ever built, until 1899, when the 704 foot liner *Oceanic* was launched. The *Oceanic*, however, had a smaller displacement, by six thousand tons.

The first ship to exceed the *Great Eastern* in size was the *Lusitania*, in 1906 – half a century later. The *Great Eastern* was powered by a screw and paddle wheels, and also had six masts for sails. The technology of the day did not allow for sufficient power from a single screw.

I K Brunel, in front of launching chains of the *Great Eastern*

The ship which Brunel dreamed of in 1851 would cost a huge amount of money, far more than any other ship or project yet attempted. To raise money for it, he claimed that it would pay for itself in a few voyages. Brunel was also an excellent salesman, and his reputation as the greatest engineer of the day was at its peak. He persuaded a group of capitalists to put up £600,000 to build her, and the work was begun.

The ship was built in the port of London, on the Thames River. It was built on the sand along a turn of the river; the plan was to move it into the river sideways, because the river was not wide enough at that point to acomodate a ship of its length.

The ship took six years of construction to be ready for launching, using up all of its initial capital and considerably more, and even then was still not completely ready. Her initial launching was scheduled for November 3, 1857. It was an embarrassing failure.

In full view of a crowd of thousands – grand stands had been built for the show, and some estimated the crowd at 100,000 – who had come to see the launching of the largest moving object ever built, the ship began to slide down towards the river sideways, but when the windlass crews attempted to check her speed, she stopped, and they were unable to start her sliding again. They were unable to get her into the water that day.

After several weeks of trying, the ship was finally eased into the river with the help of a high tide in January, 1858. The launching was estimated to have cost £120,000, or about £1,000 per foot. In 1850, £1,000 was a respectable upper-middle class annual income.

length	693 feet
width	120 feet, including paddle wheels
displacement	22,500 tons
structure	no ribs; double iron hull
hull composition	30,000 wrought iron plates, avg. wt. 1/3 ton each
innovative interior feature	12 watertight compartments
where built	Greenwich, on Thames River
power sources	iron screw; paddle wheels; sails. 1 power plant for screw, 1 for paddle
paddle wheel size	58 feet diameter, largest ever for ship
screw	24 feet diameter, largest ever built before nuclear submarines
power plants	paddles: 3,800 horsepower; screw: 6,200 horsepower
speed	12 knots, maximum
masts	six for the sails
exhaust funnels	5, most ever for a steamship
launching	1857-8; launched sideways

Great Eastern **Facts**

In 1858, finally in the water, the *Great Eastern* was still not completed; it was estimated that the owners needed $600,000 to finish her.

Thanks to overruns in the cost of the construction and the excessive cost of the launching itself, the company which had been formed to build the ship went bankrupt. She was still not finished, and additional capital to complete her and finance her initial voyages was needed. The original investors lost some $3 million.

Brunel organized a new company to take her, which bought her for $800,000, a fraction of what had already been invested to build and launch her.

The *Great Eastern* made several voyages across the Atlantic, but was never used for the purpose for which she was originally created, the voyage to India and the most distant parts of the British Empire. Due to her huge size, she was able to withstand a hurricane sized storm in the Atlantic, but her new owners failed to make a good use of her.

She might, for example, have been able to profit carrying grain and other products back to England from the United States, or in carrying some of the hundreds of thousands of immigrants leaving Europe for the US, but her directors failed to see the possibilities in this.

The *Great Eastern* continued to be plagued by hardship, bad luck, and failures throughout much of her life. Perhaps the greatest of those misfortunes was the death of her creator, I. K. Brunel. He was always a man with a great passion for his work, and the construction of the ship took its toll. Though he was only fifty-one when it finally launched, his friends noticed that he had aged considerably. On the day before its initial voyage, he visited the ship, and planned to go with her on the voyage, but he collapsed with a stroke, and died eight days later.

Brunel had a scientific philosophy which would be considered strange in today's world of patents and lawsuits. He did not believe in patenting inventions, and made no attempt to protect his many ideas. He said, "Most good things are being thought of by many persons at the same time. If there were publicity and freedom of communication, instead of concealment and mystery, a hundred times as many useful ideas would be generated."

Some months before his death, Brunel had met Cyrus Field by chance on a train, and had invited Field to see his ship under construction. As recounted earlier, Brunel had said, "There is the ship to lay your cable, Mr. Field." Though Field might not have thought so at the time, and Brunel did not live to see it, the day was coming when his words would be proven true.

Chapter 10
Putting the Pieces
Together – Again

Patience and perseverance have a magical effect before which
difficulties disappear and obstacles vanish.
–John Quincy Adams (1767-1848), sixth president of the U.S.

After the failure of the cable in late 1858, the company's directors were
very discouraged. The initial success, the great celebrations on both sides
of the Atlantic, followed by the seemingly sudden catastrophe naturally
caused a tremendous feeling of gloom and discouragement on the part
of most involved. A huge capital investment lay useless at the bottom of
the Atlantic. It takes time to recover from a disaster of such magnitude.

The next year, 1859, an attempt to lay a cable in several segments to
India was made by a different company. Unfortunately, its engineering
was poorly planned – for example, the cable was stretched very tautly
on the bottom of the seas – but the British government guaranteed
interest on the capital for twenty years. The failure of this cable on
top of the Atlantic cable failure led to the inquest, with the findings
published in 1863.

The United States broke out in a bitter and costly civil war in 1861,
which would last four years, until the spring of 1865. This was by
far the bloodiest war of the nineteenth century in the western world.
This was the first major war in history in which the use of modern
telecommunications played a major part. On both sides, the use of the
telegraph for communication was critical. Lincoln spent a great deal of
his time communicating with his generals through the telegraph.

For the duration of the war, neither the U.S. government nor most
Americans had time or interest to think of a cable across the Atlantic.
Cyrus Field was an exception; he did not give up on the cable, and
continued making trips to England, maintaining relations with the directors and attempting to raise capital for a new attempt.

Britain had an extensive trade with the southern states, buying cotton from them for its factories, and declared neutrality. A couple of incidents served to aggravate relations between the U.S. and Britain. One, called the Trent Affair, almost caused war. A U.S. warship, the *San Jacinto*, commanded by Charles Wilkes, stopped the British ship *Trent* in international waters, and forcibly removed two Confederate agents. This was a violation of international law which angered the British.

The British government ordered troops to Canada and began making preparations for war. This could easily have affected the outcome of the war. Lincoln, deciding that one war at a time was enough, released the Confederate agents, and disavowed the action. The London *Times* wrote that "we nearly went to war with America because we had not a telegraph across the Atlantic."

Field tried to exploit the situation, and wrote a letter to secretary of state William Seward, saying,

> The importance of the early completion of the Atlantic telegraph can hardly be underestimated. What would have been its value to the English and United States governments if it had been in operation on the 30th of November   . . . ? A few short messages between the two governments and all would have been satisfactorily explained. I have no doubt that the English government has expended more money during the last thirty days in preparation for war with this country than the whole cost of manufacturing and laying a good cable between Newfoundland and Ireland.

Seward wrote a letter to the U.S. minister in London, Charles Francis Adams, instructing him to advise the British government that the U.S. government would be pleased to join it in promoting a new Atlantic cable.

Field returned to England, and met with English officials, who were still interested in helping. The importance of undersea cables was much better understood in Britain, an island nation with an empire to administer. The British government raised their guaranteed payment to £20,000 per year, provided that the cable worked. Field also encouraged the directors of the company to renew the project.

Also while in England, Field also began contacting companies who might construct the new cable. One company, Glass, Elliot and Co. replied to him on February 17, 1862, that "we are so confident that these points can be connected by a good and durable cable, that we are willing to contract to do the work, and stake a large sum upon its successful laying and working."

Later in the year followed another letter from the same company:

London, October 20, 1862
Cyrus W. Field, Esq., Atlantic Telegraph Company:

Dear Sir: In reply to your inquiries, we beg to state, that we are perfectly confident that a good and durable Submarine Cable can be laid from Ireland to Newfoundland, and are willing to undertake the contract . . . We are so confident that this enterprise can be carried out, that we will make a cash subscription for a sum of twenty-five thousand pounds sterling in the ordinary capital of the Company ... Annexed we beg to hand you, for your guidance, a list of all the submarine telegraph cables manufactured and laid by our firm since we commenced this branch of our business, the whole mileage of which, with the exception of the short one between Liverpool and Holyhead, which has been taken up, is at this time in perfect and successful working order. The cable that we had the honor to contract for and lay down for the French Government, connecting France with Algeria is submerged in water of nearly equal depths to any we should have to encounter between Ireland and Newfound- land . . . The cable that we would suggest for the Atlantic will be an improvement on all those yet manufactured, and we firmly believe will be imperishable when once laid.

We remain, sir, yours faithfully,
Glass, Elliot & Co.

The pieces were beginning to come together, once again. Field now had commitments from both governments, and a company offering to construct the cable which was confident enough of success to invest a large sum of money in the endeavor. Much had been learned from the experiences of 1857-8 as well as from other submarine cable projects; the technology had advanced enough that success seemed quite possible. But there remained an important problem: the raising of capital.

Field continued his mission to raise capital for another attempt in both countries. It must have been quite discouraging, but he never stopped trying. Henry Field described some his attempts to raise capital on the U.S. side of the Atlantic:

> The summer of this year (1862) Mr. Field spent in America, where he applied himself vigorously to raising capital for the new enterprise. To this end he visited Boston, Providence, Philadelphia, Albany, and Buffalo, to address meetings of merchants and others.

> He used to amuse us with the account of his visit to the first city, where he was honored with the attendance of a large array of "the solid men of Boston," who listened with an attention that was most flattering to the pride of the speaker addressing such an assemblage in the capital of his native State. There was no mistaking the interest they felt   in the subject. They went still farther, they passed a series of resolutions, in which they applauded the projected telegraph across the ocean as one of the grandest enterprises ever undertaken by man, which they proudly commended to the confidence and support of the American public, after which they went home, feeling that they had done the generous thing in bestowing upon it such a mark of their approbation. *But not a man subscribed a dollar.*

Field's reception in other cities in the U.S. was similar, other than in New York, where most of the wealthy knew Field personally and liked him. There, Field did manage to raise about $330,000; but "even those who subscribed, did so more from sympathy and admiration of his indomitable spirit than from confidence in the success of the enterprise."

By 1863, the company's board was finally regaining its confidence. Enough time had passed to recover from the bitter disappointment of 1858, and much had been learned in the meantime as well. The inquest report, the experiences of other cable operations, the willingness of both governments to cooperate, and Field's determination to carry on all contributed.

Though sufficient capital had not been raised yet, in August of that year, the company advertised for proposals for a cable suitable to be laid across the Atlantic. The advertisement, or "request for proposals" in modern vernacular, did not dictate what material should be used, but only specified a working speed of eight words per minute. The advertisement specified what they wanted, but not the specifics of how to do it. The company directors wisely wanted to leave themselves open to new inventions or advancements in cable technology.

The company received seventeen proposals in a few weeks time. The offers were submitted to a consulting committee. Samples of the cables which the offers proposed were also provided, and these were tested extensively. The result was a unanimous recommendation that the Board should accept the offer made by the Glass, Elliot and Co. – the same company which Field had consulted with the year before.

The technology of cables was in place, the company was ready to try again, and a suitable manufacturer had been found, but there was still the question of paying for it. In January, 1864 Field once again sailed for England. He met a new potential investor, Thomas Brassey.

Brassey was born in 1805, had begun life as an apprentice surveyor, and soon became a railroad contractor. He showed an exceptional ability to manage and grow the railroads, and obviously to invest money, and by the 1860s had made himself into one of the wealthiest men in Britain.

When Field called on him, Brassey subjected him to an interrogation which must have reminded Field of some earlier experiences in getting money from investors. As Field put it a few months later,

> When I arrived in this country, January last, the Atlantic Telegraph Company trembled in the balance. We were in want of funds, and were in negotiations with the government, and making great exertions to raise money.
>
> At this juncture I was introduced to a gentleman of great integrity and enterprise, who is well known, not only for his wealth, but for his foresight, and in attempting to enlist him in our cause he put me through such a cross-examination as I had never before experienced. I thought I was in the witness-box. He inquired of me the practicability of the scheme – what it would pay, and every thing else connected to it; but before I left him, I had the pleasure of hearing him say that it was a great national enterprise that ought to be carried out, and, he added, I will be one of ten to find the money required for it.

From that day to this he has never hesitated about it, and when I mention his name, you will know him as a man whose word is as good as his bond, and as for his bond, there is no better in England.

Brassey's commitment was a big step forward, and encouraged Field and the other directors greatly. Field later said, "The words spoken by Mr. Brassey in the latter part of January, 'Let the Electric Telegraph be laid between England and America,' encouraged us all and made us believe we should succeed in raising the necessary capital . . ." His commitment served as the initial push to help Field get other investors involved, much as Peter Cooper's had done a decade earlier.

Shortly later, Field met with another investor, John Pender, who was a member of the House of Commons. On hearing Field's request that he match Brassey's offer of support, he agreed to do so immediately.

A few days later, in April, 1864, the Gutta-Percha Company merged with Glass, Elliott & Company. The Gutta-Percha Company was the same which had manufactured the core and insulation for the 1857 cable, and Glass, Elliott was one of the companies which had man- ufactured the armor. This created a powerful company which would be the dominant one in submarine cable building and laying for the next several decades. The chairman of the new company was John Pender.

It had been calculated that £600,000 of capital was needed for the new cable, of which £285,000 had been raised. The new company, the Telegraph Construction and Maintenance Company, now offered to finance the remaining £315,000, and to take shares in the Atlantic Telegraph Company as their payment.

Now most of the pieces were in place. One of the last remaining pieces, however, was the question of a ship to carry the cable.

Daniel Gooch was a member of the Board of Directors of the new cable manufacturing company, and he was also the chairman of the board of the Great Western Railway. He had known Brunel earlier: in 1842, he shared the controls with Brunel when Queen Victoria rode a train for the first time. He had also formed a syndicate which had become the third owner of the *Great Eastern*, having bought her for just £25,000.

Gooch now offered her to the Atlantic Cable Company, for the carrying of the cable, for a payment of £50,000 in stock, payable on the successful completion of the laying of the cable. Field accepted, saying, "In all my business experience I have never known an offer more honorable."

On March 15, 1864, Field invited the directors, friends and others involved in the cable project to a dinner at the Palace Hotel to celebrate the tenth anniversary of his involvement with the cable enterprise. The next day the annual meeting of the board of directors was held, and the chairman, James Stuart Wortley, thanked Field for his contributions to the Atlantic cable: "Without saying anything to detract from my deep source of gratitude to the other Directors, I cannot help especially alluding to Mr. Cyrus Field, who is present today, and who had crossed the Atlantic thirty-one times in the service of this Company, having celebrated at his table yesterday the anniversary of the tenth year of the day when he first left Boston in the service of the Company."

At a meeting on May 5, 1864, the board of directors made their appreciation of Field an official resolution:

> *Resolved*, That the sincere thanks of the Board be given to Mr. Cyrus W. Field, for his untiring energy in promoting the general interests of the Atlantic Telegraph Company, and especially for his valuable and successful exertions during his present visit to Great Britain, in reference to the restoration of its financial position, and prospects of complete success.

With the financing in place, and a suitable ship to carry it chosen, final decisions on the cable – exact specifications, manufacture, loading on the ship, preparing the ship to carry and pay out the cable, exacting landing points on both coasts – needed to be made. This time the company made every effort to make the cable the best quality possible. The advice of Professor William Thomson and Sir Charles Bright, the recommendations of the inquest committee, and the experience of the cable manufacturing company with other cables were all considered.

The final specifications provided that the cable would be the best submarine cable ever manufactured, and also considerably better than what was thought necessary for the job. Every part of the cable was improved over the cable of 1858, from the copper core to the outer sheathing. In addition, and just as important, the cable was to be extensively tested throughout the phases of manufacture, to ensure that any faults were detected, isolated and corrected as soon as possible.

The copper core was again to be made of seven strands, but the wires were thicker, weighing three hundred pounds to the mile, almost three times as heavy as the old core. More importantly, the copper was to be the purest available, which would make it the best possible conductor, and would be extensively tested before being coated with insulation.

Surrounding the core was to be four layers of gutta-percha, rather than three. Further, inside each layer of gutta-percha was a coating of Chatterton's compound. This chemical had been recently invented, and helped strengthen the insulating properties of the gutta-percha. The insulation of the cable weighed four-hundred pounds to the mile, about half again as heavy as the old cable.

trait-cable	1865	1857-8
core	copper, best quality, 7 strands, 300 lbs/mile	copper, 107 lbs/mile 7 strands
insulation	gutta-percha, 4 layers, Chatterton's comp., 300 lbs/mile	gutta-percha, 261 lbs/mile, 3 layers
armor (sheathing)	steel; each strand hemp soaked in tar, pitch; stronger, less dense	iron, hemp, tar
diameter	1.1 inches	0.625 inch
weight, lbs/mile	3,575	2,000
length-naut.mls	2,300	2,500
breaking point, miles of cable	10 miles	5 miles

Cable Specifications

The armor, or sheathing, which surrounded the core and the insulation for its protection was also greatly improved. Improvements in manufacturing had made a type of steel cheap enough to be used, called charcoal iron, and this was coated with hemp soaked with tar and pitch. The hemp protected the wires from contact with the sea water, improved the flexibility, and also increase the bulk of the wire without increasing the weight by much. This meant that, though the cable was heavier, it was less dense, and would sink into the sea more slowly than the previous cable, making a less sharp angle as it trailed the ship. This helped decrease the pressure on the cable, making a rupture less likely.

Once the cable was designed and its manufacture begun, Field returned to the U.S. for the winter. The directors of the New York, Newfoundland and London Telegraph Company welcomed him as a hero.

Next, he made yet another trip to Newfoundland, this time for the purpose of finding a new landing spot. The spot used before, Bull's Arm, was too shallow for the *Great Eastern*, which drew thirty-four feet of water. Accompanied by British Captain Orlebar on the survey ship Margaretta Stevenson, Field found a new spot for the cable, on

the eastern shore of Trinity Bay, which was close enough to the deep
water and had a suitable beach. There was a small village at the new
spot, known as Heart's Content. He returned to Britain in March of
the following year.

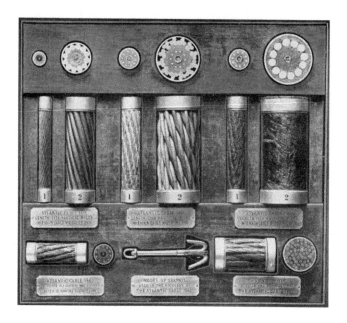

Cables of 1858, 1865, 1866

The manufacturing of the cable began in September, 1864, in Greenwich. The depth of the river there was too shallow for the huge *Great
Eastern*, so she waited about twenty miles downriver, at Sheerness. As
the cable was fabricated, two older "hulks," the Iris and the *Amethyst*,
would alternately take on a load of the cable, in two hundred fifty ton
batches, and carry it downriver to the *Great Eastern*.

The loading of the cable onto her had to be done with great care, to coil
it in such a way that no damage would be done, either when loading
it onto the ship or when it was to be paid out. The huge weight and
bulk of the cable also increased the difficulty. As a result, the loading
was done at a rate of about two miles per hour, twenty miles per day,
taking a total of about five months. The first batch of cable was ready

in January, 1865. The last mile of cable was manufactured in late May, and loaded in early June.

In addition to the cable itself, the *Great Eastern* had to take on a load of about 8,000 tons of coal. Provisions for food included a cow for milk, a dozen oxen, twenty sheep, and numerous ducks and geese. In addition to the livestock, hundreds of barrels of other food provisions were loaded. It was estimated that the total load on board, including the equipment for paying out and picking up the cable, was 21,000 tons.

About five hundred people were selected to go on the voyage. The chief engineer was Samuel Canning, the same who, years earlier, had laid the cable across the Cabot Strait. C.V. de Sauty, whose name had been the subject of ridicule by the newspapers in 1858, was the chief electrician. Professor William Thomson and Cromwell Varley were also along as electrical consultants. The only American on board was Cyrus Field, and he was also the only man on board with no specifically designated task.

Loading the 1865 Cable at Sheerness

The ship's commanding officer was Captain James Anderson. He was a highly respected and experienced commander of the Cunard steamers. He was known for his vigilance and sense of responsibility. Past experience had taught Field and the company's directors the importance of choosing the vessel's captain carefully, and Anderson would not disappoint them.

Although numerous newspapers wanted their correspondents on board, only one was permitted, William Howard Russell. He was a correspondent for the *Times* of London, and was probably the most famous newspaper writer in the world. He had achieved fame with his reporting of the Crimean War, and for this was often called the first war correspondent. Later in life, he became one of the few journalists ever to be knighted.

By July, the ship and its load were ready, and on Saturday, July 15, the ship weighed anchor and set sail for Valentia Bay, the cable's eastern landing point. The anchor was a Trotman, considered by most to be the best type of anchor in the 1850s, weighed seven tons, and the links of the chain which held it weighed eighty pounds each. It took nearly two hundred men working together to lift it from the mud.

It had been seven long years since the bitter failure of 1858. Cyrus Field had never given up, and finally all was ready to make another attempt, and the expedition was far better prepared this time than ever before.

Chapter 11
Another Try: 1865

'Tis a lesson you should heed,
Try, try again;
If at first you don't succeed,
Try, try again;

Then your courage should appear,
For, if you persevere,
You will conquer, never fear;
Try, try again.

Once or twice, though you should fail,
All that other folk can do,
Why, with patience, should not you?
Only keep this rule in view,
Try, try again.

—William Edward Hickson

As the *Great Eastern* began her voyage, she was led down the river channel to the sea by the *Porcupine*, the same ship which had guided the *Niagara* up Trinity Bay, Newfoundland, seven years earlier. On reaching the English Channel the escort dropped back, and the *Great Eastern* continued her voyage down the channel towards Ireland. Near Falmouth, she caught up with the steamer *Caroline*, which was carrying the heavy shore cable. The *Great Eastern* took her in tow, pulling the steamship along as if it were a lifeboat in tow, and the two continued on around the southern coast of Ireland.

The landing spot was about five or six miles up the shore from the previous spot in Valentia Bay. It was a place called Foilhommerum Bay, where huge cliffs came up to the ocean. Crowds of peasants had gathered all around the area to witness the great event.

Due to her deep draft, the *Great Eastern* had to remain well offshore, so she returned to protected Bantry Bay while the Caroline and a line of smaller boats brought the heavy shore cable to land. The landing was accomplished on Saturday, July 22.

The land end was put onshore and made secure, and the Caroline began to pay the cable out into the Atlantic. The landing cable was twenty-seven miles long, all of which had been paid out by ten-thirty P.M. that night. The end was buoyed and word sent to the *Great Eastern* that all was ready, and she arrived the following day, around noon.

The splicing of the two cables was carried out, a difficult task which took several hours. Late that afternoon, Sunday, July 23, she began her voyage westward, destination: Heart's Content, on Trinity Bay, Newfoundland, 1610 nautical miles to the west.

The sun was just setting. Russell, the *Times* reporter on board, described the scene: "As the sun set, a broad stream of golden light was thrown across the smooth billows toward their bows, as if to indicate and illumine the path marked out by the hand of heaven."

The British government had provided two warships to accompany the huge cable ship on her mission, the H.M.S. *Sphinx* and the H.M.S. *Terrible*. The ships were needed as scouts, to warn off any other ships in the area as the *Great Eastern* crossed the Atlantic. The *Sphinx* was also provided with sounding equipment.

Captain Anderson was pleased with the timing of the departure: he had hoped for either June 23 or July 22, in order to time the arrival in Newfoundland with the full moon. The ship's crew was also pleased with the departure on a Sunday, which they considered a good omen. During the first night at sea all seemed to go well, and most of those on board were in their bunks around midnight.

However, early the next morning, around three A.M., the sound of the alarm gong was heard. They were seventy-three miles from shore, and had paid out eighty-four miles of cable. Captain Anderson ordered the ship's engines to halt, though the ship's momentum carried her forward a considerable distance.

A leak in the flow of electricity had been detected. Professor Thomson's sensitive galvanometer had detected a distinct weakening in the current. The line was not dead, but there was clearly a problem which needed to be resolved. It was determined that the faulty part of the cable had already been paid out, so it was decided to reel the cable back in until it was found. Then it would be cut out, the cable respliced, and the mission began anew.

Fortunately, the need for reeling in the cable had been considered, and the ship had been equipped with a machine for doing so. Unfortunately, however, the "picking up" machine was placed at the bow (front) of the ship, while the paying out machinery was placed at the stern (rear).

This meant that to reel in the cable, it would have to be cut at the stern, moved around to the bow – the ship was almost seven hundred feet long – and the ship turned around. This was quite a job, requiring much care not to drop the heavy cable into the ocean. Further, the reeling in machine operated very slowly, only pulling out the cable at about one mile per hour.

However, the ship had not yet reached deep water: the depth was only about four or five hundred fathoms. (One fathom is equal to six feet.) This made the task much simpler than it would be later, in deep water.

The cable was cut and moved, attached to the "donkey" – this was the name given to the reeling in machine, in reference to its speed – and the reeling in work began. The reporter, Russell, wrote that the huge ship daintily picking up the cable made one think of an "elephant taking up a straw in its proboscis." On Tuesday morning, around seven A.M. – about ten miles of cable had been reeled back in – the problem was found. Henry Field described it:

> It is found to be a small piece of wire, not longer than a needle, that by some accident (for they did not then suspect a design) had been driven through the outer cover of the cable till it touched the core . . .It was this pin's point which pricked this vital chord, opening a minute passage through which the electricity, like a jet of blood from a pierced artery, went streaming into the sea. It was with an almost angry feeling, as if to punish it for its intrusion, that this

insignificant and contemptible source of trouble was snatched from its place, the wounded piece of cable was cut off, and a splice was made and the work of paying out renewed.

It was four P.M. Tuesday afternoon that the ship was able to resume paying out the telegraph cable. Almost two days had been lost because of a small piece of wire stuck into the cable.

Apparently, no investigation was done at the time to determine how the wire had gotten into the cable. The ship's crew and captain all seemed relieved to have found it, and were eager to resume their mission of laying the cable. If the cause could have been determined at this early stage, considerable heartache might have been avoided later.

The next three days passed by very smoothly, with both the ship and the paying out equipment doing their job beautifully. Communication through the cable with the land terminal in Ireland was constant, and even improved as time went by. Much of Britain was informed through the papers on a daily basis of the progress of the ship. No news could reach North America, of course, until her arrival.

On Saturday, July 29, early afternoon, the alarm again sounded. The cable had again lost its flow of electricity, and this time the flow was completely dead. Tests again indicated that the faulty cable had already been paid out into the ocean, so there was nothing to do except begin the process of reeling it back in.

This time, the work was much more difficult than before, because the ship was now in waters more than two miles deep. After about nine hours of labor, the faulty portion was found. On Monday, a careful examination of the faulty cable indicated that once again, a piece of wire had been driven into the core.

This time, there was serious concern that someone on board had deliberately sabotaged it. The same crew had been working below on both occasions. Captain Anderson questioned the crew, and the crew members themselves agreed that it appeared to have been deliberate, even knowing that this pointed the finger at one of themselves.

The sabotage of a submarine cable was not without precedent. A cable in the North Sea had once been rendered useless by a nail deliberately driven into it, destroying the insulation. The man who did it was caught and tried in English courts, and had confessed to doing it in the pay of a rival company.

As a result, it was decided that a watch be placed on the men. This was unpleasant to all involved, but most, including the men themselves, agreed that it was necessary.

The paying out of the cable resumed and continued for the next few days. Another five hundred miles of cable were paid out, and the ship passed the midpoint of the Atlantic. The electrical signals still operated perfectly, in fact, were operating better in the sea than they had on the ship.

As Field put it, "With every lengthening league it grew better and better. It seems almost beyond belief, yet the fact is fully attested that, when in the middle of the ocean, the communication was so perfect that they could tell at Valentia every time the *Great Eastern* rolled."

The next difficulty, a seemingly minor one, occurred on Wednesday, August 2. The ship was now in water 2,000 fathoms –12,000 feet, more than two miles – deep. Nearly 1,200 miles of cable had been paid out, and they were now less than six hundred miles from the Newfoundland coast. Two more days would have brought them to the continental shelf, into much shallower waters.

Field was keeping watch on the crew in the tank below, and the same crew was on duty as when the earlier problems had occurred. A grating sound was heard, and a warning was passed to the deck to watch the cable, but apparently the warning was not heard. Soon afterwards, another fault was detected in the electric flow, but as with the first time, there was still a (weakened) signal.

It was an annoyance, but this had occurred twice before on the voyage, and captain and crew knew what to do. No one was unduly alarmed. The cable would have to be cut, brought around to the bow and retrieved, the fault found and cut out, the cable respliced – as had been done twice before.

As Canning and the others were discussing the action to take, a worker came up from the tank below. He was carrying a piece of wire identical to those which had called the previous faults. It was from the brittle charcoal iron sheathing. Somehow, the wire from the sheathing had been punched into the cable, causing a leakage of electricity. There had been no sabotage, after all.

The process was begun. The cable was cut and brought around to the bow, connected to the "donkey," and the reeling in started. It was a little after noon, and most of the crew and officers were eating lunch.

Shortly after reeling in process started, a strong breeze came up, which caused the ship – her engines were turned off – to drift over the cable, which chaffed it. Just as the damaged part of the cable was being brought on board, it broke, and the cable vanished into the Atlantic.

Samuel Canning, the chief engineer, and Cyrus Field saw it happen. Russell, the *Times* reporter on board, described it.

> [The cable] flew through the stoppers and with one bound leaped over the intervening space and flashed into the sea   . . . Suddenly Mr. Canning appeared in the saloon, and in a manner which caused every one to start in his seat, said, "It is all over! It is gone!" then hastened on to his cabin.

> Ere the thrill of surprise and pain occasioned by these words had passed away, Mr. Field came from the companion into the saloon, and said, with composure admirable under the circumstances, though his lip quivered and his cheek was blanched, "The cable has parted and has gone overboard." All were on deck in a moment, and there, indeed, a glance revealed the truth.

In America, nothing was known of this until later, but in Britain, where there had been continuous communication with the *Great Eastern*, with its five hundred on board and two accompanying vessels, the sudden break in communication caused much consternation and speculation as to what had gone wrong. The *London Times* reported:

> At Valentia, on Wednesday last, the signals, up to nine A.M., were coming with wonderful distinctness and regularity, but about that time a violent magnetic storm set in. No insulation of a submarine is ever so perfect as to withstand the influence of these electrical phenomena, which correspond in some particulars to storms in the ordinary atmosphere . . .

In Britain, it was known immediately that something had gone wrong, but exactly what had gone wrong would not be known for another two weeks. One of the rumors which circulated was that the *Great Eastern* had hit an iceberg and foundered.

Samuel Canning was not ready to give up. He wanted to fish for the cable and pull it back to the surface. A sextant reading had been taken at noon, shortly before the cable broke, so the location where the break occurred was known to within about a half mile.

Canning suggested that they try to "fish" for the cable and retrieve it. They had on board about five miles of wire rope which could be used, more than enough to reach the bottom, nearly two and one-half miles below. To the end of the rope grapnels were attached. These had five arms, looking similar to an anchor, and it was hoped these would "hook" the cable on the bottom.

The ship retraced its path back a few miles, and also to the south for several miles, to be sure not to miss the cable. The grapnels and the rope were thrown overboard, at about three P.M. It took two full hours for the grapnels to reach bottom. The *Great Eastern* then turned to the north and began sailing slowly, dragging the hook along the bottom.

In the early morning, the rope quivered – as a fishing line does when when a fish is hooked – and the bow of the ship turned slightly. The grapnel had hooked something, but was it the cable?

The answer was soon determined to be 'yes,' because the weight of whatever was being pulled in became heavier and heavier. If it had been some object on the bottom, the pulling in would have gotten easier as it came up. Further, the object had been hooked at exactly the point where the position calculations indicated the cable should be.

Unfortunately, the wire rope had not been designed to carry such a heavy weight. It was not a continuous wire rope, but a series of ropes of about a hundred fathoms each, shackled together, and the shackles proved to be the weak point.

When the cable had been raised up about three quarters of a mile, a shackle broke, and the cable plunged back to the bottom, taking about two miles of rope with it.

Three more attempts to hook the cable and retrieve it were made. On two of these, the cable was successfully hooked and lifted some distance from the bottom, but again the shackles gave way before it reached the surface.

On the other occasion, the cable was not hooked because the flukes of the grapnel had become entangled in the rope. The last attempt was made on Friday, August 13. Following this break, there was not enough rope left to reach the bottom, leaving the expedition no choice but to return to Britain, its mission still unfulfilled.

The goal had not yet been attained, but it had been so near, that the feeling of the men on board was not one of failure, but of having come very close to the accomplishment a great mission, and certainty that they would be able to accomplish it. One more attempt would be necessary.

Cable Breaks, 2 August 1865

Chapter 12
One More Try: Preparation

Very often it is not the best athlete who wins the majorraces, but the best prepared athlete.
–Arthur Lydiard (1917-2004), legendary New Zealand athletics coach

While the *Great Eastern* was on her way back to Britain, a paper was written and signed by the company and ship officers on board, which summarized the accomplishments which had been made up to that time. It had twelve points which are summarized and paraphrased below:

1. The expedition of 1858 had proven it possible to lay a cable from Ireland to Newfoundland and transmit telegraphic messages through it.
2. The cable insulation is improved by the cold water of the Atlantic.
3. The *Great Eastern*, from her size and constant steadiness, made it safe to lay a cable in any weather.
4. It was proven possible to hook and retrieve a cable over two miles deep.
5. The paying out machinery worked perfectly.
6. A speed of more than eight words per minute was achieved.
7. There was never an excessive strain on the cable (in paying out).
8. It was possible to moor buoys in the deep Atlantic waters and use them to hold the cable.
9. More than four miles of cable had been retrieved from depths of over two miles.
10. The 1865 cable was insulated more than 100 times better than the 1858 one.
11. Electrical testing detected faults very quickly after they occurred.
12. If a steam engine were connected to the paying out machinery, then the cable could be recovered more quickly after the detection of a fault.

The paper was signed by the chief engineer, Samuel Canning; the captain, James Anderson; Daniel Gooch, William Thomson, Cromwell

Varley, Willoughby Smith and Jules Despecher. It indicated clearly their confidence that a cable could be laid.

Soon after the *Great Eastern* returned to Britain, a meeting of the board of directors took place. The mood was so optimistic that they decided to not only return and finish the 1865 cable, but to also build and lay a new one, as well.

The Telegraph Construction and Maintenance Company – which had manufactured the cable – next made an offer to construct and lay a new cable across the Atlantic for £500,000, which was their estimated cost, the payment contingent on the successful laying of the cable. Of the £500,000, £100,000 would be paid in stock of the Atlantic Telegraph Company, upon completion of the cable. Included in this offer, the company would also carry along equipment for grappling and retrieving the old cable, and sufficient cable for completing it, including the cable which was left over from the 1865 expedition.

While this was a generous offer, it should also be recalled that the Telegraph Construction and Maintenance Company also had a very large investment in the old cable, and it was also in its own best interest to get that cable raised, spliced and completed.

With this, the directors of the Atlantic company decided to raise an additional £600,000 to finance the new cable, by issuing preferred stock, which would pay a 12% dividend, payable before the dividends due to other shareholders. One hundred twenty thousand shares would be issued to the public at five pounds each. The proposal of the construction company was accepted, and work was began on the new cable.

These arrangements were all made by September, 1865 – scarcely a month after the return of the *Great Eastern*. As all seemed to be in order, Field returned to the United States for a visit with his family, and in particular to attend the wedding of his daughter. In November, Captain James Anderson wrote him, writing that there was a problem. "I am sorry you are not here," he wrote. "Somehow no one seems to push when you are absent."

Field returned back to England in December, arriving on Christmas Eve, to find the company in yet another difficulty, this time a legal one. The attorney general had ruled a few days earlier that the company's offer of preferred stock at twelve percent was illegal, and could not be done without an act of Parliament.

Parliament had already adjourned for the holidays, and there was no way that such an act could be carried out in time for the cable to be ready for the following summer: it took several months to manufacture, and the manufacture had been halted due to the ruling, and what money had already been raised through the new preferred shares had to be returned to the investors.

However, Field and the directors had overcome many difficulties before, and they were not about to allow a legal ruling stop them without looking for a way around it. As Henry Field put it, "They had seen dark days before, and were not to give it up without a new effort."

Field discussed the situation with Daniel Gooch. Gooch, it may be recalled, had offered the use of the *Great Eastern* for the cable expedition, and was a director with the Telegraph Construction and Maintenance Company.

Gooch suggested that the best way around the problem was to organize a new company, which could then raise its own capital for the construction of the cable, and contract this to the Atlantic company. The directors of the new company would be essentially same as with the Atlantic company, so in effect the two companies would act as one.

Thus, the Anglo-American Telegraph Company was organized. Gooch subscribed £10,000 of initial capital, and offered another £10,000 if necessary; and Field subscribed another £10,000; Thomas Brassey, subscribed £10,000, and offered to put in as much as £60,000, if necessary. Seven other capitalists committed to £10,000 each. The Telegraph Construction and Maintenance Company also committed to £100,000 in capital. Several other smaller private investors subscribed, raising £230,500 of the capital, or more than one-third, very quickly. The remainder of the capital was raised by sales to the public.

Thus the work on the cable resumed in early 1866. The 1866 cable was largely the same as the 1865 one, but there were some important improvements in the sheathing. The wire in the armor was to be galvanized, covered with molten zinc. This made it rust-proof, and more flexible. This meant that the hemp did not have to be soaked with pitch.

Because of this, it was a lighter color, and much less sticky. The "not sticky" part was a very good thing, because loose iron wires would be less likely to adhere to it, causing the problems which had occurred the year before. The new cable also weighed less, by about four hundred pounds per mile.

The shore end of the cable on the Irish side was made a total of thirty miles, in three different weights. The first eight miles were very heavy; the next eight, moderately heavy; and the last fourteen miles, less heavy. For the Newfoundland side, where there was much less ship traffic, only five miles of heavy shore cable was used.

Several improvements were also made on the ship and its equipment. The ship's huge screw was fitted with a cage to cover it, to prevent the cable becoming entangled in it. The hull of the ship, which was covered with barnacles and mussels two feet thick, was given a good scrubbing. This was no easy task, considering the huge size of the hull.

The ship also was loaded with twenty miles of rope for grappling with the undersea cable, which would bear a weight of thirty tons – certainly the longest and strongest "fishing line" ever used.

The paying out machinery had operated perfectly on the previous voyage, but could not reel in the cable. This was resolved by adding a seventy horsepower steam engine to power it, along with the capability of reversing direction, should it be necessary to reel in the cable. This eliminated the need to cut the cable and carry it around to the other end of the ship, saving time and labor, and, most importantly, decreasing the danger of another accident.

The paddle wheels of the ship were also modified so that they could be disconnected from each other quickly. This would make it possible to use them to keep the ship in position or more easily turn it around, both of which could be necessary when fishing for cable.

In yet another precaution, the crews were to wear a uniform which was a canvas suit, which buttoned up from the back and had no pockets. The reason for this was to make it nearly impossible for one with malicious intentions to hide a knife, wire or other tool in a pocket.

The cable was loaded on board as it was manufactured, as had been done the year before. Due to the very heavy load, it was decided to only load her coal tanks to about two-thirds of her full capacity, and to finish loading them at Berehaven. This was because the ship drew so much water that she might have difficulty getting through the shallow channel waters.

The *Great Eastern* set sail from the Thames estuary at noon on June 30, passed through the Dover Strait, then headed down the English Channel, then around to the coast of Ireland. She was accompanied by the H.M.S *Terrible*, as she had been the year before; but the British government could spare no other Naval vessels. The company chartered three other ships. The *William Correy* carried the heavy shore end of the cable to Valentia. The *Albany* and the *Medway* were chartered to accompany the expedition.

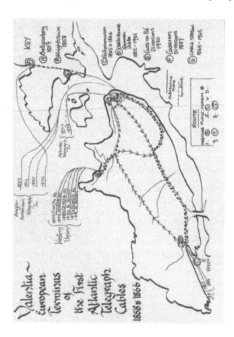

Valentia Island, showing Cable Terminal Locations

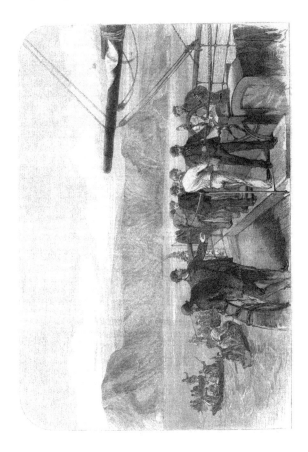

Landing the Shore Cable at Valentia, July 1866

The *Great Eastern* anchored at Berehavan for a few days, to finish filling her coal tanks. The *William Correy* continued on towards Valentia, carry and lay out the very heavy shore cable. The shore cable weighed eight tons per mile, and it was the strongest yet made. She arrived on July 7, with the shore cable. As the charter ship brought the cable to the harbor, a line of about forty fishing boats formed a bridge to help bring the cable to the shore. Once the cable had been brought ashore it was tested and found good. The heavy shore cable was paid out thirty miles to its end and buoyed, and word sent to the Great Eastern that all was ready.

Chapter 13
Victory at Last: 1866

O lonely Bay of Trinity,
  O dreary shores give ear!
Lean down unto the white-lipped sea,
  The voice of God to hear.
From world to world His couriers fly,
  Though-winged and shod with fire;
The angel of His stormy sky
  Rides down the sunken wire ...
For lo! the fall of ocean's wall
  Space mocked and time outrun,
And 'round the world the thought of all
  Is as the thought of one!
– John G. Whittier (1807-92)

The atmosphere was quite different from the previous year. It was described by the *Illustrated London News*:

> In its leading features it presented a striking difference to the ceremony of last year. Earnest gravity and a deepseated determination to repress all show of the enthusiasm of which every body was full, was very manifest. The excitement was below, instead of above the surface.

> Speech-making, hurrahing, public congratulations, and shouts of confidence were, as it seemed, avoided as if on purpose. There was something far more touching in the quiet and reverent solemnity of the spectators yesterday than in the slightly boisterous joviality of the peasantry last year. Nothing could prevent the scene being intensely dramatic, but the prevailing tone of the drama was serious instead of comic and triumphant.

> The old crones in tattered garments who cowered together, dudeen in mouth, their gaudy colored shawls tightly drawn over head and under the chin; the barefoot boys and girls, who by long practice walked over sharp and jagged rocks, which cut up boots and shoes, with perfect impunity; the men at work uncovering the trench, and winding in single file up and down the hazardous path cut by the cablemen in the

otherwise inaccessible rock; the patches of bright color furnished by the red petticoats and cloaks; the ragged gar- ments, only kept from falling to pieces by bits of string and tape; the good old parish priest, who exercises mild and gently spiritual sway over the loving subjects of whom the ever popular Knight of Kerry is the temporal head, looking on benignly from his car; the bright eyes, supple figures, and innocent faces of the peasant lasses, and the earnestly hopeful expression of all, made up of a picture impossible to describe with justice.

Add to this, the startling abruptness with which the tremendous cliffs stand flush out of the water, the alterations of bright wild flowers and patches of verdure . . . the mountain sheep . . . and few scenes will seem more important and interesting than that of yesterday.

On Friday, July 13, the shore cable was spliced to the ocean cable. The ships had to sail out thirty miles to where the end had been buoyed. The weather was foggy in the morning, and this took some time. The *Medway* spotted the buoy first, and fired a gun to signal the others.

The cable was brought up and lashed to the side of the Great Eastern. Then the ends of the shore cable and the ocean cable on board were stripped, for a foot or so, of all their sheathing and insulation, to get to the seven-strand copper core. The strands of the two cables were then wrapped together tightly, to insure a good electrical connection.

Next, this core at the splice was again re-covered with gutta-percha insulation, hemp, iron wires, and the whole very well wrapped in bands to insure that all would hold together.

Finally, the splicing complete, electrical testing of the cable throughout its entire length of more than two thousand miles was carried out. This confirmed that the splice had been done correctly. It was about three P.M. when the splice was complete.

The splice done, the expedition began that same day, Friday, July 13. As in the year before, the destination lay some 1610 nautical miles to the west, at Heart's Content, on the Trinity Bay, in Newfoundland. This time, Cyrus Field and the entire crew intended to make it.

The *Great Eastern*, loaded with the 1866 cable, leaving
Sheerness

Some of the ship's crews wanted to wait until the next day to start;
sailors were often superstitious, and Friday was considered an unlucky
day. However, it was pointed out that Columbus had sailed from Spain
on a Friday, and had discovered the New World on a Friday. As things
turned out, this expedition would also sail from the Old World and reach
the New one on a Friday. The H.M.S. *Terrible* led the way, the *Great
Eastern* followed. She was flanked by the *Albany* and the *Medway*.

It had been decided to follow a course parallel to that of the previous year, but to the south by thirty miles. The separation between the cables would avoid confusion as to which was being grappled for. It had also been decided to maintain a slower but steady speed of approximately six miles per hour. The paddle wheels provided more than enough power for this speed, so the ship's screw was disengaged.

As in the year before, there were about five hundred on board. Most were the same people. Once again, Cyrus Field was the only American. Reporter Russell of the *Times* was not along, as he had been sent to cover the Seven Weeks War between Prussia and Austria. Captain Anderson was again the skipper, and Samuel Canning the chief engineer.

The fog and rain of Friday morning cleared, leaving a beautiful day for the start. The first few days went very smoothly. John Deane, secretary of the Anglo-American Telegraph Company, wrote in his diary that Monday, July 16, was "so calm that the masts of our convoy were reflected in the ocean ... A glorious sunset, and later, a crescent moon, which we hope to see in the brightness of her full, lighting our way into Trinity Bay before the days of this July shall have ended."

On Wednesday, a problem occurred when the cable got badly entangled in the after tank. But Captain Anderson stopped the engines at once and used the paddles and screw to hold the ship in place, while Canning calmly directed the crew disentangling it.

Of this difficulty, Deane wrote in his diary, "During all this critical time there was an entire absence of noise and confusion. Every order was silently obeyed, and the cable men and crew worked with hearty good-will. Mr. Canning has had experience with foul flakes before, and showed that he knew what to do in an emergency."

The paying out resumed, the voyage continued. The halfway mark was passed on Saturday, July 21, and continued going smoothly. On Sunday, July 22, Deane wrote: "Cable going out with unerring smoothness, at the rate of six miles an hour. There had been great improvement in the insulation. This remarkable improvement is attributable to the greatly decreased temperature of, and pressure on, the cable in the sea."

The ship was paying out more than a hundred miles of cable a day. On the first Wednesday, when the cable got entangled, 105 miles were paid out, despite the problem. Most other days, from 115 to 128 miles was paid out.

The tension grew. There was growing feeling of optimism, but all well knew how quickly disaster could strike. Daniel Gooch was on board, and wrote in his diary, "I now hear the rumble of the cable overhead in my cabin, and am constantly listening to it. This stretch of the nerves day after day is hard work, and the mind has no change; morning, noon and night it is all the same – cable, cable, cable."

On Monday, July 23, Field telegraphed back to Valentia, asking for the latest news, to be delivered in Newfoundland on arrival. On Tuesday, the 24th, they passed the point at which the previous year's cable had broken. There had been no problems with faulty signals, or with wires getting stuck into the cable. Apparently the changes in the cable and/or the equipment had resolved them. Nor had there been any necessity to reel the cable back in – though they were prepared for that problem also.

On Wednesday, the 25th, the weather, which had been favorable throughout most of the voyage, began to change to rain and fog. The fog gradually became so dense that the ships sounded whistles to insure that they did not collide. Off the coast of Newfoundland, the warm Gulf Stream meets the cold Labrador current, which results in much foggy and rainy weather. The change in weather was confirmation that the expedition was approaching the coast of North America.

The British admiralty had ordered Sir James Hope, admiral in charge in North America, to send out an escort ship thirty miles off the entrance to Trinity Bay, to guide the telegraph fleet into it, where the weather is often foggy. The waters there often have icebergs, even in summer. Indeed, an iceberg was sighted on this trip, which rose fifty feet above the water line. Forty-six years later in these same waters a huge ship carrying more than two thousand passengers, traveling at reckless speeds, would tragically collide with one.

On Thursday, July 26, signs of land appeared. The water was much shallower, and birds were seen. The *Albany* was sent ahead to look for the British escort ships. Early Friday morning, around six A.M., British escort ships met the telegraph fleet, with cheers. Deane wrote, "Here we are within ten miles of Heart's Content, and we can scarcely see more than a ship's length." Later that morning, the fog began to lift, and the shores of Trinity Bay came into view.

At Heart's Content, a tiny village of less than one hundred houses, no news of the telegraph fleet had been heard since before it left Ireland, two weeks earlier. Its inhabitants and visiting American reporters had been rather eagerly awaiting it. It is not every day that the largest ship the world has ever seen visits a tiny fishing village, making telecommunications history in the process. Henry Field described the scene:

> It is Friday, the twenty-seventh of July. They are up early and looking eastward to see the day break, when a ship is seen in the offing. She is far down the horizon. Spy-glasses are turned toward her. She comes nearer—and look there is another and another. And now the hull of the *Great Eastern* looms up all glorious in that morning sky. They are coming!

> Instantly all is wild excitement on shore. Boats are put off to row toward the fleet. The *Albany* is the first to round the point and enter the Bay. The *Terrible* is close behind. The *Medway* stops an hour or two to join on the heavy shore end, while the *Great Eastern*, gliding calmly in as if she had done nothing remarkable, drops her anchor in front of the telegraph house, having trailed behind her a chain of two thousand miles, to bind the old world to the new.

The shore cable was brought in and connected to the main one, and the cable was done. The company directors went on shore into the little village church to give thanks. The little village broke out in celebrations. Daniel Gooch wrote, "There was the wildest excitement I have ever witnessed. All seemed mad with joy, jumping into the water and shouting as though they wished the sound to be heard in Washington."

England and Europe had followed the progress of the expedition from the day it left Valentia, and knew of the success immediately. New York, however, which was much closer, still knew nothing. The cable over the

strait between Newfoundland and Nova Scotia had been broken by a
ship's anchor.

Cable Expedition in Heart's Content, July 27, 1866

Field had asked the directors of the New York, Newfoundland and
London Telegraph Company to have it repaired, but they had decided
to wait until they were sure that the trans-Atlantic cable would succeed.
Thus, New York did not learn of the success until two days later.

Field ordered that a ship be sent to fish out the broken cable and repair it; in the meantime, he chartered a boat to carry cable traffic back and forth across the strait to Nova Scotia, where it was telegraphed the rest of the way.

On Sunday morning, the twenty-ninth, a cable from Field reached the Associated Press in New York City: "Heart's Content, July 27. We arrived here at nine o'clock this morning. All well. Thank God, the cable is laid, and is in perfect working order." From that moment, the news spread rapidly throughout America.

Field's family were up the Hudson River at Newburgh. As they returned home from church on Sunday, they saw a riverboat decorated with flags. It brought a cable from Field to his wife with the good news, and which said, "Now we shall be a united family." For twelve years the head of the family had been absorbed with the cable. Now the family would be together. But, not just yet. There remained one more task: find, raise and finish the laying out of the 1865 cable.

On August 1, five days after the cable had been landed, the *Terrible* and the *Albany* sailed for that point in the Atlantic, six hundred miles to the east, where the previous year's cable had broken. The point had been marked by buoys, but the year's weather had long since carried them away. They found the point, however, by astronomical observations.

The *Great Eastern* had to refuel. To provide it with coal, six ships had been sent from Wales. One had foundered at sea. The remaining five had arrived shortly after the cable was landed, and the job of refueling her began. The remaining six hundred miles of cable from the previous year also had to be transferred onto the *Great Eastern* from the *Medway*. The two sailed from Heart's Content on August 9, and the four ships met at sea on Sunday, August 12.

As had been learned the previous year, it is not an easy task to lift a cable from an ocean bed more than two miles deep. The grapnel was thrown overboard, and took nearly two hours to sink to the bottom. The cable was hooked and lifted a number of times, but in each case something went wrong.

On one occasion, the cable was lifted to the surface and was in sight for about five minutes, but then broke before the crew was able to secure it. On some days, the weather was too stormy to work. Throughout the rest of August, the ships and their crews struggled to find and raise the cable. Many times it was hooked and raised partially, but the grappling rope or the cable itself would break. Towards the end of August, the *Terrible*, which was running out of food, had to return to Newfoundland. The cable-grappling expedition had by now been at sea longer than the entire cable laying voyage.

The three remaining ships tried a different tactic. They sailed eastward, about eighty miles, where they expected the water to be slightly shallower. The date was August 31, and the sea was calm. The grapnel was thrown overboard, for the thirtieth time. Around midnight, the cable was again hooked.

This time it was raised very slowly for about five hours, until it was about halfway to the surface. The cable was buoyed at this point, and the *Great Eastern* moved westward about three miles. When the cable was hooked again at this point, the *Medway* moved another two miles to the west, where she also hooked the cable, and began raising it slowly to the surface. The plan was for the *Medway* to raise in all the way in – if possible – or to break it. The cable broke.

Next the *Great Eastern* began pulling in the cable slowly. On one side the break lessened the pressure, and on the other side the buoy did the same. The process had begun Friday; it was now Sunday morning, September 2. Two men were lowered from the high deck of the *Great Eastern,* near to sea level, where the cable was expected to surface. As soon as the slimy cable appeared, they grabbed it and secured it with ropes. Finally, the cable was gently raised to the deck of the ship.

There was still no cheering. There remained the most important question of all: was the cable still good, or could it have been damaged and made useless? The cable was hauled into the electrician's room, where it could be tested. There was about an hour of preparation.

Robert Dudley, the artist of the expedition, described the dramatic scene:

And now, in their mysterious, darkened haunt, the wizards are ready to work their spells upon the tamed lightning . . . Professor Thomson, be sure, is here, a worthy 'Wizard of the North'; Cyrus Field could no more be absent than the cable itself . . . The core of the cable is stripped and the heart itself – the conducting wire – fixed in the instrument ... The ticking of the chronometer becomes monotonous. Nearly a quarter of an hour has passed, and still no sign! Suddenly Willoughby Smith's hat is off, and the British hurrah bursts from his lips, echoed by all on board with a volley of cheers.

The reply from Valentia had come. The scene at the Irish end, at Valentia, was described vividly by a London paper, the *Spectator*:

Night and day, for a whole year, an electrician has always been on duty, watching the tiny ray of light through which signals are given, and twice every day the whole length of wire – one thousand two hundred and forty miles – has been tested for conductivity and insulation . . .

The object of observing the ray of light was of course not any expectation of a message, but simply to keep an accurate record of the condition of the wire. Sometimes, indeed, wild incoherent messages from the deep did come, but these were merely the results of magnetic storms and earth-currents, which deflected the galvanometer rapidly, and spelt the most extraordinary words, and sometimes even sentences of nonsense.

Suddenly, last Sunday morning, at a quarter to six o'clock, while the light was being watched by Mr. Crocker, he observed a peculiar indication about it ... The unsteady flickering was changed to coherency, and at once the cable began to speak, to retransmit the appointed signals which indicated human purpose and method instead of the inarticulate cries of the illiterate Atlantic – the delirious mutterings of the sea . . . The words 'Canning to Glass' must have seemed like the first rational words uttered by a high-fevered patient, when the ravings have ceased and his consciousness returns.

The entire message was, "Canning to Glass. I have much pleasure in speaking to you through the 1865 cable. Just going to make the splice."

Several months later, Field gave a speech in London, in which he described his feelings at that time:

> Never shall I forget that eventful moment when, in answer to our question to Valentia, whether the cable of 1866, which we had a few weeks previously laid, was in good working order, and the cable across the Gulf of St. Lawrence had been repaired, in an instant came back those six memorable letters, "Both O.K." I left the room. I went to my cabin, I locked the door; I could no longer restrain the tears.

The splice was made, and the crew began paying out the remaining six hundred miles of cable. A storm blew in, and Field went to the electrician's room to take shelter. As he sat there, a message came in over the cable for him, which said that his family was well and were praying for his safe return.

The message had been sent from New York to Newfoundland, over the 1866 cable to Ireland, and relayed back to the ship through the 1865 cable, which they were now paying out. That message was a second confirmation that both cables were in order. *The fact that on the high seas, in the middle of the Atlantic, Field could receive a message from his family, sent from New York, was an event that never before, in the history of mankind, could have taken place.*

The storm passed, and the rest of cable was paid out until nearly at Heart's Content, when a fault occurred. The instruments had detected it so quickly that the fault had not yet been paid out. It was quickly found – as had occurred several times before, a loose wire had become embedded in the insulation – and cut out, the cable respliced, and the expedition continued.

As the fleet came into Trinity Bay on Saturday, September 8, the little village of Heart's Content was ready to greet them. The village already knew, through communications with Valentia, that they had succeeded in raising the cable the previous Sunday. Numerous small vessels came out into the bay to greet the *Great Eastern.* Crowds cheered and hoisted Field and Canning. The shore cable was grabbed and dragged in by willing hands. Cyrus Field's dream of twelve years earlier had finally been realized.

The victory won, it was soon time for the victors to go their separate ways. The *Great Eastern* and her crew would return to Britain, Field to his family in New York. It was with emotion and regrets that he shook hands and said farewell to his comrades on the high seas, many of whom had been with him on several of the expeditions. When he left the ship for the last time, Captain Anderson shouted, "Give him three cheers!" The cheers were given – and received, no doubt – with much feeling.

In a speech given a few weeks later, Field said: "It has been a long, hard struggle. Nearly thirteen years of ceaseless waiting and anxious toil. Often my heart has been ready to sink. Many times, when wandering in the forests of Newfoundland, in the pelting rain, or on the decks of ships, on dark stormy nights – alone, far from home – I have almost accused myself of madness and folly to sacrifice the peace of my family, and all the hopes of life, for what might prove after all but a dream."

Chapter 14
The Overland
Telegraph Project

The least initial deviation from the truth is multiplied later a thousand-fold.
–Aristotle (384-322 B.C.)

During the years in which Cyrus Field and his companions worked to connect North America with Europe by an undersea cable, another attempt was made to connect the continents, via a very long distance overland telegraph, and a short-distance undersea cable.

In 1861, the president of Western Union, Hiram Sibley, was approached by Perry McDonough Collins with the idea of a Russian-American telegraph line. The line would run up the west coast through British Columbia and Russian America (now Alaska). Then it would cross the Bering Strait, which was to be the only underseas cable part.

From the Bering Strait, it was to run into Siberia, southward to the mouth of the Amur River. There it would connect with a trans-Siberian telegraph which was already under construction from St. Petersburg.

The trans-Siberian line would stretch for a distance of about seven thousand miles, and was already about three-fourths finished. The line would be almost entirely overland, except for the short distance across the Bering Strait, and would also have the potential of connecting with lines further south into China.

Sibley was quite enthusiastic with the idea. In a letter to Collins in October, 1861, he wrote, "Our men are pressing me hard to let them go on to Behrings' Strait next summer . . . If the Russian government will meet us at Behrings' Strait, and give us the right of way, etc., through their territory on the Pacific, we will complete the line in two years, and probably in one . . ."

Sibley thought that the project was quite feasible. Professor Morse also, in a letter to Collins, also declared the project to be feasible, and that no serious obstacle could be expected from climatic or geographic considerations. But while these plans were being made, the U.S. broke out into a long and difficult Civil War, and for a time the project was placed on hold, though not forgotten.

In late 1863, the war was nearing its conclusion, and on September 28 Collins submitted a proposal for the construction of a Russian- American telegraph to the Western Union board, with the approval of President Hiram Sibley. The proposal included a payment of $100,000 to Collins for the work on the project he had done up to that time,   and a 10% interest in the project. In exchange he would transfer all the rights to the line to Western Union.

The board considered that the Atlantic Cable project might succeed, which would be damaging or fatal to the project, but they considered that, after so many unsuccessful attempts, the probability that the cable would succeed was small, so they decided to take the risk.

To finance the project, a separate corporation was established, called the Western Union Extension, with Hiram Sibley as its president. Stock was authorized, up to 100,000 shares to be issued for $100 each, for a total of ten million dollars. However, only five percent of the price was required to be paid at the time of subscribing; additional assessments as necessary would be called for by the secretary of the company.

Western Union shareholders were given priority on the purchase of the shares. The entire stock was promptly taken, bringing in five percent of the total, or $500,000. It was expected that only about twenty percent of the assessment would be needed to finish the line.

In other words, investors paid five dollars for a share with a one-hundred dollar face value, and with it there was an implied commitment to pay additional investments as necessary; but with the expectation of paying no more than about twenty dollars per share. This was quite a contrast from the method of raising capital done in Britain, where the amount paid was the value of the share.

The project was supported by the Secretary of State, William Seward, and a bill was signed into law on July 1, 1864, giving the company the needed rights of way in U.S. territory. The act provided land to the company for its telegraph stations along the way, and provided for support by the U.S. Navy in the coastal waters. It also provided for protection by government troops along the route.

The responsibility of the construction was given to Colonel Charles Bulkley, a former superintendent of military telegraph. In December, 1864 he sailed to San Francisco from New York to begin the organization of the work crews.

The entire line was to begin in New Westminster, British Columbia, where it would connect with a line under construction from California, and run through that colony to Russian America, which is now Alaska. This traversed a distance of approximately 1,200 miles.

Then it would run another nine-hundred miles to the Bering Strait. Crossing the strait into Asia by a short submarine cable, it would then run for another 1,800 miles to the Amur River, where it would join the trans-Siberian line.

Thus, nearly four thousand miles of telegraph line (as then estimated) would need to be constructed through largely unknown and mostly uninhabited country, which suffered from some of the most extreme weather on the planet. At that point, it depended on another seven thousand mile line to St. Petersburg, Russia, and from there would cross Europe to connect to Britain.

Cyrus Field once remarked that he had no idea of the magnitude of the project he was getting into, when he embarked on the Atlantic telegraph project. The same may be true of this, the Western Union overland telegraph project.

On his arrival in San Francisco, Colonel Bulkley organized the work into three major areas: British Columbia, Russian America, and Siberia. Three exploring parties were organized. One exploring party under the command of Major H. L. Pope was sent to British Columbia. The second, led by Major Robert Kennicott, was sent to Russian America, and a third under C. L. McRae was landed in Siberia, just across the Bering Strait.

During the winter and spring of 1865-66, these parties made extensive exploring trips, seeking out a route for the construction of the line, and gathering as much information as possible of the country and the people which inhabited it.

At the end of 1865, Colonel Bulkley reported excellent progress on the explorations to the officers of Western Union. Routes through the land were being found, suitable for the telegraph lines; the land contained sufficient trees to provide poles for the telegraph; and the Indians along the way were friendly. In fact, construction had already begun in British Columbia on the line, and he promised a "spirited offensive," all along the lines on the arrival of spring, 1866.

As promised, Bulkley's telegraph "army" – which numbered more than one-thousand men – began its "great offensive" in the spring of 1866. Construction began, poles began to be set, lines strung. But as might be expected with such a huge project, difficulties were encountered.

For one, the crew stringing wire in British Columbia did not follow the route which had been mapped out for it, and instead began stringing wire closer to the coast, in unexplored territory. This continued for three or four hundred miles, until it reached impassable mountains. Major Kennicott, leading the Russian American crew, was in poor health, and died on May 13, 1866.

Another difficulty, "unavoidable delays" kept the Siberian-Asian crew in San Francisco until June, when they finally were transported to their starting point in Siberia, across the strait from Russian America.

During this same spring, the *Great Eastern* was taking on a load of more than two thousand miles of heavily insulated undersea cable. The president of Western Union once met the president of the Atlantic cable in London, and said, "I would give $50,000 to know if you are ever going to succeed. I hope you will; but I would like to know for certain before we spend any more in Russia."

Clearly, many were still quite skeptical as to whether or not the cable would ever succeed. But as described earlier, it was successful, and arrived in Heart's Content, Newfoundland at the end of July, 1866.

This signaled the end of the overland telegraph project. It was clear to the Western Union management immediately. Close to three million dollars had been invested in the project, most of it by the Western Union directors. They did not want to lose their money.

So, throughout the fall of 1866, the Western Union management sought to lead the general public into believing that progress on the line was still going forward. The obvious purpose of this was to keep the price of the stock up, as long as possible. But with the exception of the Siberian line – where news of the Atlantic cable had not yet arrived – this was simply not true.

The British Columbian crew, on hearing of the completion of the cable, had stopped work and left, "leaving their tools, stores, and materials to the tender mercies of the Hudson Bay trapper and the native red man." Major Pope, in charge of that division, resigned at once, saying, "I did not want to be banished to the ends of the earth if nothing was to come of it."

As of September 15, 1866, assessments of twenty-five percent of the capital stock on the project had been made, or 2.5 million dollars. But the directors sent out a circular which called for an additional five percent assessment on the stock – another five dollars per share – but also provided that up until February 1, 1867, the assessment could be converted into a Western Union bond at the favorable rate of a one dollar bond for each ninety cents of stock. The bond would pay 7% interest per year until 1875, when it would be repaid in full. In other words, an investment of ninety cents in the Russian American telegraph project could be converted into a $1 Western Union bond before February 1, 1867, which would pay a 7% interest rate. Similar provisions were also made for investments already paid in to be converted into stock.

By the deadline of February 1, 1867, about 3.1 million dollars in Western Union bonds had been taken out, that is, virtually all of the money which had been invested in the overland project. Then, on March 9, 1867 the Commercial and Financial Chronicle published the following brief announcement: "It was decided at a meeting of Directors of the Western Union Telegraph Company last week that in view of the successful working of the Atlantic Cable, it is not advisable to spend any more money in the Russian extension at present."

The directors of Western Union thus appear to have committed fraud against their own company, that is, against the Western Union shareholders. The editor of *The Telegrapher* wrote: "We would like to inquire if there was any warrant for the issuance of these bonds, whereby the stockholders of the Western Union are compelled against their will to accept the gigantic expense of the huge failure? Mr. Collins made money, and the directors of the enterprise have saved themselves a huge loss, but what do the stockholders of the Western Union company have to gain?"

A Boston Traveler editorial said, "The impression is very general that the affairs of the company are managed solely with a view to the interests of a few, large stockholders who are represented in the Direction, and that although the net earnings, as shown by the balance sheet are large, the smaller stockholders are not likely to realize much from them."

In the meantime, the Siberian crews continued to work on their part of the line throughout the winter and spring of 1867. George Kennan was with them, and was recording the progress. Several work crews were in the field, and plans were made to hire several hundred natives to help in the work. The entire route was mapped out, and thousands of poles were cut. The men working on the line expected to complete their part of the line by 1870.

But on May 31, 1867, a ship, the Sea Breeze of New Bedford, Massachusetts, was sighted. The next morning, Kennan and several of his party boarded the ship and met with the skipper, Captain Hamilton. Hamilton asked if they were shipwrecked. They explained that they were working on a telegraph cable project.

"A telegraph line! Well, if that ain't the craziest thing I ever heard of. Who's going to telegraph from here?"

Kennan asked him about the Atlantic cable: "Does it work?"

"Works like a snatch-tackle," the Captain replied. "The Frisco papers are publishing every day the London news of the day before. I've got a lot of 'em on board I'll give you."

On returning to shore, the telegraph builders read the papers. It quickly became clear to them that both Atlantic cables were functioning, and that their own project was dead. Kennan and his associates sold what they could of their wires, pickaxes and other equipment to the natives, but there was far more than the local population was able to use. Kennan and his party finally closed shop and went home.

The huge expenditure, while a total loss to the Western Union Company's shareholders, was not completely in vain. The money spent stimulated the local economies for a while, providing jobs to the workers. Considerable knowledge was gained of British Columbia and of Russia America. In October, 1867, Russian American was purchased by the United States and renamed Alaska.

Chapter 15
Summary

The world as yet does not know how much it owes to you, and this generation will never know it. I regard what has been done as the most marvelous thing in human history. I think it more marvelous than the invention of printing,or,I am almost ready to say, than the voyage of Genoese.
–John Bright (1811-89), British statesman, letter to Cyrus Field

The impact which the trans-Atlantic cable had on the world was immediate, profound, and permanent. The worlds of finance and news, to mention just two examples, were transformed deeply, never again to be the same as before.

Numerous honors were bestowed upon those responsible. Queen Victoria ordered that knighthoods be conferred upon Captain Anderson, Professor William Thomson, Samuel Canning, and William Glass; and that baronetcies be conferred upon Curtis Lampson and Daniel Gooch. She expressed her appreciation of Cyrus Field, and specifically, once again, expressed regret that she was unable to confer a knighthood on him, because he was not a British subject. Congress passed a resolution of appreciation for him, awarding him with a gold medal. He did not receive it until about two years later, however, due to a bureaucratic mixup.

A number of banquets were given on both sides of the Atlantic in honor of Field and the others, especially Charles Bright, Samuel Canning, Captain Anderson, and Professor William Thomson. As with many such endeavors, it was a project carried out with the help and cooperation of many. But the role played by Cyrus Field was widely recognized and appreciated by the most important players. Sir William Thomson, later Lord Kelvin, wrote a letter to Field which said, "I am sorry that I had not an opportunity of saying in public how much I value your energy and perseverance in carrying through this great enterprise, and how clearly you stand out in its history as its originator and its mainspring from beginning to end."

Dr. W. H. Russell, the famous war correspondent of the *Times*, who had accompanied the 1865 expedition, said in a book on the cable: "Mr.

Field may be likened either to the core, or the external protection, of the cable itself. At times he has been its active life; again he has been its ironbound guardian."

When asked to name the persons most deserving of honor for the laying of the cable by the Secretary of the Privy Council, prior to the conferring of the Queen's honors, Sir Charles Wheatstone named Field, Glass, Canning, Anderson, and Thomson. He wrote a paragraph recommending Field for honors, which mentioned his "indomitable perseverance." A part of the letter reads, "Through good and through evil report he has pursued his single object undaunted by repeated failures, keeping up the flagging interest of the public and the desponding hopes of capitalists, and employing his energies to combine all the means which might lead toward a successful issue."

The cable had an immediate impact on the world's financial markets. Where before there was a nearly two week delay between New York and London, communication was practically instantaneous. News of wars, elections, important events, all could now be known within a day or so of their occurrence. Political and business leaders of countries could now communicate in a day what previously took weeks. The news from London could be read in New York, and San Francisco as well, the next day. There were predictions that wars would be no more because of the new communications medium.

Other submarine cables soon followed, connecting all the continents of the world.

The success of the cable brought Field financial wealth, once again. He had invested almost all of his money in the cable. For the many years it took the project to succeed, his family had been forced to live very frugally, much more so than many knew. Now, for a time, they were able to enjoy to fruits of his successes in a financial sense also.

The cable's success brought Field worldwide fame. He received honors and letters from presidents, royalty, and prominent statesmen. He was honored at numerous banquets on both sides of the Atlantic.

Some of Field's strongest qualities, which were his openness and honesty, and his willingness to trust others, were those which inspired and motivated others to help him. These same qualities were also his weaknesses when he carried them too far, such as when he assumed others to be as honest and trustworthy as himself. In the 1880s, he engaged in speculative investing on Wall Street. Following the advice of others, he put much of his money in risky investments. On one horrible Wall Street day, June 24, 1887, he lost most of his wealth, around six million dollars.

Unfortunately, his last days were not lived out in comfort, nor in the way his friends or family would have wished for him. One of his daughters suffered from mental illness, and one of his sons, Edward, was found to have engaged in stock fraud. His beloved wife, Mary, passed away soon after their fiftieth wedding anniversary. Cyrus followed her, just a year later, on July 12, 1892, at the age of seventy-two. Though he had lost his fortune, his fame endured, as well as his popularity, and his legacy. His funeral service in New York was attended by hundreds, the rich and famous as well as the common people. His body was then taken to Stockridge, Massachusetts, where he had grown up, where a service was held in the same church where his father had once preached. He was buried there and his tombstone reads:

Cyrus West Field
To whose courage, energy and perseverance the world owes the
Atlantic telegraph

It is a simple eulogy, and some may think he deserved more; but, as one of his contemporaries said, "Every message that flashes through the Atlantic cable is his eulogy." Today, a century and a half later, the same could still be said of the millions of messages flashing through the optical fiber cables which now carry voice and internet traffic under the worlds' oceans, for Cyrus Field was one of the earliest pioneers in the telecommunications revolution which is still underway.

Conclusions

The Telegraph. Telegraphs were invented in several different places and times, independently, by several different individuals. Most never were made into viable businesses. It is quite possible that others have invented telegraphs which are not mentioned in this book.

Cooke and Wheatstone invented a dial-needle telegraph and started a successful telegraph business in Britain, prior to Morse in the U.S. Their telegraphs were built alongside rail lines from the early days, and the advantages of using telegraph lines for train coordination became clear earlier in Britain than in the U.S.

Morse conceived of a telegraph in 1832, but it took him until 1844 to develop his idea, get capital, and build the first major U.S. line, a 44-mile link between Baltimore and Washington, D.C.

Morse's telegraph had an important advantage over most others in the sim- plicity and use of his code. Only one wire of minimal quality was needed; the circuit was closed by the ground. Iron wires were used, which were sturdier than copper ones. Cooke and Wheatstone's telegraph used five wires; various combinations of current in the wires caused a dial to point to a letter of the alphabet, making a code like Morse's unnecessary.

One of Morse's major struggles was in obtaining capital to build a telegraph network. This struggle took many years. The lack of capital, and the difficulty in obtaining it, delayed telegraph development in the U.S. Once it got started, however, and the world saw what it could do, the telegraph spread very rapidly.

In Britain, Cooke and Wheatstone had much less difficulty in raising capital; Britain was a much richer country in 1840, had a better developed railroad system, and much less total land area to cover.

An important early issue was whether the telegraph would be controlled by private companies or by the government. In the U.S., it remained in private hands, despite the preference of Morse and many others for government control. In Britain, it started out as a private venture, but was taken over by the government in 1870. In most European countries, the telegraph was controlled by the government from its earliest days. Though there were some advantages to government control, a business in private hands is generally more responsive to change and adjusts more quickly to advances in technology.

A related issue was that of monopoly. In the early days there was much competition, and many of the early telegraph lines went bankrupt or were bought out for little by others. There was also a great deal of needless waste caused by unnecessary disputes, duplication and quarrelling between the Morse patent holders, and with others.

One of the biggest obstacles to Morse was F. O. J. Smith, a former Congressman who had helped him get the initial government grant, but soon thereafter became a lifelong enemy. Smith still tried to discredit Morse, even after Morse's death. Eventually Western Union emerged as the first great industrial monopoly in the U.S. Its high prices and profits caused a great deal of opposition, but the invention of the telephone and the eventual rise of AT&T, as well as competition from wireless gradually weakened its monopoly position.

Despite all its weaknesses, the telegraph made a huge and lasting impact on the world, both in the U.S. and elsewhere. When Morse died, the Louisville *Courant-Journal* called him "the greatest man of the nineteenth century;" the New York *Herald* said that he "was, perhaps, the most illustrious American of his age." A memorial ceremony was held in the U.S. House of Representatives, and was attended by President U. S. Grant, his cabinet, and members of the Supreme Court.

The Atlantic Telegraph Cable. Soon after the telegraph took hold in both Britain and the U.S., businessmen and engineers began to imagine the possibility of connecting the Old World and the New. It was Cyrus Field, an American businessman, who actually set out to achieve it. The difficulties he encountered were far greater than he or anyone else had ever imagined. From the time he first set out to do it until it was finally achieved took a dozen years – the same time from Morse's conception of the telegraph (1832) to the first major U.S. line (1844).

The Atlantic Cable project was, by far, the biggest electrical engineering project the world had ever seen. A huge amount of capital, international cooperation, and numerous technical advances were necessary to achieve it. Many disappointments had to be overcome. It took five tries – one in 1857, two in 1858, another in 1865, and in 1866 – before the cable was finally laid successfully.

While Field initiated and inspired the project, with the help of American investors and the cooperation of the Newfoundland government, it took investors, engineers and scientists from Britain, which had to come in and provide the capital, the engineering and scientific know-how, the industrial capability, and the ship to carry the cable. The British government provided a great deal of support.

William Thomson, a Scottish professor who later became Lord Kelvin, provided a key invention, a super-sensitive detector which used a mirror hung from a thread to detect and measure a weak electrical current. Along with several others, he was knighted for his contribution to the cable project. British capitalists provided most of the money. A famous British engineer, Isambard Kingdom Brunel, built the ship to carry the cable, and British companies manufactured it. On the 1866 voyage which finally laid a cable successfully, there were five hundred on board; Field was the only American.

The great cable project also had a significant impact on the electrical engineering discipline. The early failures of the cable led to an inquest, and this led to the standardization of many of the units of electrical measurement such as Watt, Volt, and Ampere. The inquest also set a precedent, that of conducting a serious investigation after a major disaster, which has been followed many times since.

The successful laying of the Atlantic telegraph cable probably made an even greater impact on the world than had the land telegraph. One British newspaper, for example, called it the greatest advance by mankind since the discovery of the New World by Columbus. A prominent British statesman, John Bright, wrote that he regarded it as "as the most marvelous thing in human history." Neither the telegraph nor the cable, however, would have as much impact on the world without the other.

Finally, this book is one with many heroes. The tremendous hardships which Morse and Field had to endure would have caused most to give up. Morse's young wife died when he was away, and was buried before he knew of her death; had his own future invention been in existence, he could have been wired. He experienced obstacles and opposition at practically every step of the way, as he tried to get his telegraph funded and built.

Field lost a four year old son while he was preparing for one of his many trips to England. He suffered public rejection and ridicule when the 1858 cable failed. During the twelve years of his project, he made more than fifty voyages by ship between England, Newfoundland, and New York; each voyage took about ten days in each direction.

Many others contributed, too numerous to name them all here, but all had a part in bringing modern communications to the world.

All these endured personal tragedies and hardship, and overcame obstacles to achieve their goals, and as a result made a lasting impact on mankind. They refused to give up on their goals despite hardship and setback after setback. There is a lesson here for all of us.

As Winston Churchill said many times and in several different ways, "Never give up. Never, never give up."

Bibliography

Introduction

Forbes, Esther, *Paul Revere and the World He Lived In*, Houghton Mifflin Company, Boston, 1942, 1969, ISBN 0-395-08370-2.

Part 1 The Telegraph

Andrews, Frederick T., "The Heritage of Telegraphy," *IEEE Communications Magazine*, August 1989.

Denton, Jeremiah, *When Hell Was in Session*, Reader's Digest Press, 1976.

Harlow, Alvin F., *Old Wires and New Waves*, NY: D. Appleton-Century Company, 1936.

Hochfelder, David, "Joseph Henry: Inventor of the Telegraph?" The Joseph Henry Papers Project, Smithsonian Institutional History Division.

Mott, Edward Harold, *Between the Ocean and the Lakes: the story of Erie*, New York, 1899.

Munro, John, *Heroes of the Telegraph*, London, 1891.

New York *Times*, "Obituary. Sir William F. Cooke," July 1, 1879, and "Obituary. Sir Charles Wheatstone," October 21, 1875.

Parsons, Frank, *The Telegraph Monopoly*. C. F. Taylor, Philadelphia, 1899.

Silverman, Kenneth, *Lightning Man: The Accursed Life of Samuel F. B. Morse*, Alfred A. Knopf, ISBN0-375-40128-8, 2003.

Standage, Tom, *The Victorian Internet*, Berkley Books, New York, 1998, ISBN 0-425-17169-8.

Thompson, Robert Luther, *Wiring a Continent: The History of The Telegraph Industry in the United States*, 1832-1866, Princeton University Press, Princeton, New Jersey, 1947.

Part 2 The Atlantic Telegraph Cable

Bright, Charles. *The Story of the Atlantic Cable.* New York: D. Appleton & Co., 1903.

Burns, Bill. "History of the Atlantic Cable and Underseas Communications." Web site, *http://atlantic-cable.com.* (Wealth of photos and information on submarine cables.)

Burns, Bill. "Early Cable Instruments," from the website Atlantic-Cable. com, based on a talk at the 2009 Antique Wireless Association Conference in Rochester, New York, August 20-23, 2009.

Dugan, James. *The Great Iron Ship.* New York: Harper & Brothers, 1953. 252 *The Telegraph and the Atlantic Cable*

Encyclopaedia Britanica, 1929: "Field, Cyrus West," and "Field, David Dudley."

Field, Henry M. *History of the Atlantic telegraph,* New York: Charles Scribner & Company, 1866.

Gordon, John Steele. *A Thread Across the Ocean,* Walker & Company, New York, 2002.

MacDonald, Philip B., A Saga of the Seas: *The Story of Cyrus W. Field and the Laying of the first Atlantic Cable.* New York, Wilson-Erikson, 1937.

Russell, W. H., *The Atlantic Telegraph.* Nonsuch Publishing Ltd, 2005, ISBN I- 84588-074-9; first published, 1866.

Thompson, Robert Luther. *Wiring a Continent: the History of the Telegraph In- dustry in the United States 1832-66,* Princeton University Press, Princeton, New Jersey, 1947.

The Telegrapher: a Journal of Electrical Progress, July 18, 1874, pp. 169-70.

Index

About the Author

Bert Lundy is the founder and director of a tutoring business called *Learn for Excellence*, which he started in 2010, in Watsonville, CA. The business is now located in Salinas, CA. The enterprise tutors children grades 1-12 mathematics, English, geography, history, and other areas. As the name implies, the intention is to train children to become *excellent* in mathematics, English and other areas.

He was a professor in the computer science department at the Naval Postgraduate School in Monterey, California from 1988 until 2014. His teaching and research were on computer and telecom networks, including formal models for protocol specification and analysis, protocol testing, military applications, and network economics and policies. He has published a number of research papers on protocol specification, analysis and testing. He also taught classes in other areas of computer science, including programming, algorithms, network security and computer architecture.

Having a strong belief that graduate students and professors also should study the practical side of networking, he developed and taught a class on the business side of telecommunications, including a bit of the history. This led him to conceive the idea of this book, *Telegraph*, *Telephone* and *Wireless*, and over a number of years to write it.

In the 1990s he wrote a business plan and put together a management team for a startup telecom company in Mexico. The plan was to build an optical fiber network, to provide the people of that country with modern and economical telecommunications. During this project, he visited Mexico numerous times, and also learned to speak Spanish. The project eventually failed due to lack of capital and other factors.

From 1984-88, he was a research assistant at Georgia Tech in Atlanta, leading to the PhD in 1988.

From 1981-84, he was a software engineer in Dallas, Texas, where he worked on large software engineering projects. Those projects involved the writing and testing of complex software programs, often written in machine language, for the controlling of satellites orbiting the earth.

In addition to his regular classes, Prof. Lundy has taught short classes on networking in Puebla, Mexico; Madrid, Spain; and Osaka, Japan. He has given talks at AT&T (later Lucent) Bell Laboratories, and at numerous conferences in many cities, including London, England. He has also given talks at numerous universities throughout the U.S., Mexico, and Spain.

From 1977-81 he served as an officer in the U.S. Army at Ft. Ord, California. During that time he served as a systems analyst for a major software project, developing real-time software for military systems.

In addition to the Ph.D., he obtained an M.S. in computer science from the University of Texas at Dallas, and a B.A. in mathematics, minoring in history and German, from Texas A&M University. He is an avid sportsman, having climbed Mt. Whitney (el. 14,505 ft.) and completed numerous marathons. For more recent information on author and book, see *bertlundy.com*.

Milton Keynes UK
Ingram Content Group UK Ltd.
UKHW020635041223
433752UK00017B/956